MARKIEVICZ
A Most Outrageous Rebel

MARKIEVICZ
A Most Outrageous Rebel

LINDIE NAUGHTON

Waterford City and County
Libraries

MERRION
PRESS

Published in 2016 by
Merrion Press
10 George's Street
Newbridge
Co. Kildare
Ireland
www.merrionpress.ie

© 2016 Lindie Naughton

British Library Cataloguing in Publication Data
An entry can be found on request

ISBN: 978-1-78537-081-6 (Paper)
ISBN: 978-1-78537-082-3 (Cloth)
ISBN: 978-1-78537-084-7 (Kindle)

Library of Congress Cataloging in Publication Data
An entry can be found on request

Design by www.jminfotechindia.com
Typeset in Minion Pro 11.5/14 pt
Cover design by www.phoenix-graphicdesign.com
Front cover image: Seated studio portrait of Constance Markievicz,
c.1915. (Image Courtesy of the National Library of Ireland & NLI Logo)
Back cover image: Lissadell House, Co. Sligo. Photo by the author

Printed and bound in Great Britain by TJ International Ltd. Padstow

Contents

Acknowledgements and
Note on Sources

For a woman of her stature, Countess Constance de Markievicz has received remarkably little attention from biographers.

The first biography, written by Seán O'Faoláin and published in 1934 – seven years after her death – was criticised by her friends for its patronising tone.

It took another thirty-three years before any other writer was prepared to tackle the subject. Then two came along in the same year. Jacqueline Van Voris's *Constance de Markievicz in the Cause of Ireland* was published by the University of Massachusetts Press in 1967, while Anne Marreco's *The Rebel Countess: The Life and Times of Constance Markievicz* came out in London that same year.

Twenty years later, in 1987, came Diana Norman's *Terrible Beauty: A Life of Constance Markievicz, 1868–1927*, and then, in 1923, Anne Haverty's *Constance Markievicz: An Independent Life*, which has recently been republished. This last was the first biography of Markievicz written by an Irish woman. In more recent years have come four more books. In 1998, Sari Oikarinen's *A Dream of Liberty: Constance Markievicz's Vision of Ireland 1908-1927* provided the first close examination of Markievicz's political and social philosophy, and in 2003, Joe McGowan edited *Constance Markievicz: The People's Countess* for the Constance Markievicz Millennium Committee in Sligo. Patrick Quigley published a biography of Casimir Markievicz called *The Polish Irishman – the Life and Times of Count Casimir Markievicz* in 2012. Finally, in 2016, came Lauren Arrington's *Revolutionary Lives: Constance and Casimir Markievicz*.

The ground-breaking work done by these previous biographers cannot be underestimated and we owe them our thanks.

Bringing Constance to life as a warm, witty and kind-hearted woman were the prison letters she wrote to her sister, Eva, later assembled by Esther Roper, Eva's lifelong companion, in book form. The originals are held at the National Library of Ireland, complete with sketches and drawings. A big thank you for their help to the staff in both the main reading room and the manuscripts section of the library. Thanks also to the staff at Blackrock Library, through which many out-of-date books were located, and to the National Museum at Collins Barracks, where Constance's 1892 diary is held.

The papers of the Lissadell estate were donated to the Public Records Office of Northern Ireland in Belfast; another invaluable resource, made easily accessible by the excellent staff. Lissadell House itself is now owned by Constance Cassidy and Edward Walsh and open to the public for much of the year. Sligo Library also holds a small archive of letters and other memorabilia relating to Markievicz, as does Kilmainham Gaol in Dublin.

We are indebted to the Bureau of Military History for digitising and releasing a treasure trove of witness statements and pension details relating to 1916, the War of Independence and the Civil War online. These have helped bring to life the history of Ireland in the early twentieth century.

Big thanks to my family and friends for their encouragement and support while writing this book. Let me also record my gratitude to Colm Kennedy and the staff at Vayu Energy for their support; to my eagle-eyed agent Jonathan Williams; and to everyone at Merrion Press for their professionalism and efficiency.

My late mother Jessie Naughton read – and corrected in her inimitable style – the early chapters of this book while she was in hospital with her final illness. This book is dedicated to her memory.

Prologue

On Sunday, 30 April 1916, with the six-day Irish rebellion that became known as the Easter Rising almost over, a nurse called Elizabeth Farrell was driven to Grafton Street in Dublin by a British army officer. From there, she walked to the Royal College of Surgeons on St Stephen's Green carrying a white flag and a surrender order.

Farrell went to the side door of the college and, when it opened, she asked for Commandant Mallin. Since he was sleeping, Farrell gave the surrender order to Countess Markievicz, his second-in-command and one of only two female officers in the Irish Citizen Army.

'Surrender? We'll never surrender!' said the Countess, before waking Mallin. Despite her fighting words, there was no alternative but to surrender and so Mallin and Markievicz led the small group of exhausted rebels out of the college and on to the street, where they surrendered to Captain de Courcy Wheeler of the Kings' Royal Rifle Corps. After smartly saluting the captain, Constance kissed her revolver before handing it over.

De Courcy Wheeler offered Constance transport to Dublin Castle, which she refused, preferring to march with Mallin and her comrades down Grafton Street and into Dame Street. By now, crowds were lining the streets, with many waving Union Jacks and celebrating the end of the six days of misery they had endured during an insurrection that had devastated their city.

On 4 May, Constance was tried for her part in the Rebellion and sentenced to be shot, a sentence that was commuted to life imprisonment on the grounds of her sex. By then, the swiftness and savagery of the British response to the insurrection was changing public opinion and the rebels were on their way to becoming revered as martyrs for the Irish cause.

After women were finally given the vote in 1918, Constance – from Holloway prison – would become the first woman in Britain or Ireland to be elected to the House of Commons and, later, only the second female cabinet minister anywhere in the world. In 1926, realising that the political posturings that followed 1916 were leading nowhere, she became a founding member of Fianna Fáil, supporting her friend Éamon de Valera.

She had come a long from way from her origins as a privileged member of the landlord class in Sligo, rejecting not only the 'black English blood' that ran through her veins, but throwing off the conventions of her class and her sex.

As any Jane Austen reader knows, a woman's success or failure in life was entirely dependent on whether she found herself a husband, and any husband, however ugly or old, was better than none. The fight for women's equality began with the arrival of convenient birth control. With her life no longer circumscribed by continuous child-bearing, women in the late nineteenth and early twentieth centuries had the time and energy to begin the fight for their rights to a proper education, for work and for the vote.

It would be a long, hard battle, and it is far from over today. Women in the public eye were viewed with suspicion. They were attention-seekers, derided as shrill and even hysterical. Their views could not be trusted, because – as everyone knew – women were flighty, unreliable and inconsistent.

That, certainly, was how Markievicz was seen. Begrudgers, such as Seán O'Casey, berated her for playing the revolutionary. Others, like James Connolly and Patrick Pearse, recognised her brilliance as an organiser and motivator. Her outstanding contribution to the fight for Irish freedom was the Fianna – a boy's brigade formed with the specific purpose of training boys to take arms against the English. By the time of the Easter Rising, these boys were disciplined and organised young men, trained in the use of arms. Had the Fianna not been formed in 1909, there would have been no Volunteers in 1913 and no Rising in 1916, Pearse later said.

Ordinary Dubliners saw Constance for what she was – an immensely open-hearted and generous woman – and she won their lasting respect. When the woman they affectionately called 'Madame' died in 1927, they gave her one of the biggest funerals ever seen in Dublin. 'Official' Ireland stayed away.

She had died, officially of appendicitis, at the relatively early age of fifty-nine, worn out by too many hard battles and a succession of arduous jail stretches. Although she had famously avoided execution and lived for eleven years after the terrible events of 1916, she gave up her life for her country, as surely as her friends James Connolly, Patrick Pearse, Thomas MacDonagh, Tom Clarke and Francis Sheehy Skeffington.

Her vision of a kinder, better society, where all men and women were equal, where resources and wealth were shared, where no one starved or died of the cold, and where all children were cherished remains a worthy aspiration.

CHAPTER ONE

Alien Class, Alien Race

When Countess Markievicz was sentenced to death for her part in the 1916 Rebellion in Ireland, she risked putting half of Debrett's into mourning – or so said her husband. Her social awareness, her generosity and her kindness were firmly rooted not only in her privileged background but in her native County Sligo. All her life she cursed the drop of 'black English blood' that ran through her veins. She was never to forget the great wrongs her ancestors had committed against the native Irish and, from the age of forty, making amends became her life's work.

Her family had come to Ireland in Cromwellian times but, by the 1860s, when Constance Gore-Booth was born, its great days were numbered, along with those of the Ascendancy class in Ireland. At a time of rapid industrialisation and mechanisation, the Irish economy was stagnating and, since the Act of Union in 1800; it was closely tied to a rapacious British economy that saw Ireland purely as a market to be exploited.

When cheap manufactured goods from Britain flooded into Ireland, thousands of craftsmen, particularly textile workers, were left without work. At the same time, rural workers were hit hard by the rapid advances in agricultural machinery, which made farming less labour-intensive. With work scarce, those living on the land could barely feed their families, much less pay their rent or leave anything to their children. Unlike the rest of the United Kingdom, Ireland had few big industrial centres outside Belfast and Dublin and, with nowhere else to go, these two cities became magnets for impoverished families desperate for work. This situation was not helped by a growing population; with early marriage and large families the norm, the Irish population increased by 75 per cent between 1780 and 1821.

Even before the Great Famine of the mid-1840s, Irish men, women and children were starving; in some areas, infant mortality was a staggering 50 per cent. The steady stream of emigration began and, in the thirty years between 1815 and 1845, nearly a million Irish emigrants – twice the total for the preceding two hundred years – packed up their meagre possessions and went in search of the better life that newspaper articles and advertising promised in countries such as the USA, Canada and Australia. Later on, the land wars took their toll and, like other land-owners, the Gore-Booths had to work hard to make the estate pay. It was a troubled country to which the infant Constance returned after her birth in London in 1868; her grandfather's cousin, Captain King, had been murdered during that year's election campaign and Lissadell, the family home, was turned into a fortress, with windows sandbagged and guns mounted on the roof.

Sligo was solidly unionist, with a high proportion of Protestants in its population and four military barracks. Loyalists controlled business and commerce, forming the Sligo Association as early as 1688. William Butler Yeats described Sligo, home to his mother's people, the Pollexfens, as a place where 'everyone despised nationalists and Catholics'. When jobs were advertised, notices often baldly stated that 'No Catholics need apply'. Meetings of the local Orange Order branch were held in Lissadell House.

> You saw the landlords in their big demesnes, mostly of Norman or Saxon stock, walled in and aloof, an alien class, sprung from an alien race; then there were the prosperous farmers, mostly Protestants and with Scotch names, settled in snug farmsteads among the rich undulating hills and valleys, while hidden away among rocks on the bleak mountainsides, or soaking in the slime and ooze of the boglands or beside the Atlantic shore, where the grass is blasted yellow by the salt west wind, you find the dispossessed people of the old Gaelic race in their miserable cabins.

So wrote Constance in a 1923 article for *Éire* newspaper.

Her ancestors, the Gore family, had come to Ireland during the seventeenth century in the aftermath of the Nine Years' War. When the English made their first major push to dominate Ireland, Sir Paul Gore, a successful soldier of fortune, was part of a cavalry troop led by the Earl of Essex, and was granted land in Donegal and at Ardtarmon on the shores of Drumcliff Bay, about two miles west of the present Lissadell House. The name Lissadill or Lissadell referred to the O'Daly hereditary poets, who had lived in the area since the twelfth century; the full name in Irish is *Lios an Daill ui Dálaigh*, meaning 'O'Daly's Court of the Blind'. Reminders of more ancient times included a round tower and carved high cross from the monastery founded by St Columcille in 574 at Drumcliff. The estate amounted to 32,000 acres spread over forty townlands in the parishes of Drumcliff and Rossinver.

In 1711, a marriage between Nathaniel Gore and Letitia Booth brought with it considerable estates in Manchester and Salford belonging to the Booth family. With this marriage, the Sligo family added 'Booth' to its surname. Constance may have inherited her vivacity from her wild and wilful great-great-grandmother. Legend has it that Letitia plunged to her death along with her coachman when she forced him to drive around the rim of the Derk of Knocklane, a fearsome semi-circular chasm with a sheer drop into the Atlantic Ocean about 200 metres below, located above the Yellow Strand about six kilometres to the west of the current Lissadell House. The wailing sound visitors hear over the chasm is reputed to be that of Letitia, the Banshee Bawn.

Around this time, Ardtarmon Castle burned down and the original Lissadell House was built close to the location of its current, more recent replacement. Robert Gore-Booth, Constance's grandfather, was born in the original house on 25 August 1805 and, though still a boy, succeeded his father in 1814. At the age of twenty-one, he took over the estate at Lissadell, which was in bad shape. A tall man with a red beard, Robert was a Cambridge graduate who enjoyed the finer things in life, including gardening and playing his Stradivari cello, as well as hunting with horse and hound. He had become interested in architecture while travelling abroad and was determined to upgrade the Lissadell estate, using the income from the family holdings in England.

By 1833, he had doubled the size of the estate by acquiring land twenty miles to the south of Lissadell (including the town of Ballymote) for £130,000. This land was used for cattle grazing. Annual income from about 1,000 tenant farmers amounted to £15,000, which meant Sir Robert was considerably wealthier than most of his neighbours. About 300 of his tenants paid £4 a year each for a few acres of poor land, from which they scratched a paltry existence. The average yearly wage at the time for a farm labourer was between £15 and £18. Typically, any cash a tenant acquired went towards paying the rent, often to an absentee landlord living abroad in some splendour.

After the Act of Union abolished the regional parliament, the large estates did well, but little changed for the ordinary Irish and both the native Irish and the country's administrators became passive and lethargic. The Industrial Revolution barely touched Ireland, although towards the end of the nineteenth century Belfast and the surrounding areas were allowed to develop heavy industry providing it did not interfere with profits on the larger island. For the majority, still living off the land, survival was a struggle and the dominance of the potato in the diet, favoured because it could feed an entire family from a small plot, was storing up problems for the future.

Between 1834 and 1835, Sir Robert began work on building a new and more splendid house at Lissadell. When, four months after coming into his inheritance, he had married Caroline King, daughter of Viscount Lorton, he received a marriage portion of £10,000, which he decided to put towards a new house. His wife died in childbirth soon after, but Sir Robert remained closely linked to the King family, with his sister Anne marrying Robert King in 1829. He had much admired the neo-classical style of Rockingham, his father-in-law Viscount Lorton's home, overlooking Lough Key in Boyle, County Roscommon, which had been designed by John Nash.

In 1830, Sir Robert remarried; his bride was Caroline Goold, a renowned beauty. After the wedding, he commissioned the London architect Francis Goodwin to come up with a design for a new house; Goodwin had designed the town halls of Manchester and Salford. With the building works underway, Sir Robert and his wife embarked on a Grand Tour of Europe, collecting seventeenth-century Italian paintings and other items they would use to furnish their new home.

The house, two storeys over a basement with forty-eight rooms, was the last house built in Ireland in the Greek revival style. Standing at the end of a long avenue, its box-like exterior was relieved by a bay window the height of the building on its south side. Three large windows on each floor gave magnificent views of Knocknarea, the legendary burial place of Maeve, Queen of Connacht. Other rooms looked out on Sligo Bay and Ben Bulben. On the north facade was an unusual *porte cochère* entrance, large enough for vehicles to pass through; this Goodwin thought necessary because of the exposed position of the house.

Building materials included limestone from Ballysadare, the setting of Yeats's 'Salley Gardens'. Black Kilkenny marble was used for the floors, columns and staircase in the entrance hall, while ornate, Egyptian-style chimneypieces of Italian marble added grandeur to the other principal rooms. Family rooms were positioned on either side of a long gallery, supported by thick pillars and lit from above; the gallery contained an organ and Sir Robert's art collection. Lighting for the house came from a local gasholder – Lissadell was the first house in Ireland lit by its own gas supply. In the basement, the servants' quarters included a butler's pantry, kitchen, bakery, wine cellar and china room, as well as sleeping quarters for the butler, the housekeeper and the maids. There was, however, no smoking room; Sir Robert abhorred the habit.

The setting was idyllic, as Constance recognised:

> Behind the gray barrack-like house, ranges of mountains lay like a great row of sphinxes against the sky and shut us out from Ireland. Trees and glades sloped down to the bay, across which Knocknareagh rose, crowned by the great queen's cairn. The bay slipped into the Atlantic, somewhere behind black cliffs, and the Atlantic was the end of the world. Brave fishing boats tempted the outskirts. But there it lay, impassable, unfathomable, incomprehensible, beyond might be Heaven or Tír na nÓg, for the farther away your eyes pierced the more it glittered and dazzled and broke up into coloured lights and blue mysteries.

Sir Robert maintained the family tradition of living in Ireland, and the rents he collected went back into the estate. As a working farm requiring energetic management and a big staff, Lissadell bustled with life. Because horse riding was so important to the estate's management,

Sir Robert built a riding school for his children and it was here that the infant Constance had her first riding lessons. Inspired by his travels, Sir Robert introduced many new ideas and innovations, such as the planting of hardy grasses near the seashore to save the land from the pummeling of the Atlantic Ocean. He experimented with harvesting oysters and used the vast quantities of seaweed that grew on the coast to help enrich the soil.

From the time he took over Lissadell, Sir Robert showed an acute awareness of the problems caused by the sizes of the leases taken out by his tenants; they were extremely small, for the most part, which made it difficult for tenants to survive and for him to collect a decent rent. The Irish tradition of subdividing land among the sons in a family exacerbated this problem. On his Boyle estate, Viscount Lorton, father of his first wife, had begun offering leases of no less than sixteen acres. Following his lead, Sir Robert started encouraging his bigger tenants to increase their holdings, a move that, at the very least, caused some misunderstanding, since he was under no obligation to look after the evicted tenants.

Compared to some of his neighbours, Sir Robert was considered a 'good' landlord, committed to the local community and serving as magistrate, grand juror and lieutenant of the county before his election as an MP following the Great Famine. His tenants were encouraged to drain their land, while slates were provided for roofs and timber for new houses. Each year, before 1 April, all tenants were required to whitewash their houses. Improvements were financed by a £4,000 loan fund from which tenants could borrow at a favourable rate.

For this reason, the controversy that arose following his acquisition of 8,780 acres in 1833 at the 'Seven Cartrons' in the townland of Ballygilgan, east of Lissadell, is somewhat surprising. Sir Robert was continuing his father's work in expanding the demesne. He had planted 52,100 trees within the demesne and had closed an old public road on the perimeter of the estate, replacing it with a new public road farther north and west. When he acquired the large estate in Ballymote, he funded this purchase, like that of Ballygilgan, with the sale and mortgage of family property in Manchester.

At the time, the British colonies of Australia, South Africa and Canada, as well as the United States, were attempting to attract settlers from Britain and Ireland. The big ports of Liverpool, London and Glasgow and smaller ones at Limerick, Waterford, Dublin and Belfast never had it so busy, with good reason. Like many other landlords, Sir Robert considered emigration a possible solution to the chronic shortage of land and, following the famine of 1831, arranged for fifty-two families to emigrate to Quebec in Canada, most of them leaving holdings of no more than two acres. He paid each person £2 for disturbance, £4 for every acre of good land they left, and sea passage to Canada. His aim was to increase all holdings to at least five acres, just enough to sustain a family and provide him with a rent. He was to pay compensation of £196.58.04 to tenants for 'giving up possession' in 1834, and again in 1835. The few families opting to stay at home were given land elsewhere. He paid £273 in passage money to America in 1839 and a further £148 in 1841, as well as providing thousands of pounds to provision the ships.

The alternative version of the story suggests that about one hundred families were summarily cleared from their homes, mostly by Sir Robert's agent, Captain George Dodwell, who had a reputation for ruthless evictions and chicanery. For those who chose to emigrate, a ship called the *Pomano* was – allegedly – chartered; the boat was not registered on any list and was in poor condition. It sank long before reaching its destination and all aboard were lost. A ballad was composed about the disaster.

The story of the *Pomano* remains controversial, especially since the stories about the disaster were collected many years after the alleged shipwreck. In the period 1833 to 1834, many ships sailed from Sligo Bay and Ballyshannon; a brig called the *Zephyr* made several voyages, as did another called *Britannia*. A registered ship called the *Pomona* sailed from London on 4 April 1834 and arrived in Quebec on 11 May; it – or a ship with a similar name – made regular journeys across the Atlantic after that, most notably one from Sligo to Quebec on 31 May 1839. The name *Pomano* and variations such as *Pomono* and *Pomone* were popular ships' names and it could be that the *Pomano* story has become confused with the tragic story of the *Pomona*, which set sail for the USA from Liverpool on 27 April 1859 with 373 passengers and thirty-five crew on board, many of them from the Sligo area. Battling gale-force winds in the Irish Sea, it hit the Blackwater Bank off Wexford and quickly sank.

Hundreds of bodies were washed ashore over the next few days and, of the 400 or so on board, only twenty-three survived. It remains the sixth worst shipping disaster to have occurred in Irish waters.

Compared to others, the Gore-Booths responded well when Ireland was devastated by the Great Famine of the mid-1840s. Sir Robert's wife Caroline became a familiar figure locally, riding out on her pony with panniers filled with food. The British Liberal government had failed to take decisive action, blaming the widespread starvation on the irresponsibility and selfishness of the local landlords. Yet, under a clause enacted by the British government, tenants who owned more than a quarter acre of land were not eligible for relief.

Between 1845 and 1851, the population of Ireland dropped from about eight million to just over six million. A million died and many more left in a wave of mass emigration, mostly for North America. By the time of the Easter Rising in 1916, some twenty million Americans counted themselves as Irish.

During this terrible time, Sir Robert and his family fed their remaining tenants as best they could. With the help of his ship-owning brother, Henry, Sir Robert was credited with importing Indian corn directly from America in 1847 at a cost of almost £35,000; it is also alleged that he mortgaged the Lissadell estate for £50,000 to help with famine relief. However, these claims are disputed. The records show that the £50,000 from the mortgage went not on famine relief but to pay off the balance of the Ballymote purchase, leaving the estate debt-free; Sir Robert argued that this allowed him to continue with famine relief schemes and work programmes. The Indian corn he imported was a commercial transaction: he bought it for £13 to £14 per ton and sold it for £15 to £16 per ton.

Sir Robert was alleged to have made more clearances from the September of 1849, with the eviction of thirty families from Lissadell. When they returned to the broken-down walls for shelter, they were arrested and brought before the magistrate at Teesan Court just outside Sligo town, and released only when they agreed to leave the land. Between 1847 and 1851, over 30,000 people emigrated through Sligo port. Allegations of forced emigration would continue to haunt Sir Robert, who was forced to defend himself before a House of Lords Select Committee in 1848. In his notes for this hearing, he recorded that 'eighteen families got farms on my estate elsewhere and many others were offered land at Ballintrillick but preferred going to America'. In 1847, he had sponsored the emigration of about a thousand to North America, which some have seen as 'dumping' the problem on the colonies. One of the ships used was the *Æolus*, owned by his brother Henry, who was importing Canadian timber to Scotland at the time.

A report from the Government Emigration Agent at St John, New Brunswick, paints a stark picture. Of the large number of those who arrived on the *Æolus*, 500 of them 'exported by their landlord Sir Robert Gore-Booth' would become 'a public charge, from their inability to work, and utter destitution'. The agent was not impressed: '... this shovelling of helpless paupers, without any provision for them here, if continued, will inflict very serious injury on this colony'. He recommended that the treatment of the passengers 'should, without delay, be noticed and condemned'. Not everyone agreed with this harsh judgement. In a note of thanks from passengers on the *Æolus* who had safely arrived in St John, Sir Robert is described as 'always kind to his tenants'.

The Famine proved a turning point in Anglo-Irish relations. A landlord class that considered itself the representatives of the hated Crown could hardly expect loyalty from its Irish tenants. They had not helped their cause by distancing themselves from their communities, shipping their boys off to public schools in England and their daughters to the London court where, with luck, they would acquire an English husband. Most ignored Irish culture and history and spoke with a peculiar 'West British' accent all their own.

After the famine eased, a sadly shrunken population found it easier to survive. With good prices paid for farm animals and dairy products, rents became easier to pay. In 1850, Sir Robert was elected to the House of Commons and he held the seat until his death in 1876, buying 7 Buckingham Gate, close to Buckingham Palace, as his London residence. Despite the campaign of vilification when he stood for re-election in 1852, he topped the poll, assuring the Sligo electors of his support for tenants' rights. He had an undistinguished record at Westminster, with only five mentions in *Hansard* over twenty-six years in the Commons; his interests were always more local.

By 1871, his second son, Henry, born in 1843, had taken over the management of the Lissadell estate following the death of Sir Robert's land agent. He would inherit the estate when Sir Robert died in 1876. On 29 October 1861, Robert, the older brother and heir, had died aged thirty. There are two accounts of his death: one that he succumbed in Madeira from the after-effects of fighting with the 4th Light Dragoons in the Crimean War; the second that he died in a boating accident near his home. Earlier, in September 1848, Robert had narrowly escaped death after a boating accident on Drumcliff Bay, in which Sir Robert's brother-in-law Francis Goold had drowned; these two incidents may have become confused. What appears to be true is that he left a young wife who stayed on at Lissadell until her second marriage.

On 27 April 1867, Henry married Georgina Mary Hill of Tickhill Castle in Yorkshire, a granddaughter of the Earl of Scarborough. Through this marriage, the Gore-Booths developed family links with Baron Bolton, the Earl of Bradford, the Marquess of Zetland and the Duke of Westminster.

A year later, on 30 April 1868, Constance Georgine was born at 7 Buckingham Gate, the family's London home. She was followed by a son, Josslyn, in February 1869 and by Eva in 1870. In 1874, a third daughter, Mabel, was born and, in 1878, a second son, Mordaunt.

After taking over the management of the estate, Henry had introduced accounts and book-keeping practices unusual for the time, as well as setting out a fair table of rents. The rents he charged were below those recommended by Griffith's valuation; his tenants paid between twelve and fifteen shillings an acre. This compared to the forty shillings – plus extra for the right to gather seaweed – charged by the neighbouring Ballyconnell estate. Many of the tenants supplemented their income by working on the Lissadell farm, in the wood or garden. In the days when few people travelled far, Lissadell was the centre of their universe and it was to Sir Henry that they came when they needed advice on family problems, on finalising wills or on marriage settlements. When lightning struck the roof of the nearby Maugherow Catholic church, Sir Henry paid for the repairs.

Despite his dedication to the estate, Sir Henry, like his father before him, was frustrated by the small size of the holdings, which could barely feed the families living on them. He escaped these day-to-day frustrations of running the estate as often as he could, leaving it in the capable hands of his wife, Lady Georgina. Sir Henry was a keen amateur scientist, explorer and sailor, having developed an interest in boats when he used to sail around Sligo Bay with his older brother Robert in a yacht called *Minna*. Thomas Kilgallon, who later gained a formidable reputation as butler at Lissadell, had joined the staff at the estate and helped the brothers repair and maintain the boat. While at home, Sir Henry loved to hunt, shoot and fish and had even ventured farther, spending three summers sailing and fishing in the icy waters of the Arctic as a young man. In 1873, he sailed with a friend as far north as Spitsbergen, the traditional starting point for expeditions to the North Pole and, in 1879, he joined Captain A.H. Markham on the Norwegian schooner *Isbjorn* for a journey around the Barents and Kara Seas, an area then opening up for the first time. For this voyage, Sir Henry received the thanks of the Royal Geographical Society.

With Thomas Kilgallon, Sir Henry would sail his own forty-foot ketch, the *Kara*, on a voyage to rescue a friend, Benjamin Leigh Smith, who was marooned in Franz Josef Land in 1882. The *Kara* was purpose-built for the Arctic with stout cross-beams and steel plates to help it withstand the pressure of the shifting ice floes. After sailing from Tromso in Norway on 4 July, they found Smith alive and well at the Matochkin Shar where the ice had crushed his ship.

Despite the best efforts of his wife – who had an artificial lake built at Lissadell to provide him with fish – Sir Henry would continue to voyage for the next fifteen years. Packed into glass cases in Lissadell were the souvenirs of those adventures: a variety of birds, a great salmon, a bear that had nearly killed Kilgallon, walrus tusks and the skull of a bottle-nosed whale. Constance grew up with these souvenirs and, according to her stepson Staskou, regarded her father as the 'beau idéal'.

Although a man of great energy, Sir Henry was no politician. In spite of this, he dutifully played his part in the local community, serving on juries, presiding over the annual agricultural show and spending many years on the board of guardians for Sligo. He was happy to accept the status quo. In the gilded world of the Anglo-Irish, it was the unscrupulous landlords who gave the system a bad name; the system itself was neither questioned nor discussed.

In the winter of 1879, when Constance was twelve, famine returned to Ireland after thirty years and many starving tenants were evicted. Sir Henry reduced rents and, with his wife and the three older children, he visited all his tenants, providing food, clothing and even hay for bedding. If any tenants were forced into the workhouse, he would keep their cabins safe for them. He maintained that this was all he could do and stated that there were only six evictions at Lissadell, all of them of 'idlers who would neither work nor pay'. His attitude may have been paternalistic, but his children, especially the older three, grew up with a solid sense of their obligations to society. Still, times were changing.

Earlier in 1879, in neighbouring County Mayo, Michael Davitt had begun a campaign for land reform that would result in the Irish National Land League. In that year alone, over 6,000 tenants were evicted from their homes; a year later the figure stood at 10,457 and, in the four years following, 23,000 were forced from their homes. Protesters inevitably ended up in jail.

The Land League, led by Charles Stewart Parnell, a charismatic young Protestant landlord from County Wicklow, held its first conference in October 1879. The Land League's aims were simple: they would defend tenants threatened with eviction and would force the government to subsidise tenant buy-outs of their land. They would organise and create a fuss – a philosophy later embraced wholeheartedly by Constance Gore-Booth.

The Land League's first meeting in County Sligo took place at Gurteen, part of the Gore-Booth estate, on 2 November 1879 and attracted 8,000 men and women. Michael Davitt was one of the speakers, along with James Daly, a newspaper owner, and James Boyce, a barrister. All three were subsequently arrested for sedition. 'The Gurteen Three' returned to Sligo on 25 November for their trial, when all charges were dropped.

In the land war of 1879 to 1892, the tenant farmers of Ireland, resentful of their 'foreign' landlords, showed their defiance for the first time. A new word was added to the English language when Captain Boycott of Lough Mask House, County Mayo, was ostracised for his opposition to the Land League. At times, the agitation erupted into violence and outrage, with ordinary law ceasing to function; the occasional estate agent or landlord was shot. Even Sir Henry, who, as a 'good' landlord, was invited to attend a Land League 'Monster Meeting' in Ballymote in 1880, received threatening letters from one of the many secret societies that flourished at the time.

The Land League, like Sinn Féin later on, set up its own courts and government and, with Davitt preaching that women should take over while men were in jail, the Ladies' Land League was founded, with his sister, Anna Parnell, as secretary. When the Land Act was finally passed in the House of Commons in 1881, it guaranteed the three Fs: fair rent, fixity of tenure and freedom of sale. That was not enough for Charles Parnell and the Land League and they opposed the bill on the grounds that Irish tenants should not have to pay rent to foreign-based, absentee landowners. Parnell was arrested and the Land League declared a rent strike, with Anna and the Ladies' Land League helping keep the organisation active. For the first time, women became involved in public life, attending mass meetings and taking over from their fathers, brothers and husbands. This was often to the mortification of the men, who feared ridicule for their reliance on mere women. Under the Coercion Act, Parnell and other leaders were arrested in October 1881, and both the Land League and the Ladies' Land League were banned. The women were arrested under statutes designed to curb prostitution, one of the few existing laws relating to women.

British political leaders had realised that the landlord system could no longer be defended and, under the Kilmainham Treaty of March 1882, which was agreed between the British Liberal prime minister, William Gladstone, and Parnell, prisoners were released and the agitation came to an end. The more moderate Irish National League was founded without a women's section. By then, Sir Henry was remarking that his tenants were less trustworthy and also less friendly. Yet at Lissadell, in January 1887, a meeting of Sir Henry's tenants decided to go on paying rent to the estate since 'Sir Henry always held at heart the welfare of the people'.

The troubles were by no means over. After Parnell was released, Lord Frederick Cavendish was sent to Ireland as Chief Secretary to inaugurate what everyone hoped would be a new period of peaceful co-operation. On 6 May 1882, the day of his arrival, while walking in Dublin's Phoenix Park, Cavendish and his under-secretary, Thomas Henry Burke, were murdered by members of 'The Invincibles', a radical splinter group from the Irish Republican Brotherhood. Although Parnell condemned the murders, Gladstone immediately passed a new Coercion Act. Three days later, despite much opposition, he brought in the Arrears Bill that allowed tenants of land worth less than £30 a year to cancel their arrears. The number of agrarian crimes dropped.

Parnell saw the ending of landlordism as a step towards the overthrow of English rule in Ireland. In the general election of 1885, the Irish National League won every seat except East Ulster and Dublin University. When re-elected, Gladstone, recognising 'the fixed desire of the nation', put forward the first Home Rule Bill in 1886. It was greeted with howls of disapproval by the Conservatives, as well as by the aristocratic landlords of the Liberal Party, who saw it as a betrayal of the British Empire.

The bill was defeated and Gladstone lost office in the ensuing general election, the first to be fought in Britain on the Home Rule question and a turning point in Britain's relations with Ireland. Supporting Home Rule did not help the Liberal cause – in the next twenty years, the Liberals were to hold office for only one period of three years between 1892 and 1895. Ireland was to dominate the public debate in Britain until the First World War began in 1914.

Constance grew up in this politically charged atmosphere and she never lost her attachment to her Sligo roots and its troubled history:

> and history had laid her fingers on each mountain wall, and trusted her secrets with each little blade of grass pushing up to life from the blood-drenched soil that was the burying place of generation after generation with their dreams of freedom and peace; their lives of battle and pain. The mighty tomb of Medb, up among the storm winds of the mountain-top, the great raths and druid stones on the plains called to you in the voice of Ireland's great ones. The voices of the *sidhe* murmured of imperishable glories, white hands beckoned and unearthly music drew you into the secret and holy places haunted by shadows and dreams of the splendour of that Ireland that is unconquered and unconquerable.

On her native province she would write:

> And this was Connaught, the Connaught whither Cromwell banished the tradition of the Gael in all its splendour when he and his horde of barbarians trampled the ancient beauty that is Ireland

into the mud with blood-stained feet, and with incendiary torch and dripping blade and with – oh, mockery! – the words of the Prince of Peace on his lips, brought ruin to a world-old civilisation, and misery to a helpless people.

Her attachment to the land was visceral and fundamental.

CHAPTER TWO

Under Ben Bulben

For the young Constance, life at Lissadell was idyllic. The Gore-Booth children, with their Wynne cousins from the neighbouring estate of Hazelwood, spent their summers sailing, fishing and riding. In winter, they learned to shoot and to hunt. The family showed horses at the annual agricultural show and sometimes at the Dublin Horse Show, which, for the Ascendancy class, was the social highlight of the year. In Constance's early childhood, the household included her grandfather, who died in 1876, and the formidable Aunt Augusta, her father's sister, known as 'Wee Ga' because of her diminutive size; Constance's mother was known as 'Ga'.

Constance would grow up 'intimate with the soft mists and the coloured mountains'. Each morning she awoke 'to the sounds of the wild birds' or 'the wake of the corncrake that told how the summer sun was risen'. In the local fields, she could rejoice in a 'tossing multitude of big white daisies, swaying and bending, taking colour and a shining joy from the kiss of the sun, and shrinking away into a dim, opalescent mystery under each passing cloud'.

Like her mother and aunt, Constance soon became a fearless and skilful rider. Her father gave her a pony when she was four years old and instructed one of the Lissadell staff to lead her out to the lawn at a gentle trot. She was soon kicking the pony to make it go faster and she galloped away on her own. She won her first pony race when she was fourteen at the County Sligo Hunt and rode side saddle with the County Sligo Harriers hunt every Tuesday and Friday during the winter. She learned to drive a coach-and-four. Locals remembered her galloping across Moffet's Burra from Lissadell to visit the Ashleys at Classiebawn Castle.

From her father, she inherited a love of adventure and an ability to handle guns. He would bring her on shooting parties chasing pheasant and woodcock at the Mountain Plantation at Ben Bulben or in the nearby bogs. He taught her to stalk the deer he had introduced to the estate.

Later, the poet William Butler Yeats remembered her gallant and daring horsemanship in his poem 'On a Political Prisoner':

> When long ago I saw her ride
> Under Ben Bulben to the meet,
> The beauty of her country-side
> With all youth's lonely wildness stirred,
> She seemed to have grown clean and sweet
> Like any rock-bred, sea-borne bird.

Constance was a much-loved and happy child; she was outgoing, healthy, quick-witted and intelligent. She enjoyed being the centre of attention and worked hard at anything that interested her. Her brother Josslyn, next to her in age, was more serious, while her sister Eva was quieter and more introspective and never to enjoy good health, although she was as fearless a horse rider as her sister. Since Sligo was one of the most 'planted' of Irish counties, there were plenty of neighbours of her own class to visit and hunt with. As well as the Wynne cousins, other relatives lived nearby. Lord Shaftesbury and the Leslies, frequent guests of Lord Palmerstown at Classiebawn Castle, were family friends.

Constance's kindness and good heart were obvious from an early age. The son of a groom at Lissadell remembered the young Constance insisting on taking over when his mother, who was heavily pregnant, was washing clothes in a tub in the kitchen. On another occasion, she sat up all night with his father who was suffering from pneumonia. With Eva, she would ride out and visit tenants in their homes, and both of them were liable to give away the clothes on their backs to those in need.

On those visits, sitting around the turf fire, the 'country people', as they were always called, told them stories of the fairies, of Queen

Maeve, and of Irish heroes such as Wolfe Tone and the men of 1798. Later, Constance would say that her first political inspiration had come from her own 'desolate home county' and the 'dispossessed people' she grew up among. There is a story that, as a young woman, she called a strike of her father's tenants and encouraged them not to pay their rent. When asked why, she pointed out to her father that they needed the money more than he did. In this small world, visiting Sligo, only ten miles away, was an event. It was a lively town, with a population of 11,000 and plenty of shops and a busy harbour, visited by an estimated 500 ships every year; the town hosted regular regattas and rowing races.

In August came the annual trip to Dublin for the Horse Show. In those pre-car days, such journeys were undertaken by train, since the railway had arrived in Sligo amid great fanfare in 1862. At the Horse Show, horses were bought and sold and, for all ages, there were riding and show-jumping competitions, as well as sideshows, handcraft displays, balls and parties. An occasional visit to London, 'the centre of the Universe!', as Constance described it, caused almost unbearable excitement.

Autumn brought the annual 'Harvest Home' for workers and tenants, held from the 1840s in the 'Riding School', a large barn used for exercising horses indoors. After tea, served by members of the Gore-Booth family, came a sing-song and other entertainments and then a final supper before everyone left at around 11pm. In winter, the flocks of barnacle geese arrived on their annual retreat from the freezing Arctic; during the summer, there was cricket on the lawn and trips to Knocknarea.

Constance would later observe that

> In Ireland, as I dare say in other countries, people live in air-tight compartments. They rarely seem to get outside the particular gas they are born in, and those who do so find it very difficult, once they have extricated themselves, to thrive and develop in the new atmosphere. So it was with me.

Like most girls of their class, Constance and Eva were educated at home by governesses, with Miss Noel, or 'Squidge' as she was known, the most enduring of them. The brothers were sent to boarding school in England. Before Squidge arrived, the girls' learning had not stretched much beyond music, poetry, French, drawing and the recitation of verse from books. 'Twenty Minutes' by Harriet Child Pemberton, a collection of drawing-room dialogues, was a favourite. Both Constance and Eva inherited their mother's love of drawing and sketching. Constance's favourite subjects initially were her beloved horses, soon followed by drawings of local people going about their business. Squidge introduced them to the classics and attempted to extend their education beyond the conventional. Constance admitted to the limits of her education later on: 'No one was interested in politics in our house. It was rare that anyone mentioned them'. The status quo was accepted 'almost as if it had been the will of God'. It was there 'just like the mountains and the sea were, and it was absurd to try and alter it for that led nowhere and only caused trouble'.

Nor did the girls learn much of history: 'Irish history was also taboo, for "what is the good of brooding over past grievances?" But history is being written on every fence and boundary wall'. Although a restless child, Constance applied herself enough to learn German and later Italian, as well as French. She could quote large chunks of Schiller, Heine, Goethe and Dante, a habit she continued into adulthood, as a fellow prisoner in Aylesbury jail later remembered.

Constance grew into a tall, attractive, willowy young woman, slender but robust, with thick, waist-length, brown hair. She was full of vitality and attracted the admiration of all who knew her, despite her direct manner and occasional lapses into tactlessness. Her lifelong interest in the theatre was ignited by the amateur dramatics enjoyed by the family in the long winter evenings. Sir Henry stage-managed, Lady Georgina and Aunt Augusta provided the musical accompaniment on piano and violin, and the children, along with any guests, played the parts. They wrote their own pieces for performances, such as a sketch written by Eva called *A Daughter of Eve, or Alphonso's Bride*, which was based on the Bluebeard story.

Constance witnessed at first hand a darker side of Irish rural life when, in the wet and chilly summer of 1879, the potato harvest failed and the Lissadell tenants faced starvation. When Lady Georgina set up a food distribution centre at Lissadell, her children worked with her.

When Constance was twelve and Eva ten, the artist Sarah Purser came to Lissadell, at the invitation of Lady Georgina, to paint portraits of the family. After the Lissadell commission, Purser became a popular society artist, going through the British aristocracy – in her own words – 'like the measles' – and making a good living through her art. She remembered Constance as a lovely child, 'idolised and spoilt and always so good-hearted in her absurdities', although she preferred the more reserved Eva, who was easier to manage. In her portrait, the sisters pose in the open air as if gathering flowers, with Constance, the future warrior, sitting and wearing a hat, and Eva, the future poet, kneeling at her feet.

Around this time, Constance was driving through the local village of Cliffoney with her father when a Land League meeting was taking place. Stopping the carriage to see what all the excitement was about, she heard Parnell's secretary, Thomas Sexton, later a local MP, addressing a large crowd near Cummin's Hotel. She heard him tell the story of her grandfather Sir Robert Gore-Booth and of how he had 'banished the people of the Seven Cartrons and sent them to sea on a rotten boat'. Sexton's speech made a deep impression and turned her into an ardent supporter of tenants' rights.

Middle- and upper-class girls from a Protestant background were fortunate to have role models such as Anna Parnell and her sister Fanny, as well as Isabella Tod, Anna Haslam and Anne Jellicoe, all active campaigners for women's educational and legal rights at the time. Catholic girls had few such role models; their choices in life were between a good marriage or retreat to the convent.

Life for Constance revolved around the twice-weekly hunts. Her first horse, Max, given to her by Aunt Augusta, was named after a hero in German literature. According to Edward Rowlett, master of the Sligo Hunt Club, the fearless Constance was 'altogether outside the ordinary realm of competition' as a horsewoman and never took 'a bad toss'. She had the gift of light hands and Max enjoyed a comfortable old age without a scar to show for his earlier days galloping over the hedges and ditches of County Sligo. Constance loved a practical joke and Rowlett – her willing sidekick in many adventures – remembered a jape when she planned to blow up a munitions magazine belonging to the Sligo Militia at Rosses Point; bad weather scuppered the idea.

Then there was her interference in a local argument between the Church of Ireland and the Methodists, involving the use of the school hall for Methodist services. The vicar, hardly likely to promote the services of his rivals, was not happy. So Constance, Mabel, Eva and Edward attached an announcement of the Methodist services to the steeple of the church, with the precarious climb up the collapsible ladder left to Rowlett. After the incident, Constance sent him an anonymous blackmail note demanding money. If he wished his part in the adventure to remain secret, he should come to the road from the church between midnight and 2am. On his way, Rowlett met two figures he thought were Constance and Mabel dressed as policemen. He pursued them only to discover that they were members of the Royal Irish Constabulary.

From their regular visits to their tenants' houses, Constance and Eva were familiar with the tales of the 'little people' or *sidhe*, who, on significant days such as *Bealtaine* (1 May), *Lúnasa* (1 August) and *Samhain* (1 November) were unusually active. To keep them at bay, gifts of flowers, such as primroses, gorse or hawthorn blossoms, were gathered before dawn and placed in bundles on door posts. One *Bealtaine*, Constance concocted an elaborate charade, with her sister Mabel dressing as a prince and she herself as a princess. They knocked on the door of a local family and, after they were let in, danced to the accompaniment of a musical instrument described as 'numerous gadgets dangling'. The seven girls and three boys of the house cowered behind their mother in terror at the sight.

Another adventure, recorded in her diary for 1893, concerned a bet she made with two young men staying at Lissadell that she would beg from them on the high road and that they wouldn't recognise her. 'My grand joke comes off. Armed with an old ass, a child (Mickey Mashy) and much broken crockery, we arrange the tableau on the high road.' The donkey was saddled with panniers whose bottoms opened at the touch of a lever. As the men approached, she tipped the lever and the crockery fell out. After enduring much wailing and hand-wringing, the lads gave her money to replace the crockery. Having won her bet, Constance returned the cash to them later that day.

On another occasion, she came to the back door of Lissadell dressed as a beggar woman and was turned away. On another occasion, also dressed as a beggar, she accosted a man she considered unkind to poor people. As she expected, he let fly at her and she then made herself known. It was not the only time she embarrassed a man she felt was behaving badly. At dinner one evening she found the wandering hand of an older admirer on her knee. 'Just look what I have found in my lap!' she proclaimed, picking up the offending hand.

She had a tandem of her own invention that she attached to the ponies Kelpie and Storeen, and from which she could dump an unsuspecting passenger. At one time, she had a pet monkey; she also had a tame snake she liked to wear around her neck. She was the centre of attention: threading oranges for the Christmas tree she always decorated, elected as Beauty Queen of the West at a charity do, sailing her little boat, galloping around the estate and, in quieter moments, reciting poetry while lying on the hearthrug. A favourite room in Lissadell House was the 'Glory Hole', an anteroom situated between the drawing room and the dining room, where Constance painted and read and sometimes dined with friends. She cut her name into the pane of glass, along with some of the other children. Her bedroom was a small room leading out of the nursery, looking south over Drumcliff Bay to distant Knocknarea.

In 1886, Constance went on the 'Grand Tour' with Squidge, spending six months travelling. She especially loved Florence – the Duomo, San Miniato and Fiesole – and devoted her time to copying old masters, taking private drawing lessons, learning Italian and tormenting Squidge with practical jokes. Later she would say that she soon tired of the 'intense respectability' of the tour and its associated social round. Around this time, she became secretly engaged to one of her hunting friends, Philip Dudley Perceval of Temple House in Ballymote. Since he had no fortune to fall back on, he took himself off to Australia and the romance fizzled out; he would later marry her cousin Muriel Wynne.

On her return from Europe, all that was left was an introduction to society in London and Dublin, with the goal of finding a suitable husband. Only the grandest members of the Irish aristocracy attended the London season. The year 1887 saw Queen Victoria's jubilee celebrations and, when Lady Georgina called a meeting to decide on a gift for the Queen from the town of Sligo, Constance attended and helped to collect funds.

In the other Ireland that year, William O'Brien, the Parnellite editor of the *United Irishman*, was jailed under Balfour's Coercion Act after organising a rent strike in Mitchelstown, County Cork. Demonstrations at his arrest led to the police shooting dead three tenant farmers. In prison, O'Brien refused to wear convict clothes and lay in bed naked for weeks before a sympathetic warder smuggled in a suit.

Such disturbances barely touched the lives of the better off. The 'season' officially opened in mid-February with the Lord Lieutenant's Levee, followed by the Ladies' Drawing Room the next day. It ended with the St Patrick's Ball on 17 March, which was attended not only by 'the Castle set' but also by the professional classes. By the 1880s, thanks to a period of relative prosperity in the country, Dublin had smartened up. According to Elizabeth Bowen, 'Viceregal hospitality was lavish, private hospitality kept the pace, and there were memorable regimental balls.'

An admirer of Constance at the time was Sir Alexander Godley of the Royal Dublin Fusiliers whose family came from nearby Killegar, County Leitrim. He included Constance in a list of local beauties and recalled a weekend at Lissadell, when the charming eldest daughter of the house made the men throw their caps in the air so she could shoot at them.

On St Patrick's Day, 17 March 1887, Constance made her formal entry to society when she was presented to the Queen in London. Her sponsor was the Countess of Erroll, lady-in-waiting to the Queen and a cousin of Lady Georgina. In the society columns, Constance was described as 'the new Irish beauty'. She was now officially eligible for marriage and four months of frivolity followed – balls and parties at night; luncheon parties, shopping and horse-riding by day. At Ascot, she wore a pale-blue gown draped with old lace; on another occasion, a more daring red dress slashed with black stripes, and topped by a hat with three ostrich feathers provoked much comment. It was a stiff and formal world and something of a trial for a wild Irish woman who preferred the outdoors.

On 22 June, the final day of Victoria's jubilee, a committee of Irish women, led by the vicereine, Lady Londonderry, presented the Queen with an Irish bog oak casket containing over 150,000 signatures of loyalty from her Irish subjects. Lady Georgina's work was done; she and Constance returned to Ireland in late July in good time for the annual Horse Show Week, where a highlight was a garden party at the Viceregal Lodge in the Phoenix Park.

Lord Londonderry was followed as viceroy by the more diffident Lord Zetland, who was married to a cousin of Lady Georgina; they would remain in Ireland from 1889 until 1892. His wife started a fashion for theme balls, such as a White Ball, and for the season, Lady Georgina would borrow a house at Harcourt Terrace, known then as Joly's Buildings, from her cousins the Coffeys. When on the run in 1798, the Irish rebel Lord Edward Fitzgerald had used a dried-up well in the garden as a hiding place.

Since Lady Georgina was often unwell, the redoubtable Elizabeth, Lady Fingall chaperoned Constance when she came to Dublin. Although only three years older than her charge, Lady Fingall was considered a respectable married woman. She remembered Constance as 'a wild beautiful child and all the young men wanted to dance with her ... she was the life and soul of any party'. She was also 'a stormy petrel from the beginning to the end'.

A typical incident occurred when, returning from a ball at Dublin Castle to Harcourt Terrace, Constance and Lady Fingall found a drunken soldier clinging to the house railings and singing loudly. After assuring her companion that she could handle drunks, Constance persuaded him to move on. He wandered off but soon the serenading resumed. This time, the two ladies, by then wearing dressing gowns, slippers – and in Lady Fingall's case, a tiara – succeeded in getting the drunken soldier to go away. There was no question of calling the police. 'She had sympathy with him, even then. For he must be absent without leave, and would get into trouble,' wrote Lady Fingall in her memoirs.

By the time Lord Zetland was appointed Lord Lieutenant, the Parnell scandal had split Ireland in two and even the Gore-Booth children were aware of it. In her sketch *A Daughter of Eve*, or *Alphonso's Bride*, Eva had referred to both Parnell and his deadly rival Timothy Michael Healy.

> Let's go and listen at the door ... If it's Mr Parnell himself
> He mightn't enjoy being put on the shelf
> If it's Mr Healy, he'll rage and shout ...

In 1890, when Parnell was at the peak of his powers, Captain William O'Shea obtained a divorce from his estranged wife Kitty on the grounds of her ten-year liaison with Parnell. This relationship was a marriage in all but name, which had produced three children and had not troubled O'Shea until this point. The ensuing scandal was a gift to Parnell's opponents in Dublin Castle and the British Conservative Party and the effect, both on Parnell's career and on Irish politics, was devastating. British Liberals, who had rallied to Gladstone's crusade for Home Rule as a great moral issue, took the view that Parnell was no longer a fit person to lead the Irish Parliamentary Party. Gladstone reluctantly suggested that he resign. Parnell's refusal forced a bitter split in his party, led by the cantankerous Healy. Parnell continued to fight for the leadership until his sudden death, aged only 45, on 6 October 1891, five months after he had married Mrs O'Shea. Irish politics would take over a decade to recover.

In March 1891, just a few months before his death, Constance and Eva shocked locals when they rode at the head of a procession escorting Parnell through the streets of Sligo as he campaigned for the North Sligo by-election. Another version of the story has them borrowing two horses and riding secretly to the meeting at Grange, just north of Lissadell. Their motives were unclear. Lady Zetland was staying at their house and they may have wished to shock her; they may have seen Parnell as a tragic hero, or they could have been motivated by mere curiosity.

Judging from her diary of the time, Constance, now aged twenty-three, remained indifferent to national politics although sensitive to local matters and always taking the side of the underdog. The diary, kept sporadically for 1892, begins on 1 January with a description of a shooting party attended by her cousin Lord Dunraven and a neighbour, Wilfred Ashley, to whom she was attracted. After he left on 3 January she wrote: 'Such a dull lonely feeling waking up and knowing the friend is gone. What is it that makes me so fond of him, something deep down somewhere in both of us that meets and meets.'

Wilfred returns to Lissadell between 9 and 14 January for a play called *Pilot Rosalie*. She is 'in the blues' after mortally offending him in some way she clearly did not quite understand. Whatever she did, Wilfred refused to dance with her. Next day, they avoid each other 'with determination' until, out shooting, he offers her a piece of chocolate; all is forgiven. On her twenty-fourth birthday, they went fishing for trout in a collapsible boat 'with scores of cushions and rugs'. 'We rowed into the mud to steady ourselves and fixed our little ship steady by sticking an oar into the mud and ate our frugal meal *tête-à-tête*. It was an idyll.' Because he sprained an ankle, Wilfred stayed longer than expected. When he left on 6 February, she missed fussing over him. 'It is so good to have someone to look after ... seek out stray draughts for and run messages for. It's rather nice to be indispensable to someone.' Her feelings were not reciprocated. Later Wilfred would become a Conservative MP and Minister of Transport. His daughter Edwina married Lord Mountbatten.

In February, Constance was in London as the guest of her cousin Josslyn, Lord Muncaster, in Carlton Gardens. Josslyn brought her shopping and gave her 'many pretty things'. She attended the Victorian Exhibition, which she found vulgar and tasteless, and went dancing at 'the club' with her cousin Rhoda L'Estrange, later Countess of Carlisle. There was also church at St Paul's and a fancy dress ball in Malmesbury, where she met an old friend and 'danced a good deal with him'.

She read Ouida's romantic novel *Ariadne* and loved it, 'unnatural and overstrained' though it was. It made her think of love and how she had not found herself a 'god' as had her sister Mabel, who adored her fiancé Percy Foster, a 'good-hearted, thoroughly English' chap, who loved her as well as 'men do love'. Yet Constance is not sure if that is what she wants. 'Every thought a contradiction tonight ...'

Later she writes: 'Women are made to adore and sacrifice themselves, and I as a woman demand as a right that Nature should provide me with something to live for, something to die for. Why should I alone never experience the best and, at the same time, the worst of life's gifts?'

Riding horses remained a passion. On her return from the London visit on 2 April, she arranged to be met at the train station by her horse Max for the final hunt of the season. A week later, she was in the garden planting a beautiful bed of white Arabis with coloured hyacinths. Her love of gardening would endure. She was also up to her usual mischief, stealing and hiding a cow and calf belonging to the Dillon family and leaving the poor owners to wander the local roads and paths calling 'Sucky sucky'. In the spring, she travelled to Dublin for the Kildare Hunt

Races in Punchestown. This time, she stayed at the Viceregal Lodge in the Phoenix Park and attended dances, one of them at Lady Iveagh's, and visited her aunt, May Wynne, whose son Graham was an admirer.

In late May, Sir Henry was preparing for his Arctic expedition to find Leigh Smith. He anchored his newly bought ketch, the *Kara,* off Lissadell for two weeks before sailing north for Tromso and Novaya Zemlan. Constance spent several days aboard the yacht, enjoying, among other activities, an elaborate dinner, followed by songs and dances from the crew. The only damper on the night was the arrival of her mother: 'Mama came on board to sit in judgement, which stiffened our marrow and wet our spirits.' Constance showed no signs of wishing to join her father on the expedition although it was 'so dreary and sad' watching the ship sailing away and 'getting smaller and smaller'.

Inspired perhaps by Sarah Purser, Constance had decided that she wanted to study art. From the time she could hold a pencil, she had loved to sketch and doodle. In the margins of the Bible she owned as a child are sketches of her beloved horses. On her return to London for 'the season', in May 1892, she spent over four hours a day drawing and painting 'with Miss Nordgren and Miss Griffin'. Anna Nordgren was a Finnish artist, then aged forty-six, based at the Bolton Studios off Fulham Road in London. At this time, Constance decided she wanted to study abroad: 'If I could cut the family tie and have a life and interest of my own I should want no other heaven,' she says in her diary. 'If I was sure of myself and knew I could succeed for sure and make a name or more to the point money I would live on a crust. But to do all that with the chance of having to return and throw oneself on the charity of one's family a miserable failure is more than I can screw up my courage to face.'

In late July, Lady Georgina, along with Constance, Eva and Rachel Mansfield, went to Germany for the opera at Bayreuth. While listening to *Tannenhauser, Parsifal* and *The Mastersingers*, and visiting Wagner's grave and house, as well as Cologne Cathedral, Constance captured the scenes with her sketches, often attracting an audience of children. Back home, she travelled to Dublin for the Horse Show 'and for Economy went by the slow train. Damn Economy say I.' She missed Wilfred. At some point, she visited Castle Leslie in County Monaghan.

That winter, she painted and sketched, went to wood-carving classes in Sligo and hunted once the season began. In January, Eva and

Constance went to a house party in Adare, County Limerick, home of the Earl of Dunraven, a cousin of Sir Henry's. A guest at Adare was Lord Randolph Churchill who, within six weeks, would make his final parliamentary speech. There was much talk of the Irish question at Adare, but Constance made no comment. She did express annoyance that the servants' party was stopped at midnight, however, even though Lord and Lady Dunraven had said it could continue as long as they liked. Their own ball, a night earlier, had gone on until 5am. On 4 February, Constance turned twenty-five. She had a low-key day with no birthday cake and only one present.

In March, Constance was present at a unionist demonstration in Sligo Town Hall against Gladstone's Home Rule bill. She records how she 'Declined to be among the aristocracy and sat in the hall and drew caricatures of the speakers.' In April, while a guest of the Zetlands in England, she attended an anti-Home Rule meeting at Richmond in Yorkshire. Lord Zetland, who was presiding, predicted that the bill would lead to unstoppable social revolutions, while Lord Ashbourne, as principal speaker, warned of this 'calamitous bill'. Constance approved, stating: 'Lord Ashbourne a real angel, speaks splendidly.' She could still be unthinkingly unionist. On its second reading, the bill was carried by the Commons, but was defeated in the House of Lords.

In 1893, Constance enrolled at the Slade School of Fine Art at University College London. By this time, Alphonse Legros, the renowned Slade professor, had retired. Frederick Brown, a member of the New English Art Club, the avant-garde group influenced by the French Impressionists, replaced him. Among the places Constance lodged was the Alexandra House Hostel for Girl Art Students, founded by Sir Francis Cook, a great-uncle of Maud Gonne's. Inevitably, Constance got into trouble; she arrived back late one evening after a night out with a cousin, probably Graham Wynne, well past the locking-up time of ten o'clock. When she was forced to find a hotel for the night and was then told to quit the hostel, she wrote a furious letter to her father, who in turn, got in touch with Sir Francis. Despite an apology and the promise of a more lenient locking-up time of 10.30pm, she refused to go back to the hostel. Her long-suffering father set her up in a studio of her own at Stanley Chambers.

She continued to work with Anna Nordgren and exhibited with her at the Society of Women Artists. Later Anna Nordgren came to

Lissadell and the pair painted out of doors, with Constance's technique improving all the time. A letter dating from that time asks her to submit one or two sketches for the election of new members to the 91 Club of women artists, founded by Nordgren. She was duly elected.

Like many women at the Slade, she was infatuated by Henry Tonks, one of the teachers, who was ostentatiously dedicated to his art and scathingly critical of his pupils. Constance upset him with her provocative gestures – sitting astride her 'donkey' (drawing stool), winking at him across the room, taking a bun from a bag and stuffing it suggestively into her mouth. A fashion of the time was 'rinking' or roller-skating and, on one occasion, Constance managed to run into Tonks at full speed, knocking him down. She had the manners of the kitchen maid, he complained.

While in London, Constance met the poet W.B. Yeats after inviting him to Bryanston Square where she was staying with friends. They met for lunch a few times and, in 1894, he gave her an inscribed copy of his play *The Land of Heart's Desire*, which had been produced in London the previous March. Although the play was not a success, Yeats's name was becoming known and, with his long flowing cloaks and flamboyant hats, he looked every inch a poet. Like many intellectuals of the time, Yeats was dabbling in mysticism and the occult and would introduce Constance to the Hermetic Order of the Golden Dawn, of which their mutual friend Althea Gyles was also a member. The popular interest in the occult was not unknown to Constance; her grandfather had conducted séances in an attempt to communicate with the dead in Lissadell. For her part, Constance tried to persuade Yeats to fight a duel after she and Anna Nordgren were insulted by a man called Brown.

Constance returned home often, riding out with her beloved Max. She took part in a drag race of the Sligo Harriers on 27 March 1894, where she would have finished first had she not been led astray by a crowd at the final fence. Around this time, she became the only woman in Ireland to ride in a point-to-point race and she won many more admirers for her skills.

Parnell's fall had provoked widespread disillusionment with politics and, to fill the vacuum, the educated classes turned their attention to Irish culture. In 1893, Douglas Hyde, Eoin MacNeill and Father Eugene

O'Growney started Conradh na Gaeilge (The Gaelic League), a movement designed to popularise the Irish language, as well as Irish music, literature, dancing and games. Literary figures, such as Yeats, Lady Gregory, J.M. Synge and George Russell (Æ) looked to a romanticised version of their Gaelic past for inspiration.

During the winter of 1894–5, Yeats, then aged twenty-nine, was spending six months with his uncle George Pollexfen at his house, Thornhill, outside Sligo. He visited the Gore-Booths in Lissadell often, staying with them twice. 'A very pleasant, kindly, inflammable family, ever ready to take up new ideas and new things,' he wrote of the family after his first visit. At the time, Constance was collecting autographs and he supplied her with those of John O'Leary, Katharine Tynan, Douglas Hyde, Æ and Standish O'Grady. When Constance was jailed in 1916, he wrote to Eva of his happy memories. 'Your sister and yourself, two beautiful figures among the great trees at Lissadell, are among the dearest memories of my youth,' he said.

Fletcher Le Fanu, a nephew of the author Sheridan Le Fanu, and the vicar at Lissadell, invited Yeats to give a talk on Irish folklore at the school house in Lissadell. Yeats described the experience in a letter to his sister Lily: 'I lectured in the school house on fairy lore chiefly to an audience of Orangemen. It was a novel experience. I found that the comic tales delighted them but that the poetry of fairy lore was quite lost on them. They held it Catholic superstition I suppose.'

The family itself, including the ailing Aunt Augusta, were more receptive to his stories. Ghosts or spirits made occasional appearances in the lives of the Gore-Booths. At Lissadell, Mordaunt was reported to have seen a house boy in the hall, not knowing that he had died a few hours earlier. In her prison cell at Aylesbury in 1916, Constance felt the presence of a former prisoner, who never spoke but often kept her company. She wondered if he was Irish.

Yeats was collecting folklore at the time and the Gore-Booths introduced him to tenants, whose stories he adapted for his book *Mythologies*. He spent most of his time with Eva, in his view a promising poet, and told her of his unhappy love for Maud Gonne; his stories of Gonne's independent life may well have influenced the sisters. Constance sketched him one night while he sat talking to her younger sister. Josslyn hated Yeats.

Yeats passed on his impressions of Lissadell and its inhabitants. Aunt Augusta was fiercely strong-willed and, while 'mostly invisible, is always more or less there like an iron claw. She is very much a Tory and cares for nothing but horses.' Around the table, he remembered the 'talk of youth' and he was impressed by the house, especially the impressive sitting room with its 'great windows open to the south'. He wrote to Katharine Tynan that 'These people are much better educated than our own people and have a better instinct for excellence.'

Sir Henry he dismissed as thinking 'of nothing but the North Pole, where his first officer, to his great satisfaction, has recently lost himself and thereby made an expedition to rescue him desirable'.

Josslyn is 'much troubled by his wealth and almost painfully conscientious'. He was 'theoretically' a Home Ruler, not 'particularly' clever, and without much will.

This was not entirely fair to Josslyn: when it came to the management of the farm, he worked hard on improving methods of production, with mixed results. He had spent two years studying farm methods in Canada and the USA and became a keen supporter of the co-operative movement. Sir Horace Plunkett had founded the Irish Agricultural Organisation Society in 1894, encouraging farmers to band together and sell their own produce, cutting out middlemen. In June 1895, Josslyn set up the Drumcliff Dairy Society, the first of its kind in Sligo. At a fancy dress ball organised by Colonel Campbell, Master of the Sligo Hounds, Constance and Eva went dressed as Drumcliff Co-operative dairymaids.

While Josslyn was promoting co-operation among small farmers, his sisters became suffragists. Following the Reform Acts of 1832, 1867 and 1888, men with property could vote. Between 1870 and 1882, when a series of acts allowed married women to own property, the right of these women to a vote was hotly debated. In 1866, when John Stuart Mill presented the first petition seeking the vote for women, there were twenty-six Irish signatories. In 1872, Isabella Tod formed the first Irish suffrage society in Belfast. This was followed in 1874 by the Dublin Women's Suffrage Association founded by Anna Haslam, a Quaker from Youghal. In 1876 came the Irish Women's Suffrage and Local Government Association with Haslam as secretary. The movement proved slow to spread. Only the decision in 1896 to allow women to act as Poor Law guardians stirred the movement back into action. Two years later, women of property would get the right to vote in local elections.

On Christmas Eve 1896, following a private meeting to set up a local committee, Constance, Eva and Mabel Gore-Booth attended a public meeting to promote women's suffrage in the Milltown National School in Drumcliff. Banners decorated the walls of the hall: 'Who would be free themselves must strike a blow', 'No taxation without representation' and 'Liberty, Justice and Equality'. The room was packed, mostly with curious men; Sir Henry and Lady Georgina also attended. 'Amusing Proceedings' headlined the *Sligo Champion* in its report of the meeting.

Constance opened the meeting in her first recorded speech and proved herself a born rabble-rouser.

> Now in order to attain any political reform, you all know that the first step is to form societies to agitate and force the government to realise that a very large class have a grievance, and will never stop making themselves disagreeable till it is righted. John Stuart Mill said thirty years ago that the only forcible argument against giving women the suffrage was that they did not demand it with sufficient force and noise. Silence is an evil that might easily be remedied, and the sooner we begin to make a row the better.

She pointed out in Britain 247,000 had signed a petition demanding the vote for women, up from 11,000 in 1873. It proved a rowdy meeting and she showed an aptitude for handling hecklers, a vital skill for a public speaker. When one man shouted: 'If my wife went to vote she might never come back'. Constance replied 'She must think very little of you then.'

Her sister Mabel nervously spoke next, proposing a resolution to give women the vote and encouraging them by every means possible to fulfil their public duties. The motion was seconded by the faithful Edward Rowlett and opposed by a few men, who argued that giving women the vote would make them more independent, masculine and inclined to ride bicycles.

Eva reminded the audience of the good work done by the co-operative movement. 'All of us, men and women alike, besides our immediate duties to our families, have duties to our neighbours, and to our country, and to society at large. Charity begins at home but it should not end there.' A Miss Young also spoke. When the motion demanding votes for women was put to the floor, it was carried amid much noise, cheering and applause. In the Christmas spirit, one joker had hung a large branch of mistletoe over the chair where Constance would sit. She was not amused.

After Eva went to Manchester around 1897 and Constance to Paris in 1898, the North Sligo Women's Suffrage Association fizzled out. Eva's life had changed for ever following a meeting in Italy with the British suffrage campaigner Esther Roper in 1896. She would go on to spend long years working for the rights of working-class women in Manchester and the north of England with Roper.

Both the sisters were – at last – finding their voices.

CHAPTER THREE

Casi and Con

For Constance, 1897 began as normal. She rode with the local hunt and dressed as a milkmaid for a fancy dress ball at Sligo Courthouse. She spent time in Dublin, attended the Punchestown races, competed with great success at the St Patrick's Day races held near her home in County Sligo, and then took the mailboat from Kingstown to London for 'the season'.

In July, she was a bridesmaid at the wedding of her cousin Gray Wynne. A month later, she was back in Dublin for the Horse Show, where her mare Cherry Ripe received a commendation and pupils of Lady Gore-Booth's needlework classes exhibited their work. By September, Eva had left for Manchester. She was missed at the annual children's fete at Lissadell, where Constance, along with Josslyn, Mordaunt and Mabel, assisted with the races and a picnic of cakes and fruit.

Since her time in London had passed without too much drama, Constance had persuaded her parents to let her study art at the studio of Rodolphe Julian in Paris. With the London art world in the doldrums, Paris was attracting ambitious young artists from all over Europe. Her teacher, Anna Nordgren, who had worked at the studio, probably played some part in getting Constance her place, while a small legacy from an aunt boosted her finances. Her parents gave her a meagre allowance of only two francs a day, hoping that she would come to her senses and return to a more conventional life in Ireland.

During her eighteen-month stay in Paris, Constance was part of a class taught by Jean-Paul Laurens. Although there was no entrance exam, Julian insisted on high standards and had much influence in Parisian art circles. George Moore, who had studied there in 1873, described a class of around thirty pupils, eight or nine of them women, sitting in a circle and drawing 'from the model'. By the time Constance arrived, the school had expanded, with women and men taught in separate classes, although the women's fees were double those of the men.

Constance absorbed herself in her painting and enjoyed Parisian life, visiting the museums and art galleries, sitting in sidewalk cafés and travelling everywhere by bicycle. For most of her time in Paris, she lived in a modest English pension on the Rue de Rivoli, near the Louvre. On her wedding finger, she wore a ring, declaring that she was married to art. She had plenty of admirers, including a young Englishman, William Max-Muller, whom she was tempted to marry. He became a British diplomat and was envoy to Poland from 1920 to 1928. Her friends called her either 'Velo' because of her love of cycling or 'Teuf Teuf', the French equivalent of the English 'choo-choo', which could also mean party or party-goer.

The writer Violet Hunt had come to Paris and a mutual friend asked Constance to show her around. She remembered Constance as a tall, thin woman, with tawny red-gold hair, and a peering, puzzled look caused by her short-sightedness, which was at odds with her 'perfect boyish frankness and camaraderie'. She suffered some teasing, especially for her accent but, in one case at least, she cured it by grabbing her chief tormenter by the hair and ducking her under a nearby tap, as she would have done with her brothers in the past. Hunt noted that Constance avoided the expatriate community and had nothing but contempt for the Moulin Rouge, which she saw as a tourist haunt. Instead she brought her new friend to La Cigale and Le Soleil d'Or on the Boulevard Saint-Michel – altogether more risqué haunts.

One evening, Violet and her friend Camomile refused to go with Constance to the Bal des Quatres Arts in Montmartre. She arrived back at their pension at 2am, sleeping on the floor rather than taking the long walk back to her own lodgings. She put herself to sleep by reciting Swinburne's *Triumph of Time*. Violet thought her 'hopelessly generous', despite her small allowance. She was so poor that she often did not have enough to eat, which Hunt thought may have starved her brain. 'She did not think, she had no emotions which she could not work off with a dance at the Moulin de la Galette.'

Count Casimir Dunin de Markievicz, born on 15 March 1874, and so six years younger than Constance, was in every way a match for her, not least in height. He was six feet four inches to her six foot and described by Violet Hunt as a 'handsome Byronic beauty'. He came from Zywotowka, a village in the *kresy* area of east Poland; a region with a complicated history. Although annexed by the Ukraine and under Tsarist Russian rule, the Polish landowners remained the masters, with the peasant class largely Ukrainian. Until the arrival of the Bolsheviks in 1919, life in Zywotowka revolved around a privileged circle of Poles, who spent their time hunting, riding and attending parties. In this, it resembled the life of Ireland's rural landlord class and, like Constance, Casimir had spent his early life drawing, painting and devising amateur theatricals to amuse his eight siblings and their elders.

Casimir had studied law for two years in Kiev, a Ukrainian city with a large Polish community, before announcing to his parents that art was his destiny. His dream was to study in Paris and, in 1895, he enrolled at the École des Beaux-Arts. His fiancée, a frail beauty called Jadwiga Splawa Neyman, followed him to Paris soon after to study music and the pair married. A son, Stanislaus, was born in 1896 after which Casimir left Paris for St Petersburg to undertake his compulsory military service in the Russian army. He returned to France and Jadwiga a year later but, although his wife was soon pregnant again, the couple's relationship was disintegrating and Casimir was later to hint that she had found 'another'. When Jadwiga fell ill with consumption, a penniless Casimir decided to send her home to the Ukraine where she could be looked after. Jadwiga died in 1899, with her second son Ryszard surviving her only by a few months. A second version of the story had Jadwiga going into labour on the journey to the Ukraine, developing peritonitis, and dying, as did her newborn son, soon afterwards. Stanislaus, known to Constance as Staskou, was dispatched to the home of his maternal grandmother in Zywotowka.

Although enjoying bohemian life to the full, with a great deal of champagne, many love affairs and an occasional duel, Markievicz took his art seriously. A 1900 painting called *Amour* won a Medaille d'Honneur at the Paris Salon and was exhibited in Russia a year later and later again in Dublin. He charmed everyone he met and Constance – like him gregarious, popular and outgoing – was dazzled.

There are at least two versions of how they met. What is certain is that the momentous event occurred in January 1899. According to his friend, Stefan Kryzywoszewski, he and Casimir arrived late at a student ball one evening and spotted two women, both English-speaking. One was forgettable; the other was Constance – a living Rossetti or Burne-Jones, with delicate features and a proud bearing. Stefan, who was shorter than her, asked her to dance and then gallantly passed her on to his friend, who matched her in height and bearing. In a letter to her brother Josslyn, Constance gave a more sober account of their meeting. 'We met at a dance where Mrs Forbes-Robertson took me. She is a Pole and introduced me to a great many of her compatriots and we've been great pals and comrades ever since.' Mrs Forbes-Robertson, born Janina Flamm, was married to the artist Eric Forbes-Robertson.

Cycling was all the rage at the time and soon Constance and Casimir were cycling for miles along the paths and roadways near Paris, as well as strolling through the beautiful parks of Paris. Because of his size, Casimir had a bicycle made especially for him. He completed the Paris–St-Malo race, telling his son later that only a broken chain had prevented him from winning. On the sidelines cheering him on was Constance who had gone to stay with her cousin, Mrs Bryce, at St Lunière, near St Malo. A photograph of the pair wearing fashionable cycling knickerbockers and smoking cigarettes was taken after a 194km trip from Paris to Dieppe and back.

In the evenings, they could be found sitting in Left Bank cafés, drinking, smoking and discussing art, drama and poetry. It was a case of opposites attracting – Casimir easy-going and sensual, Constance fiery and restless. Since Constance did not speak Polish and Casimir's English was poor, their common language was French. They shared a love of dressing-up, theatricals and high jinks and had themselves photographed in costumes from the Napoleonic era. Their monthly allowances disappeared quickly and many of Constance's letters home contained requests for money, while Casimir resorted to washing trams at night for extra francs.

Although soon inseparable and known to their friends as 'Casi and Con', the pair were staunch companions before they were lovers. Soon after meeting him, Constance wrote to her sister Eva of her new friend. 'I think that you will like him. He fills me with the desire to do things

... I don't quite know when we shall be married but I wish it to be soon.' Constance was clearly smitten from the start and was craving the status that only marriage could bring to a woman. A few weeks after he met Constance, Casimir got news from home that his estranged wife and their second son had died. He turned to Constance for consolation and became increasingly committed to their relationship, despite a brief infatuation with a woman called Alys, of whom little is known. She was a friend of Constance's and, like Casimir's late wife, was a frail beauty. Alys married someone else but died soon after in childbirth. She left Casimir a ring.

In an undated letter to Josslyn, probably from 1899, Constance announced her engagement. 'He is an artist and very clever,' she added. She assured her family of Casimir's noble connection, giving his full name, Casimir Joseph Dunin de Markievicz, and his title '*potomsturemyj dvoranin*', which meant son of a count, whose family has been on a certain property for seven generations. A cousin had worked for the Tsarist administration and an uncle had been a general in the Russian army. She claimed that Casimir had no interest in her money and little interest in politics: 'Thank goodness he hates politics and has never meddled in any plots or belonged to any political societies.'

Other hastily scribbled letters to Josslyn followed. She told her brother that he had £160 a year and that she did not want any money from him since she had her own. 'We both paint for the love of it and we both like the same sort of amusements after our work,' she said. In another letter to her brother, she gave an abbreviated and somewhat stark account of her intended's previous life: 'He married very young and was most unhappy. His wife deceived him and there was a great scandal, her lover tried to kill her. She died of consumption a year ago.' Although Casimir developed a reputation for embellishing the truth, this tale possibly contained a grain of truth. 'When my first wife leave me she come to my room and says, "Casimir, I leave you. I love another,"' he told Constance during rehearsals for his play *The Dilettante* in 1908.

Constance's family, especially her mother, worried that the Count was a gold-digger from a part of the world best known, in her view, for producing 'barbarians' like Peter the Great and Ivan the Terrible. The argument as to whether he was a true count has raged ever since.

Members of the Polish landowning class with a certain status were in the habit of adopting titles. Concerned that his sister was falling for an exotic charlatan, Josslyn contacted the Russian embassy in London and a member of the Russian secret police was delegated to investigate. State Councillor Rachovsky reported that Mr Markievicz, a student painter with M. Bougeur at the Académie Julien, liked the 'noisy' life, with music, dancing and playing billiards and cards among his pleasures. He also spent a great deal of money and drank numerous bottles of champagne. In sum, he was a harmless and typical bohemian.

Casimir made his new friend the subject of his next major painting, 'Constance in White', which is now held at the National Gallery of Ireland, with a copy in Leinster House. He gave a more intimate and sensual view of Constance in 'Portrait of Constance Sitting on a Chair', with shoulders bare and hair pinned behind her ears.

There was a story of a duel between Casimir and a Frenchman who had slighted Constance at a masked ball. She was wearing an Empire costume with her hair piled high and sporting a monocle with a black ribbon; Casimir was dressed as Marshal Ney in French military uniform. A boisterous Frenchman flicked the monocle from Constance's eye. Casimir knocked the man down and both men drew their swords. Casimir, an expert swordsman after his year in the Russian Imperial Guard, had continued to fence as a means of keeping fit. When the Frenchman refused to apologise for his slight to Constance, Casimir challenged him to a duel. They met at dawn in the Bois de Vincennes. The Frenchman came out the worse, with a deep wound to his thigh that required a long stay in hospital. Constance's honour was upheld.

By September 1899, despite the reservations of both their families, the pair became unofficially engaged. Sir Henry and Lady Georgina Gore-Booth, on their way to the clean air of St Moritz in Switzerland, stopped in Paris, where they met Casimir for the first time. Over the next few months, Josslyn, Eva and Mabel also visited Paris at various times and met him. He effortlessly won them over.

Constance spent the Christmas of 1899 with her parents in St Moritz. After his many trips to the Arctic, her father's health was fragile and on 13 January 1900 he died of influenza, aged only fifty-six. His body was returned to Lissadell where he was buried on 23 January; whether Constance returned for the funeral is open to question. Although she had grumbled about her 'soft mild milk and water father' in her 1892 diary, she had admired his adventurous spirit and unconventional approach to life.

Josslyn, as his father's heir, was now responsible for his sister. He attempted to control her spending by refusing to send her a chequebook. In the early spring, with just three francs left, she wrote him a pleading letter asking for £10 so that she could pay her rent and buy paint and canvases. A second letter arrived in mid-April. When Josslyn warned his sister that Casimir might be after her inheritance, she jumped to her fiancé's defence, insisting that she intended to keep control of her own finances and claiming that he would inherit £160 in four years' time. Josslyn urged his sister to come home and spend a few months in Lissadell. She refused. In early May, Casimir's mother, Marya, travelled to Paris to meet Constance and, when she returned to Zywotowka, she sent the couple her blessing. Josslyn reluctantly agreed to the match.

In May, Constance and Casimir made the journey across the Irish Sea to a typical summer in Sligo – 'raining, rainin' like blue hell' in Casimir's words. It was too soon after Sir Henry's death for much entertaining but, weather permitting, the newly engaged couple spent hours painting together and exploring the local countryside on foot and horseback. With Josslyn to guide him, Casimir spent many hours shooting in the foothills of Ben Bulben. The neighbourhood was agog with stories of the dashing Polish count with the unpronounceable name who had tamed the wild daughter of the big house.

In July 1900, Constance and Casimir's engagement was formally announced; the marriage would take place in September and the couple would return to Paris afterwards. With Josslyn, as the eldest son, inheriting the estate at Lissadell, Constance sold her beloved horses and set off for London with her mother and sisters to buy her trousseau and organise the wedding – a complicated affair owing to the couple's differences in religion and nationality. The Markievicz family felt that Casimir, under Russian law, should be married in a Roman Catholic Church, while Constance, brought up in the Church of Ireland, was aware of the Catholic ruling that any children of a 'mixed' marriage must be brought up as Catholics. Although later to convert to Catholicism, at that point she was not happy about bringing up any children she might have as 'Popish' babies.

Meanwhile, Markievicz travelled to Poland before joining the Gore-Booths in London, bringing with him a cousin, Mikhail Strzalko, who would act as his best man. For the marriage, Casimir had to learn his lines. Constance later told her stepson Staskou that the pair had travelled around London on open-top buses with Constance taking the part of the priest and asking 'Wilt thou take this woman to wife?' Casimir solemnly gave his answers in a strong Polish accent, to the great entertainment of the other passengers.

The marriage took place on 20 September 1900 and involved three ceremonies. First came a civil wedding in a registry office, followed by formal registration of the marriage at the Russian embassy in Chesham Place, Belgravia, and then the religious ceremony at the Parish Church, Marylebone. The marriage settlement made no mention of Markievicz's income, but went into great detail about Constance's finances; for the moment at least, his income was less than his wife's.

Because the family was still in mourning, it was a small wedding with only fifty guests, among them, according to Casimir's own account, the future King Edward VII, then Prince of Wales. The pair made a striking couple. The groom wore his Russian court uniform – a tight black tunic with gold-braided collar and cuffs, white trousers, a long rapier and a three-cornered hat. The bride wore white satin, with a train of old Brussels lace and a garland of rosebuds. The bridesmaids – Eva and Mabel, along with family friends Rachel Mansfield and Mildred Grenfell – wore green gowns trimmed with lace. Josslyn gave his sister away and their friend, Fletcher Sheridan Le Fanu, officiated. In the service Constance promised to love and honour her husband, but left out the traditional promise 'to obey'.

Afterwards, Lady Gore-Booth received the guests in 41 Devonshire Place, near the church; this was the home of Constance's cousin Rhoda L'Estrange, by now married to the Earl of Carlisle. The bride and groom left immediately after the reception for Paris and, after a flurry of tears, goodbyes and promises, were put on the train at Victoria station. No sooner had the train reached the next station than the happy couple jumped off and sneaked back to London for a party with some of their livelier friends.

Quite where the couple spent the early days of their marriage is unclear. Elizabeth Countess of Fingall remembered them visiting her in

Killeen, County Mayo, while on honeymoon. Casimir had sat down at the piano and bellowed out a song to his own accompaniment. 'Con she is mad!' he would say. They were in London on 8 October 1900 when Constance was pondering a letter from her solicitors that pointed out that the Roman Catholic wedding ceremony the Markievicz family had been hoping for would mean that divorce would be out of the question. Fortunately, Casimir had gone off the idea of a Catholic ceremony.

At some point, they spent three weeks cycling around Normandy, staying wherever the mood took them before returning to Paris and renting a studio and four rooms in Montparnasse. After exhibiting his *Portrait of Baron Greifenfels* at the Salon earlier in the year, Casimir was getting a number of portrait commissions. The couple employed a maid, Josephine, who stayed with them for several years. In December, they were in London for the wedding of Constance's sister Mabel to Percy Foster of the Royal Scots Greys. Convention in those days demanded that the eldest daughter marry first, so it must have come as a relief to Mabel when Constance finally married. Christmas was spent in Nice.

In the autumn of 1901, Constance and Casimir were back at Lissadell where they remained for the rest of the year. With Constance pregnant, the couple spent their days reading, walking and painting. Maeve Alys – named for the legendary queen of Connacht and their late friend Alys – was born on 13 November 1901. It was a difficult birth and Constance nearly died during the delivery. She later told a friend that, because she dreaded another pregnancy, she avoided sex with her husband after the birth of their daughter. Maeve was baptised on 11 January 1902 by the Reverend Le Fanu, followed by a grand dinner at Lissadell.

A few months later, Constance and Casimir were back in Paris, preparing for a trip to the Ukraine in the summer of 1902. Their daughter was left at Lissadell in the care of Lady Georgina, who adored her. In later years, Constance would protest that they had been thinking only of the child when they left Maeve at Lissadell. Babies were prey to a variety of infections, and the bohemian environment of Paris was no place for a newborn. Children in those days were often looked after by the extended family and, indeed, Casimir had also – by modern standards – abandoned his son.

Casimir travelled to the Ukraine with his right arm in a sling after a bicycling accident at Lissadell. In those days, it took a full two weeks to travel from Paris to Zywotowka – from Paris to Berlin, then on to Warsaw, Kiev and Oratow, which was the nearest town to Casimir's home. While they travelled, Casimir entertained his new wife with the legends and stories of his country and, more crucially, told her of the uprisings of the Polish people against the Russian Empire. His elderly aunts could remember bands of insurgents armed with scythes and shotguns fighting Russian armies, much as the Irish had fought the British in 1798. Constance came to the conclusion that the Polish community living under Russian rule was in a similar position to fellow Catholics living in an Ireland occupied by the British.

After they arrived in Zywotowka, Constance immersed herself in the daily life of the Markievicz family, riding and hunting and happily dressing up in a Ukrainian costume. Her mother-in-law, the recently widowed Countess Marya, ruled the household; Casimir's eldest brother Jan managed the estate and bred horses; his wife Lena was a keen gardener. There were two other brothers and four sisters living in the area; a fifth sister had died. Constance found much in the Ukraine to remind her of home, although the poverty of the peasants was more extreme and the roads of deep sticky clay were often impassable in winter. There was hunting with borzoi hounds, rather than beagles, while the flora grew on a grand scale; huge poppies as big as saucers sprang from the ground and the sunflowers were as tall as small trees.

As an artist, she found much to interest her in this vast country. Casimir had built a makeshift studio in the park and some of the pictures she painted at this time still hang at Lissadell. One of Constance's most remarkable pictures from the visit is called *The Conscript*. It shows a young peasant sitting at a table in a cottage he clearly does not wish to leave. Casimir's impressive *Bread* was produced during this visit to the Ukraine – a triptych showing a peasant sowing seed, a woman with a sickle beside the harvested corn and finally the finished loaf on a white cloth. Constance thought it one of his best works and it would remain with her until her death.

Before the bitter cold of winter set in, they travelled to the home of Markievicz's father-in-law, forty kilometres distant. There Casimir was reunited with Stanislaus, who had lived with his maternal grandparents since the death of his mother. Stanislaus, still not six years old, was captivated by the tall, handsome father he had not seen since infancy and by his new 'mother'. 'She was tall, slim, exquisite, with a crown of soft wavy golden brown hair, the rays of the Southern sun playing upon it' he would later write in an unpublished biography of his stepmother. She smelled of perfume, paint and cigarettes and seemed like a creature from another world. He soon discovered, to his joy, that she was 'as kind as she was beautiful'.

Constance took an immediate liking to her stepson. She let him try one of her cigarettes and, when he began to choke, gave him red fruit-drops wrapped in thin paper. He remembered her adopting a badly treated Borzoi hunting dog that was about to be put down. She tended to its sores and looked after it until it recovered. On another occasion, she adopted a lame stork, left behind after the annual winter migration to warmer climates. She set his broken leg and fed him live frogs – a stork's favourite food. Afterwards, the stork would stand in the corner of the studio and answer to the call of *Ptak*, the Polish word for bird.

All too soon, it was time to pack up and go and, in the autumn of 1902, the Markieviczs returned to Paris, leaving a tearful Staskou behind. With her, Constance brought the Ukrainian costume she had been given by the Polish aunts, as well as miniature versions for her daughter Maeve and her niece Moira. She was never to forget her first visit to the Ukraine, which had stimulated her spirit and her imagination. To celebrate their return to Paris, the Markieviczs gave a fancy dress ball for 150 people, with Casimir concocting a party punch from fourteen different drinks. In December, they were back in Ireland, spending Christmas at Lissadell with their daughter.

During this visit, Casimir met the writer, poet, artist and mystic George Russell (Æ) for the first time. At the age of nineteen, Æ had started a branch of the theosophical movement at Ely Place Dublin, which helped launch the Irish literary renaissance. Although primarily an artist, poet and mystic, Æ had a practical side, working for the co-operative movement to promote a self-sufficient Ireland. Russell believed strongly that emigration was robbing Ireland of its most talented men and women, and he was doing his best to keep them in the country. He encouraged and published new writers, among them Eva Gore-Booth,

Padraic Colum and a young man with a fine tenor voice called James Joyce.

Josslyn Gore-Booth, in his own way, was as open to these new ideas as his sister. He knew that the days of the 'planted' landowners were ending and that, when ownership shifted to the tenants, landowners would have to find new sources of income, ideally in collaboration with their former tenants. At Lissadell, he planted trees, set up sawmills and created a nursery for flowers, among them daffodils, which he exported all over the world. Earlier that year, the Sligo Manufacturing Society, organised by Sir Josslyn to make shirts and other clothing, attracted over a hundred members.

Æ suggested to the Markieviczs that they move to Dublin, where they might earn a living from their art. In Paris, they were two struggling artists among many; in Dublin, they would shine. Particularly attractive to the couple was the revival of theatre in the city. When Lady Georgina offered the couple a house in the suburb of Rathgar, the decision was made. Æ, who lived around the corner, was delighted that 'the Gore-Booth girl who married the Polish count with the unspellable name' were going to settle in Dublin sometime in the summer. 'We might get the materials for a revolt, a new Irish Art Club. I feel some desperate schism or earthquaking revolution is required to wake up Dublin in art matters,' he wrote to Sarah Purser. In the same letter, he reveals that the Countess would appear as Cathleen Ní Houlihan in a one-act play by Yeats to be produced with his *Deirdre* during Easter week.

In the spring of 1903, the Markieviczs made a second journey to the Ukraine. When they returned to Ireland in October, they brought a delighted Staskou with them. Staskou always remembered the look of joy on his stepmother's face when she told him that his maternal grandparents and his paternal grandmother had at last agreed to let him come to Ireland. There were two conditions: he must remain a Roman Catholic and he must keep up his Polish. At the station in Oratow, Constance showed that she had learned some Polish herself when she leaned out of the window and shouted *Moskal swinja* (Muscovite pig) to a bemused policeman on the platform. Her political muscles were starting to twitch.

They had an adventurous trip home. Before leaving, the Markieviczs were asked to help a reluctant local conscript called Janko to escape by pretending that they employed him. After he slipped across the Russian–German border, Janko met up with the Markieviczs in Berlin and continued to Ireland with them, dressed as a servant. When they reached Paris, they packed up their belongings and said goodbye to friends. In London, Staskou was given the run of the toy shops.

They finally arrived at Lissadell, where the young boy was greeted warmly by Lady Georgina. The family, encumbered with sixty-four suitcases, would now make the long-anticipated move to Dublin. By the winter of 1903, they were installed in a house called St Mary's at 1 Frankfort Avenue, Rathgar. George Russell and his unconventional wife Violet lived nearby in Coulson Avenue; next door to the Russells was Maud Gonne. At St Mary's, there was a large garden with a rockery and a greenhouse behind the elegant one-storey-over-basement Victorian villa; a studio was soon attached to the dining room.

Dublin awaited.

CHAPTER FOUR

The Play's the Thing

At the beginning of the twentieth century, Dublin – on the surface at least – was a pleasant city with a population of about a quarter of a million. To the east and north were the sandy beaches and the cooling breezes of the Irish Sea; to the south, the rolling hills of Dublin and Wicklow. All were readily accessible, especially since the arrival in the city of the tram, the train, the bicycle and, later, the car. Dublin's centre, although split by the river Liffey, was compact, with Sackville Street and Grafton Street the main thoroughfares and magnificent buildings, such as the Custom House, the Four Courts, the old Houses of Parliament and Trinity College, adding an air of distinction. On the fringes were the elegant Georgian squares – Fitzwilliam and Merrion to the south, Mountjoy to the north.

The city, described by Joyce in one of his kinder moments as mellow, shabby and genteel, had much to attract the artist, with dozens of theatre companies, and lively 'salons' hosted by the leading writers and artists of the time. However, with political activity concentrated in Westminster after the 1800 Act of Union, Dublin had lost something of the aura that it had held as the second city of the British Empire, and many of the large houses, especially north of the Liffey, had degenerated into overcrowded tenements. Of the city's estimated population of 306,573, some 21,000 families were living in a single room. Many houses were unfit for habitation, with decaying walls crumbling under the weight of the roofs.

Poverty was rampant. At a time when twenty-two shillings was considered the minimum necessary for food and shelter, men were working seventy hours a week for fourteen shillings and women ninety hours for five shillings. Diseases of poverty, including tuberculosis, meant that the death rate was 24.6 per 1,000 compared to 13.6 in London. Child mortality was higher than in any other city of the British Isles. Those children that did survive ran wild in the streets, got little education and married young, so perpetuating the cycle. Prostitution, especially in the notorious 'Monto' area to the east of Sackville Street, was rampant.

Since washing was difficult, the stench and the filth of those tenement buildings were overpowering; the streets were open sewers. Undernourished children slept on straw, clinging to dirty rags to keep themselves warm. Cooking involved a saucepan on an open fire, and tea and bread constituted the staple diet. For the growing numbers of Irish men and women thrown off the land, Dublin could offer little in the way of work. Unlike Belfast, which could boast the thriving shipyards of Harland and Wolff and which briefly took over as the largest city on the island, the city had no industry to speak of. Most of the jobs available involved unskilled labouring and the general work of handling, carrying and carting.

On the political front, the fall of Parnell and the culture of mud-slinging and back-biting that followed caused widespread disillusionment with politics. Fortresses of the Ascendency such as Trinity College and the Bank of Ireland on College Green remained unchanged; the Union Jack flew all around the city. Douglas Hyde and others, known as the 'Irish Irelanders', feared that the Irish were growing too comfortable with their status as citizens of a nation subsumed into an entity called Great Britain.

Hyde's book *Love Songs of Connacht* helped spur the Irish revival, and culture became a means of reinforcing a sense of Irishness. From this sprung the GAA in 1884, the Gaelic League in 1893 and, later, the Abbey Theatre. Through the Gaelic League, those from the Protestant and unionist middle classes could explore their Irishness. For Irish women, it was an awakening. Social life was transformed, with men and women mingling freely at meetings, classes and *céilís*, which were seen as more 'respectable' than dances. Although the mass of Irish people were Catholic and, as yet, untouched by the Gaelic League or Sinn Féin, the views of the 'Irish Irelanders', promoted by D.P. Moran, editor of the weekly national paper *The Leader*, were having a broader impact.

Moran, who saw Ireland split between the Pale and the Gael, started a 'Buy Irish' campaign, encouraging the Irish to be self-reliant and to take pride in their national distinctiveness.

With the 1898 centenary celebrations of Wolfe Tone's 1798 rebellion, Irish nationalism found a focus. Following Queen Victoria's diamond jubilee celebrations a year earlier, Irish nationalists were intent on a celebration of their own and the initiative for a 1798 memorial committee came from John O'Leary and the Irish Republican Brotherhood (IRB), a militant and secretive nationalist organisation, founded in 1858 and closely attached to the Irish-American Clan na Gael organisation. Yet, it was the more mainstream Irish Parliamentary Party, led by John Redmond, that promoted the move to create permanent monuments to the men of '98. Thanks to the success of a popular history, written by a Catholic priest, Father Patrick Kavanagh, the 1798 rebellion was seen as a fight for 'Faith and Fatherland', a view that was at some remove from the secularist republicanism of the IRB, committed to fighting 'against the aristocratic locusts, whether English or Irish'. The centenary celebrations became a rallying point for resurgent nationalist opinion, with local committees all over the country creating an alliance of Catholic and nationalist forces committed to Home Rule for Ireland. One side-effect was that the IRB lost ground to mainstream nationalism.

Soon after this came the start of the Boer War, in which South African republicans showed that it was possible to take on the might of the British Empire. Two small Irish brigades, led by John MacBride and Arthur Lynch, fought with the Boers. In 1899, Maud Gonne, who had worked with the Land League for some years, and Arthur Griffith, a Boer War veteran, co-founded the Irish Transvaal Committee and organised a number of pro-Boer rallies in Dublin. The number of Irishmen signing up for the British forces dropped significantly.

Maud Gonne, older than Constance by two years and later a close ally, was a striking woman, considered the great beauty of her time. Like Constance, she was unusually tall for a woman, with masses of auburn hair and striking golden eyes; she was also an expert horsewoman and animal lover. Because she was independently wealthy, she could live her life as she wished. At the age of twenty, while in Paris, she had met Lucien Millevoye, a militant anti-monarchist, who not only became her lover but fired her up with the notion of fighting to free Ireland, as Joan of Arc had freed France. In 1889, she met W.B. Yeats, who fell hopelessly in love with her.

Following a somewhat mysterious mission to Russia on behalf of Millevoye, Gonne had returned to Ireland and, after making friends with Arthur Griffith, Willie Rooney, Douglas Hyde and later James Connolly, she became involved in the fight for Irish freedom. Women were asserting their rights; feminists sought to remove all the barriers that had been imposed on women by a patriarchal society, while suffragists specifically targeted the political barriers faced by women. In 1899, Griffith, who had returned from South Africa to edit the *United Irishman* at the request of Willie Rooney, had urged the women of Ireland to ban the British press and British culture from their homes. Women's influence as a force for change was becoming recognised; for a start women could persuade their sons not to join armies. Later, Griffith was jailed for two weeks after he gave a rival newspaper editor a thrashing with a South African *sjan-bok* stick for claiming that Gonne was a spy. Gonne was paying Griffith's wages of twenty-five shillings a week at the time, ensuring that the *United Irishman* stayed solvent.

When Maud Gonne discovered that, as a woman, she could not join the Celtic Literary Society, she founded Inghinidhe na hÉireann (Daughters of Erin), later described by Constance as 'the women's rebel society'. The Inghinidhe grew from a meeting of fifteen women in the Celtic Literary Society's Rooms in Dublin on Easter Sunday 1900, which fell on 15 April. While the meeting's original purpose was to organise a thank-you gift for Arthur Griffith after his stout defence of Gonne, it turned to planning a 'Patriotic Children's Treat' in response to the Children's Treat in the Phoenix Park organised earlier that April as part of Queen Victoria's three-week visit to Dublin.

Victoria's trip was unexpected and came almost forty years after her 1861 visit. Officially, the reason was to thank loyal Irish soldiers; unofficially, its purpose was to reverse the dwindling numbers of Irishmen volunteering for the British forces. Although local authorities were given less than a month's notice of the Queen's arrival, they put on a good show and she was greeted with a 100-cannon salute when she sailed into Kingstown harbour on the afternoon of 3 April. A day later, marching bands and cavalry officers on horseback accompanied Victoria and her two daughters from Kingstown through Dublin's south suburbs to the Viceregal Lodge in the Phoenix Park. At Leeson Street Bridge, she was officially welcomed to Dublin by the Lord Mayor, Thomas Devereux Pile. All along the route, children waved flags and streets and houses were decorated with bunting, Union Jacks and royal emblems.

The Phoenix Park was the venue on Saturday 7 April for the 'Children's Treat'; 52,000 children were invited and given sandwiches, biscuits and fruit donated by Dublin firms. Gonne's Patriotic Children's Treat in July was aimed at the less privileged children of Dublin. On the Sunday after the annual Wolfe Tone commemorations, some 30,000 children paraded through the streets from Beresford Place to Clonturk Park, Drumcondra, where they were treated to a picnic and anti-recruitment speeches. With the funds left over, Inghinidhe na hÉireann was founded. Its aims were to re-establish the independence of Ireland, to encourage the study of Gaelic language, literature, history and music, to support Irish industry and to discourage the circulation of English literature, music and entertainment. Soon the Inghinidhe began organising free evening classes for boys and girls in the Irish language, Irish history, music, drama and art. St Brigid was their patron and members adopted Gaelic names to conceal their identities. One of their main forms of entertainment came in the form of *tableaux vivantes*, or 'living pictures', which were easier to enact than formal dramas. Several were staged at the Antient Concert Rooms in Great Brunswick Street (now Pearse Street).

In April 1902, the Inghinidhe's drama class, in association with William and Frank Fay's Ormond Group, put on the first public performance of *Cathleen ni Houlihan*, co-written by W.B. Yeats and Lady Gregory, in St Teresa's Hall, Clarendon Street, Dublin. The play was seen as the forerunner of a new style of realistic drama based on Irish folklore and speech patterns ('I do be thinking').

Set in a cottage 'close to Killala' in 1798, the lead role of the mysterious old woman was played by Maud Gonne. She appears to the hero Michael Gillane on the eve of his wedding, telling him that she had taken to wandering because there were 'too many strangers in her house' and describing her 'four beautiful green fields', representing the four provinces of Ireland, which have been taken from her. 'Many a man has died for love of me,' she says. News comes through that the French have arrived in Killala, and a mesmerised Gillane leaves to join them and fight for Ireland's freedom. As she leaves 'with the walk of a queen', rejuvenated by Gillane's readiness to sacrifice himself, the Old Woman proclaims:

> They shall be remembered forever,
> They shall be alive forever,
> They shall be speaking forever,
> The people shall hear them forever.

From death would come new life – a concept embedded in Christian thought with its central image of Jesus on the cross, sacrificing his life to save his people. After the performance, Lady Gregory went backstage to congratulate the performers and the Fays. From this sprung the Abbey Theatre, founded by Yeats, Lady Gregory and Edward Martyn in December 1904, with the patronage of Annie Horniman.

Queen Victoria died in 1901 and, in July 1903, her successor King Edward VII, with his wife Queen Alexandra, visited Ireland. A year earlier, members of the Irish Party had refused to attend ceremonies to mark his coronation. The visitors were generally well received, despite Inghinidhe na hÉireann and other nationalists scuppering Dublin Corporation's proposal to present an address of loyalty to the king, as it had done to his late mother only three years earlier. Under the Local Government Act of 1898, 100,000 Irish women were not only able to vote in local elections but put themselves forward as candidates; the Inghinidhe urged women to vote against the address of welcome in the forthcoming municipal elections.

Politically, a view had emerged that if the land question was solved, the demand for Home Rule might die away. From 1898, the United Irish League, founded by William O'Brien, intensified the pressure on landlords. A number of progressive landlords, backed by the Chief Secretary George Wyndham, called a Land Conference in 1902. Out of the conference came the Wyndham Land (Purchase) Act in August 1903, which included a 'bonus' to induce landlords to sell. Josslyn Gore-Booth was one of the first to sell out, making 300,000 acres available to 1,500 tenants.

The Wyndham Act was the beginning of the end for landlordism, although it caused a split between the Redmondites and William O'Brien, who was accused of putting land purchase and conciliation before Home Rule. Following Wyndham's initiative, Lord Dunraven, a moderate unionist (and cousin of Constance), had founded the Irish Reform Association, a follow-on from the Land Conference that advocated a gradual devolution to Ireland of her domestic affairs.

Alarmed Ulster Unionists saw the Act and Dunraven's move as the first step towards the Home Rule they so bitterly opposed; hard-line republicans were also opposed to the Act. Wyndham was driven from office and the rift in Irish society deepened. At no time did Irish republicans consider the Ulster Unionists' point of view, nor did suffragists look to the north-east where the Primrose League, the Women's Liberal Unionist Association and the Ladies Committee of the Irish Unionist Alliance were politicising Irish women, along with the Belfast-based National Association of Irishwomen, and the Irish Women's Centenary Union.

Soon after their arrival in Dublin, the Markieviczs were on their way to a function in Dublin Castle when a small beggar girl put her hand through the window of their horse-drawn carriage, looking for a few pennies. So overawed was she by the sight of Constance's magnificent diamonds that she was rendered speechless. As the carriage moved on, Constance looked back. The sight of the child receiving a hard slap across the face from her mother for failing in her job would never leave her.

In those early days, the Markieviczs were part of the 'Castle set' attending the annual round of balls and social events, with Casimir resplendent in his military uniform court dress and Constance the picture of well-bred elegance in elaborate gowns, her hair sprinkled with jewels. For Casimir, the Castle was the perfect place to make contacts and win commissions. He was in his element, entertaining the men and flirting with the women. From the time they arrived in Dublin, the Markieviczs were regulars at Æ's Sunday night 'at home'; after he got to know her, Russell would describe Constance as 'a fine breathless character, straight as a lance, truthful, and as devoid of fear as any human being I have ever met – but in too much of a hurry'.

The adaptable Casimir became a regular in the Dublin pubs, usually accompanied by his close friends Martin Murphy, a carpenter and stage manager at the Gaiety Theatre, and Dubonsky, a diminutive Polish tailor, who was also a Jew. Murphy's name became so connected with Casimir's that he was mentioned in Joyce's *Finnegans Wake* as 'Markievicz Murphy'.

Casimir hoped his painting would support the family and, with Constance, Æ, W.J. Leech and Frances Baker, he took part in an exhibition of Young Irish Artists held in the Leinster Hall, Molesworth Street, from 11 to 23 October 1903. Constance exhibited twenty-seven pictures and Casimir twenty-four, most of the latter with a Polish theme.

A few months later, the art collector Hugh Lane – a nephew of Lady Gregory's – returned to Ireland from Rome with a collection of paintings acquired from the estate of the Scottish railway baron, James Staats Forbes; these, he hoped, would form the core collection of a new Dublin municipal art gallery. Among the paintings were works by the French artists Millet, Courbet, Monet and Manet.

Casimir and Constance were among the more prominent members of a committee set up to locate and fund a suitable building for the new gallery, with Constance acting as secretary of the Ladies' Picture League and Casimir chairing a public meeting in the Royal Hibernian Academy on 8 December 1904. George Moore and W.B. Yeats were among the speakers, with Moore giving a lecture on 'Modern Painters of the Royal Hibernian Academy'. The purpose of the meeting was to persuade the dubious Dublin bourgeoisie to buy pictures and support the proposed gallery. Artists agreed to paint portraits of prominent Irishmen to help raise funds. Casimir's portrait of Æ proved one of his best and, in 1908, when a temporary home was found for the gallery at Harcourt Street, it was one of the exhibits.

At home, life was conventional, if somewhat bohemian, for the Markievicz family. On the surface, the pair made an ideal couple and they still cared deeply about each other. They each had a private income and, since wages for the domestic workforce were low, the Markieviczs managed to keep a cook-housekeeper and two 'dailies' to ease the workload involved in running a house. Josephine, who had come with them from Paris, was succeeded in 1904 by Ellen Banks as cook and housekeeper. In 1904, Maud Gonne was in Dublin for the christening of her son Seán, and she met Constance at Æ's. She was taken to see Maeve in her bath. Years earlier, while Gonne was at a function in London, the young Constance, with her two sisters 'who were as tall as myself', had been pointed out to her. At the time, Gonne kept her distance from Constance, seeing her as part of the 'Castle set'.

From 1903 to 1907, Maeve and Staskou lived with their parents in a comfortable home filled with antiques and paintings. To help him learn English, Staskou had a tutor called Miss Pemberton. He went to the Alexandra College kindergarten on Earlsfort Terrace and later to the Jesuit Belvedere College in Dublin's city centre, which he hated. Their mother sometimes did the cooking using recipes she had collected in France. She was an indulgent parent who allowed her children more freedom than was usual in those post-Victorian times. Neighbours – and her own housekeeper – were horrified when she allowed Staskou and the Russell boys to frolic naked in the garden during a summer heat wave, spraying them with water from a hose. Maeve and Staskou became adept apple tree climbers; Constance was unconcerned that both might tear their clothes. Mrs Banks, who would stay with the family until 1910, felt that Constance was no longer leading 'a lady's life', and had little interest in managing either the house or her money.

In August 1904, during the week of the Horse Show, the Markieviczs held their second exhibition called 'Pictures of Two Countries' at the Leinster Hall on Molesworth Street with Æ. Underlining their industry, Casimir showed eighty-six paintings, Constance seventy-six and Æ sixty-three. Among the paintings exhibited were Casimir's *Amour,* with an asking price of £330, and Constance's *The Conscript* priced at £150. Most of the other paintings were on offer for between three to six guineas. The show was well received and visited by the Lord Lieutenant, while Hugh Lane bought several paintings for his planned gallery. Characteristically, Constance's work was based on intuition rather than technique. She excelled at capturing the moment. By contrast, her husband's work was technically adept, while Russell's was more whimsical and mystical. The exhibition remained an annual event until 1913, although Constance exhibited for the last time in 1908.

In 1905, Casimir received a commission from the Earl of Mayo, Dermot Robert Wyndham Bourke, for his most ambitious work to date. *The Investiture of the Right Hon the Earl of Mayo as Knight of St Patrick* shows sixty-eight members of the Most Illustrious Order of St Patrick and companions attending the investiture. Among them are the Lord Lieutenant Lord Dudley, the Irish chief secretary, George Wyndham, and the Prince of Wales, the future King George V. Constance, wearing a green mantle, sits beside the future Queen Mary. The painting was exhibited at the Royal Hibernian Academy in May 1906. Casimir was to exhibit at the Royal Hibernian Academy from 1905 to 1909, alongside the best painters of the time – John Butler Yeats, Sarah Purser, Nathaniel Hone, William John Leech and Walter Osborne. Mostly he showed portraits, which gave him a small but steady income. Constance exhibited landscapes at the academy between 1904 and 1907. She would continue to attend Castle functions, mainly for her husband's sake, even as her sympathies swerved towards nationalism.

In January 1905, the Markieviczs had made their Dublin stage debuts in a series of dramatic recitals, mostly from Shakespeare, organised by Elizabeth Young, who acted under the name Violet Mervyn. She had rented the Abbey Theatre for the occasion. Elizabeth Young was a younger sister of the poet and mystic Ella Young, a protégée of Æ's who lived at Grosvenor Square in Rathmines and hosted a popular 'at home'. That same year, the first of many dogs appeared in the Markieviczs' home – a cocker spaniel called Jack, who came from the Viceregal Lodge. Casimir had been painting a portrait when the under-secretary's wife, Lady MacDonnell, gave him a puppy, which he brought home in his pocket. A bulldog called Goggles joined the household soon after.

When the Dudleys left Ireland in December 1905, they were replaced in the Viceregal Lodge by the Aberdeens, convinced Home Rulers who had done a short stint in Ireland twenty years earlier. Constance was present at the new Viceroy's first 'Drawing Room' in 1906 where she 'presented' a friend, Mrs Maud O'Connell Fitz-Simon, owner of the cottage she was later to rent at Sandyford. In the general election of 1906, the Liberals, the party of Gladstone that, in theory at least, was committed to Home Rule, swept to victory by such a large margin that they did not need the Irish vote. Knowing that any Home Rule bill would be thrown out by the Tory-dominated House of Lords, the government proposed a return to the Devolution Plan conceived by Lord Dunraven, which impressed nobody. Redmond's motion at a national convention that it was 'inadequate in scope and unsatisfactory in detail' was passed unanimously. The Irish question was pushed to one side.

The Markieviczs attended the Aberdeen's first State Ball in 1906 and Lady MacDonnell's dance in March. Casimir had taken singing lessons and belted out Polish songs at a party given by Lady Weldon, wife of the State Steward and Chamberlain, also in March. In April, Constance had a stall at the La Floralia fete, held in connection with the Irish Horticultural Society's Spring Show, where the twin Miss Arnotts helped her. During the year, Casimir founded the short-lived Irish Fencing Club at 9 Merrion Row, just off St Stephen's Green, recruiting Lord Aberdeen as patron and a *maître* from France as instructor. Monsieur Dain became the subject of one of Casimir's best portraits, holding a sword and sporting a magnificent waxed moustache.

Although art was still the focus of her life, Constance was developing her interest in the theatre. Dublin boasted many theatrical groups and, in December 1906, Constance played the druidess Lavarcom in a revival of Æ's *Deirdre* by the Irish National Theatre at the Abbey. Máire Nic Shiubhlaigh, who played the title role, described Constance the actress as 'rather unpredictable'. On stage, her enthusiasm for the work occasionally carried her away; she could never quite sink her own vivid personality in a role. Off stage, Constance was 'a lovely woman' whose beauty had character and who was 'the most remarkable woman I have met'.

There was little love lost between Casimir and W.B. Yeats, who held differing views on the role of the theatre. At the time, the only alternative to the high-minded 'peasant plays' at the Irish National Theatre was what Máire Nic Shiubhlaigh called 'begorrah' plays at the Gaiety and old Theatre Royal, or music hall at the Queen's and Dan Lowrey's Music Hall. Casimir preferred a more cosmopolitan style of drama and he found a ready audience; Yeats wanted to create a uniquely Irish form of writing and theatre.

At the Abbey, tensions erupted in May 1906 when the theatre ceased to be a co-operative and started to pay its staff. Æ, Padraic Colum and Máire Nic Shiubhlaigh resigned in protest and allied themselves with the new Theatre of Ireland, which remained essentially 'amateur'. Constance joined the committee of the new company and she and Casimir made a donation, annoying both Yeats and Lady Gregory, who claimed that she had made off with £50 that rightly belonged to the

Abbey. Later, after the United Arts Club was founded, Casimir was to take his wife's side in an argument on the subject that erupted in the club. On another occasion, Casimir arrived at the club to find a friend of Sir Hugh Lane's preparing to give a lecture on Victor Hugo. He insisted he needed the room for rehearsals. Sir Hugh complained about the incident to his aunt, Lady Gregory, who then spoke to Yeats. As late as 1912, Lady Gregory was warning Yeats to use a long spoon when supping with the Markieviczs.

In January 1907, Eva Gore-Booth organised a suffrage demonstration at the Manchester Free Trade Hall. Manchester had long been a hotbed of suffrage activity; in 1903, Emmeline Pankhurst had founded the Women's Social and Political Union in the city, encouraging a more aggressive approach to promoting women's rights, not just in Britain but internationally. Constance spoke at the demonstration, although unlike her sister, she was never primarily a suffragist, despite certainly believing in equal rights for all. As her stepson Staskou put it: 'any struggle against authority and for those suffering injustice, appealed to Madame'. On 8 March 1907, the Women's Enfranchisement Bill had its second reading in the House of Commons. It was dropped without a vote.

A few months later, an appearance as a prancing pirate in a charity production of Gilbert and Sullivan's *The Pirates of Penzance* organised by the Irish Theatrical Club at the Gaiety Theatre in May 1907 persuaded Casimir to turn his attention to the theatre. His first effort at writing was a collaboration with Seamus O'Kelly called *Lustre* – a one-act play telling the tale of Jimmy Donnellan, who came home from a stint with the British army, attempted to steal his mother's lustre (ornaments) and caused her death. It was later translated into Polish and filmed.

With Constance, Casimir was one of 600 guests at the annual State Ball of 1907 and sang Polish songs at an afternoon party given by Lady Aberdeen, with Constance accompanying him on the piano. That year, after a tearful farewell from his parents, Staskou was sent to Mount Saint Benedict's, an elite Catholic boarding school in Gorey, County Wexford, which was modelled after British public schools; Staskou was to stay there until 1911. Also that year, Josslyn married Mary L'Estrange Malone, a cousin of the Gore-Booths who had met her future husband in Constance's house. Following the marriage, his mother moved out of Lissadell, first into rented accommodation in Ballytivnan, just north of Sligo town, and then to Ardeevin, between Sligo and Rosses Point. Maeve was dispatched from Dublin, either to keep her grandmother company, or because her grandmother had decided that she could look after her better than her mother. With no children in the house, it meant the end of normal family life for the Markieviczs.

Around that time, the Markieviczs were among the founders of the United Arts Club, an idea first mooted by Æ three years earlier and taken up by the art journalist Ellie Duncan, an ally of Hugh Lane's. In 1907, Duncan issued a circular addressed 'To All Cultivated People', inviting artists, musicians and writers to join a club where they could meet, work and socialise. Others to join included W.B. and Jack Yeats, Percy French, Padraic Colum, John Millington Synge and William Orpen. Women, as well as men, were welcome to join and Casimir remained on the club's committee for many years; in Beatrice Elvery's cartoons of club members, Casimir was always depicted as twice the size of anyone else. The dinners were lively affairs where guests had to improvise a verse of a poem or a song.

A feature of the United Arts Club, which first leased rooms at Lincoln Place, was the life art classes held every week. Page Dickinson, the artist and architect, remembers all sorts of people turning up for them. The Markieviczs helped out with lessons in drawing and draughtsmanship. Both, Dickinson felt, were good artists who could have been first rate had they not spread their energies too thinly.

In March 1908, Count Markievicz launched the Independent Dramatic Company at the Abbey Theatre with his own play *Seymour's Redemption*, a wittily written tale of a politician who has an illicit love-affair. The proceeds of the opening night went towards buying a Corot for the proposed Municipal Art Gallery. W.B. Yeats disliked the play and felt it should not have been staged at the Abbey – even worse, it had attracted bigger audiences than the serious plays he favoured.

Constance played one of the main parts with her usual verve, although her voice was shrill and her accent distinctly Anglo-Irish. Still, audiences were kind and no one could deny her sincerity. In May of that year, Constance was again on stage, this time with old friends from the Theatre of Ireland, in a two-night revival of Edward Martyn's *Maeve*. She took the lead role, working hard to improve her vocal delivery. In October 1908, the Markieviczs were busily rehearsing Casimir's society farce, *The Dilettante,* and a one-act comedy he had written with the Northern Irish actress Nora Fitzpatrick called *Home Sweet Home.* With Constance and Máire Nic Shiubhlaigh acting in the first and Fitzpatrick in the second, the plays would be staged at the Abbey in early December.

At Christmas would come the annual visit to Lissadell, with the Markievicz family bundled into cabs for Broadstone station to catch the train for Sligo. During the visit of late 1908 and early 1909, Casimir created his 'dining hall pictures' on the pilasters at Lissadell. In humorous style, he painted himself, Mordaunt Gore-Booth, Jock the terrier and Kilgallon, the formidable butler.

Around this time, Constance rented a small white-washed cottage, one of three 'Slate Cottages' beside a pool in the foothills of the Dublin Mountains at Sandyford; it belonged to her friends the O'Connell Fitz-Simons. She opted to take the smaller cottage consisting of two rooms, at the modest rent of a shilling a year. A retired laundry maid called Mary Mulligan occupied the adjoining cottage and acted as caretaker for Constance. Staskou loved it – with Æ's son Brian Russell, he roamed freely around the hills and woods of Three Rock and Fairy Castle while his mother, and occasionally his father, found sheltered spots to paint. They washed in the local stream, lived on little more than bread and cheese, and freewheeled home to Rathgar after their breaks, their bikes loaded with canvases. Constance was inspired by the panoramic views: 'The mountains seem to tower over the plains and city of Dublin regal with its triple rocky crown and its mantle of heather and golden gorse. You climb to the summit and watch the sun sinking over the plains of Meath and the moon rising over Wicklow's hills.'

Padraic Colum, the previous occupant of the cottage, had left behind copies of two newspapers, *The Peasant* and *Sinn Féin,* which featured sentimental articles on the troubled past of the Irish people. One wet day in 1908, with nothing else to read, an article about Robert Emmet caught Constance's eye. His face was familiar to her from the print she had seen on the walls of houses in Sligo, but she knew little of him. Quoted in the article was his stirring speech from the dock that – in most versions – so memorably concludes: 'I have but one request to ask at my departure from this world ... when my country takes her place among the nations of the earth, then, and not till then, let my epitaph be written.'

It was her introduction to the heroes of Ireland's past and soon she was devouring stories of Owen Roe O'Neill, Wolfe Tone and Thomas Davis:

> I awoke to the fact that Ireland had not surrendered, that there were men and women who had not acquiesced in the conquest, who had a vision and an outlook higher and nobler than that of the Parliamentary Party, who went humbly to Westminster, hat in hand, to swear oaths of allegiance and look for doles and concessions as a reward for Ireland's loyalty.

Constance had grown up in a family that, although privileged, was socially aware; her father had always felt a sense of obligation to his community. She had seen desperate poverty and deprivation at first hand in Europe as well as in Ireland. She believed strongly in equal rights for women but, until that point, had felt helpless. 'Growing children take their ideas from the people around them, and thus it is hard to understand life from a bigger point of view when your outlook has been limited by a family, a house, a demesne and a glimpse at a parish beyond.'

She felt Irish but had not questioned the status quo: 'though Irish in all one's inmost feelings, one's superficial outlook was aloof and vague. One took the conquest as a *fait accompli* and as irrevocable, and believed that "things weren't too bad nowadays". One knew no history, one realised none of the responsibilities one had inherited.'

Forming co-operatives, like her brother and Æ had done, would have proved difficult for a woman. She had listened to the arguments both for and against Home Rule, but she had no vote and no say in whether the Home Rule Bill would ever be passed. Nor were women welcome in the Irish Party; the new parties springing up would prove far more welcoming. While she loved and appreciated poetry and art, Constance was a woman of action, voluble and outgoing. Not for her the slow and patient road to reform.

She was ready to do something for Ireland and wanted to do it now.

CHAPTER FIVE

Extremists and Fire-eaters

At one of Æ's Sunday nights, Constance had met the Sinn Féin leader, Arthur Griffith. She told him she wished to join the cause. Griffith responded with suspicion: 'Mr Griffith was very discouraging to me and very cautious. I first thought that he merely considered me a sentimental fool; later I realised that he had jumped to the conclusion that I was an agent of the enemy.'

Although she agreed with his Irish-Irelander views, she never shared Griffith's political outlook. In her view 'Mr Griffith's ideal for Ireland was the status that she held in 1782, during the short period when Grattan's parliament succeeded in bringing a certain amount of prosperity to the manufacturers and tradespeople of the Irish cities. Mr Griffith was not only monarchist and capitalist in his ideas, but he disliked republicanism and did not want anyone to talk of fighting for Ireland's freedom.'

Under Griffith's regime, the Sinn Féin organisation was pacifist rather than militant, with economic independence from Britain the top priority. Its practical objectives included protection for industry and commerce; the establishment of a national bank, stock exchange and insurance system; national arbitration courts and a national civil service; control over transport, wastelands and fisheries, the reform of education, the withdrawal of all support for the British armed forces and the non-recognition of the British parliament. It was not enough for Constance: 'to me the whole scheme was rendered impossible because it did not include provision for the building up of an Irish army'.

On the night of St Patrick's Day 1908, Constance attended her last ever ball at Dublin Castle, dancing Irish reels with her husband. Eleven days later, on 28 March 1908, Constance was one of the few women to attend a meeting in the Rotunda where Griffith was speaking. She met Bulmer Hobson, who was on the executive of Sinn Féin, around this time. Hobson, born in Belfast into a Quaker family, had a small private income and, along with his friend Denis McCullough, was helping revive the Irish Republican Brotherhood (IRB). At that time, he was – in the words of Constance – 'a desperate extremist and fire-eater', inspired by the veteran Fenian Tom Clarke and by Seán Mac Diarmada.

Encouraged by Hobson, Constance absorbed the ideas of Tone, Mitchel and Lalor: 'they were the gospel – it was they who made me realise that the only freedom worth having was the freedom to root out the foreign civilisation with all its cruel and material ideals and to build up a noble civilisation on Gaelic lines'. She embraced the nineteenth-century nationalist view of war as essential in building a nation and believed that noble deeds, fearless deaths and lives of self-denial and renunciation were the essential characteristics of the Irish way of life. Hobson not only accepted Constance into Sinn Féin, but introduced her to Helena Molony, who organised Inghinidhe activities when Maud Gonne was absent in France.

On a dank and drizzly night in 1908, Constance took up Molony's invitation to attend an Inghinidhe meeting. She was coming straight from a smart society function and Sidney Gifford Czira remembered a 'radiant creature' bursting into the room. She was wearing a ballgown of blue velvet 'with a fashionable train of the period' and, in her hair, 'a diamond ornament glittered'. As the group of women took in this vision, Constance introduced herself. 'Good evening. So sorry for being late – must take off my wet shoes,' she said all in one breath, before walking over to the hob and putting her shoes there.

The cool reception she received did not faze her; she was impressed by the reluctance of the women to fawn over her and quickly joined the discussion about a proposed new monthly magazine for women. Before the end of the meeting, she had offered to sell her diamond ornament to raise funds for the magazine, which would be called *Bean na hÉireann* and was to be edited by the anarchist Nannie Dryhurst. The committee turned down her generous offer. After the meeting she walked to the tram with Czira, the train of her ballgown dragging in the mud. She was unconcerned: 'You see, I'm getting quite unused to wearing clothes like these since I joined the Movement.'

She joined the Inghinidhe, taking the name 'Macha' – the Gaelic equivalent of Epona, the horse goddess of the Greeks, except that Macha was also human and able to outrun any chariot. When writing gardening notes for Bean na hÉireann, she also used the pen-name 'Armid'. Helena Molony was 'Emer' and Maud Gonne 'Maidhbh'; 'Dectora' was Madeleine ffrench-Mullen, who edited a children's page. Gonne introduced Constance to a class of unruly boys the Inghinidhe was struggling to control. 'The Countess managed them wonderfully and we never had a day's trouble with them once she took them over. Out of that, I think, developed the idea of the Fianna.'

Through Hobson, Constance had joined the Drumcondra and Glasnevin branch of Sinn Féin. With Dr Pat McCartan, another Northern Irish firebrand, and Seán McGarry, Hobson set out to educate the new recruit and brought her to North Great Britain Street to see Tom Clarke in his newsagent's shop. Clarke, son of an Irish Protestant soldier and a Catholic mother, was one of the most impressive characters in the nationalist movement. At 18, he was forced to emigrate to the USA, where he joined Clan na Gael. They sent him to London where he was arrested 'in connection with a dynamite plot' and given a life sentence. He was to spend sixteen years in prison, a sentence that badly affected his health. After he was finally released on licence in September 1898, he travelled back to the USA, where, in 1901, he married Kathleen Daly, twenty-one years his junior. When the family returned to Dublin in 1907, he opened a small shop first in Amiens Street and later at 75a North Great Britain Street (now Parnell Street). Far from broken by his long years in a British prison, Clarke's revolutionary zeal still burned bright and he was determined that his time in jail would not have been spent in vain.

Constance would never forget that first meeting with a man who had led a 'broken and sacrificed life'. 'It stands in my memory as the first milestone ... that told me definitely and surely that somehow or other I had blundered onto the right road.' She was impressed by his kindness and intelligence. 'The thing that struck you first about him was his eyes, they were so bright and alert ... they were like a searchlight turned on you, and only afterwards you noticed the colour and found out how kindly they were and how they softened the fierce, bushy eyebrows'.

Clarke was a modest man, who rarely talked about himself and abhorred attention. 'What you got from him was interest in your schemes, encouragement for your hopes, support in your hours of despair.' Like many others, she saw him as 'the link and the living inspiration between that dead Fenian and the young, true hearts that were preparing to carry on the work'.

A young railway worker called Seán O'Casey was another member of the Drumcondra branch. O'Casey, according to one account, would sit at the back of the hall, a dour and intense figure who spoke eloquently for the cause of Irish nationalism in both Irish and English. He would later become one of the country's finest playwrights, writing three classic plays about 1916 and the aftermath. For her part, Constance would sit quietly in the middle of the room, 'ready to explode into the most unconvincingly bloodthirsty sentiments' in public, but 'speaking with a gentle charm to anyone who approached her in private'. So said Desmond Ryan in his memoir *Remembering Sion*.

She quickly realised that the Irish nationalist movement was divided into factions. At one extreme was the Irish Parliamentary Party, many of them Home Rulers, but happy to conduct their business in Westminster, although disastrously and fatally splintered after the fall of Parnell. Still, most Irish supported their policies and wished for no more than Home Rule. James Connolly, the socialist, humanitarian and defender of workers' rights, stood at the other extreme and was opposed to Home Rule. Between the two sat Arthur Griffith and Sinn Féin, separatists but firmly opposed to physical force, rebel armies and secret societies. Yet within Sinn Féin were some, like Bulmer Hobson, who had signed up with the secretive IRB. Most members were conservative on social issues.

Although their political opinions were similar, Griffith and Hobson loathed each other and Constance came to distrust Hobson, suspecting him of using her in his disputes with Griffith. At first she decided that it was a personality clash, improbable as it seemed: 'Mr Hobson seemed so much younger, almost belonging to another generation, that it seemed strange for him to be so bitterly up against an older man so infinitely more gifted than himself'.

Life was gathering speed for the countess, who had celebrated her fortieth birthday in February 1908. As well as her family, her art and the theatre, she now had Sinn Féin and Inghinidhe na hÉireann to keep her busy. In April, she visited her sister Eva who, after the Women's Enfranchisement Bill was dropped, continued to devote herself to the cause of women workers in the north of England and helped found the Manchester and Salford Women's Trade Council. While in England, Constance got her first taste of political campaigning in a by-election contested by Winston Churchill at a time when the rights of barmaids were causing much agitation.

Under Clause 20 of a Licensing Bill introduced by the government, working after 8pm would be illegal for all women – not just barmaids. Eva, as joint secretary of the Women's Trade Union Council, took up their cause and, when Churchill, a Liberal, refused to support the rights of the women workers, supported the Conservative candidate, William Joynson-Hicks. On the day Churchill spoke in Manchester, Constance caused heads to turn when she drove a coach drawn by four white horses around the city. When the coach arrived at Stevenson Square, Eva and Esther Roper climbed on its roof to make rousing speeches, while Constance handed out leaflets defending the right of 100,000 respectable, hard-working women to work. 'Con was simply splendid, driving four horses all day long and half the night. Nobody talked of anything but her beautiful driving,' Eva wrote in a letter to Josslyn. Next day, Constance spoke at a mass meeting in support of Joynson-Hicks, 'the only one who takes a straight and decent view of the barmaids' question'. Her quick wit won over the crowd. Churchill lost the election by 529 votes; a few weeks later, he stood for parliament in Dundee and was elected.

On Saturday, 13 June 1908, the National Union of Women's Suffrage Societies procession took place from Embankment to Royal Albert Hall in London, with over 10,000 women attending. With Eva, Esther and Sarah Reddish, Constance travelled to London. Eva did not attend the main event, but held a demonstration on behalf of Lancashire Women's Workers in Trafalgar Square, attended by 2,000 people. From the foot of Nelson's Column, she told the crowd that five million women were working in Britain who were not paid properly for the work they were doing, many receiving half the male wage. Constance, who had led the procession from Holborn in a four-in-hand carriage, got the crowd cheering by declaring that 'they cannot abolish woman, take away her occupation, and let her starve ... We are told that the bar is a bad place for women, but the Thames Embankment is far worse'. The barmaids won their case.

By August, Constance was back in Dublin, exhibiting her more recent paintings at Leinster Hall with Casimir, Æ and others. Her *Tinker's Honeymoon* and *Old Man in Connemara* were particularly praised. On the night her 1908 exhibition opened, Constance went to a public Sinn Féin meeting. The following day, she met members of Inghinidhe na hÉireann for further discussions on *Bean na hÉireann*. The first issue of the magazine appeared in November 1908, edited by Helena Molony after Nannie Dryhurst abruptly resigned. Constance designed the title page, showing a peasant woman against a backdrop of a round tower and a rising sun.

The paper sold for a penny a copy and men as well as women snapped it up. It attracted advertising for, among other things, Irish tweed, bicycles and gramophones. Contributors included Roger Casement, Arthur Griffith, James Connolly, Æ, Seamus O'Sullivan and Casimir under the pen name 'Seumus Cassidy'. Molony wrote 'Labour Notes', while Constance's gardening column mixed sound advice on planting and pruning with political parables.

She had always been a keen gardener, but by now all her thoughts were of Irish independence. Readers were advised to think of slugs as akin to the English in Ireland; crimson roses reminded her of Ireland's martyrs. Ireland was compared to a 'poor wee bulb' buried in the dust and dirt of English rule. Like the garden in winter, Ireland was sleeping and resting, recouping her vital powers for the struggle that would come: 'now it is our duty to till and to dig and to do all which lies in our power to aid the tender plant of nationality in its struggles for existence'.

When it came to the Inghinidhe – or 'Ninnies' as they were affectionately called – no job was too small for Constance. As well as conducting drama classes for girls, she arranged the tables and chairs for meetings, tackled correspondence and sold the paper on the streets.

Casimir's first full-length play, *The Dilettante*, presented by the Independent Dramatic Company, opened in the Abbey for three nights in December 1908. Constance played the lead role of Lady Althea, who had to tell her husband that she loves Archie, a dreamy artist, who has, in turn, fallen in love with Ella, played by Nora Fitzpatrick. In the end, the two women decide Archie is not worth it and go away together. Rehearsals led Casimir to reveal how his first wife, Jadwiga, had announced her intention to leave him.

Performed along with *Home Sweet Home*, the one-act farce written by Casimir and Fitzpatrick, the evening attracted appreciative audiences for its three-night run. While Casimir's dramas were no masterpieces, they were enjoyed by Dublin audiences and he had become quite a celebrity. Three weeks later, the company of eighteen took the two plays to Sligo for a Christmas carnival, organised to pay off the debt of the Gillooly Memorial Temperance Hall. Despite blizzards and high winds, the hall was packed for two nights and 'Miss Gore' received good notices.

While in Sligo, the Count spoke with stirring sincerity at a Gaelic League meeting on making the Irish language compulsory at the newly formed National University. As Padraic Colum had remarked, he was the perfect stage Irishman and, at the conclusion of the Christmas carnival, he belted out a version of 'The Wearing of the Green' with his wife on the piano.

In March 1909, Constance delivered a lecture to the Students' National Literary Society on 'Women, Ideals and the Nation'. It was her first piece of sustained thinking on the subject. She addressed her audience as women and as Irelanders and regretted that 'for the most part our women, though sincere, steadfast nationalists at heart, have been content to remain quietly at home, and leave all the fighting and the striving to the men.' That was so despite the magnificent legacy 'of Maeve, Fheas, Macha and their other great fighting ancestors', the women of 1798, the *Nation* newspaper, the Ladies Land League and, 'in our own day', the women who joined Sinn Féin and the Gaelic League.

Nationalist women must pause before joining any group fighting for women's suffrage that did not include freedom for Ireland in its programme. 'A Free Ireland with No Sex Disabilities in her Constitution should be the motto of all Nationalist Women.' It was up to each woman to find her own way of serving the nation. 'Fix your mind on the ideal of Ireland free, with her women enjoying the full right of citizenship in their own nation, and no one will be able to side-track you.' Drunkenness was identified as one of the great scourges of Irish life that women must fight.

Irish women were urged to support Irish-made goods.

> If the women of Ireland would organise the movement for buying Irish goods more, they might do a great deal to help their country.

If they would make it the fashion to dress in Irish clothes, feed on Irish food – in fact, in this as in everything, live really Irish lives, they would be doing something great ... 'No English goods' is the war cry ...

They must enter public life and fight for a better Ireland. 'You will go out into the world and get elected on to as many public bodies as possible, and by degrees through your exertions no public institution – whether hospital, workhouse, asylum, or any other and no private house – but will be supporting the industries of your country. Regard yourselves as Irish and believe in yourselves as Irish'. She went on:

Arm yourselves with weapons to fight your nation's cause. Arm your souls with noble and free ideas. Arm your minds with the histories and memories of your country and her martyrs, her language, and a knowledge of her arts, and her industries. And if in your day the call should come for your body to arm, do not shirk that either ... May this aspiration towards life and freedom among the women of Ireland bring forth a Joan of Arc to free our nation!

The lecture was published in the *Irish Nation* in three instalments and reprinted as 'Women, Ideals and the Nation' in 1919. Constance was, by now, a frequent and confident speaker. Around this time, she spoke to the Women's Workers Union, arguing that women could expect almost as little from men's unions as from employers. In organisation lay strength, she asserted. Within the union, women could fight together for better wages, for the vote and for Ireland. Constance urged all nationalists to support Larkin, although his republicanism was less extreme than her own. Before Larkin, she pointed out, Irish unions were controlled and organised from England 'and Irish Nationalism [was] obscured'.

Constance's interest in the theatre had by no means waned and, in April 1909, she received deserved praise for her role in a Theatre of Ireland production of Seamus O'Kelly's new play *The Shuiler's Child*. Later that year, in August, the company played in Kilkenny and, in November, they were back on the Dublin stage. Although she was, by now, a vice-president of the Theatre of Ireland, this was to be her last performance with the company. Any future productions would be with her husband's company.

By early 1909, the Irish Women's Franchise League, founded by Hanna Sheehy Skeffington a year earlier, was growing in membership. Because the Irish Parliamentary Party held the balance of power in the House of Commons, English suffragists were keeping a close watch on the fight for women's rights in Ireland. While Home Rule dominated parliamentary debate, the issue of women's suffrage was gathering pace, and a number of private member's bills on women's suffrage were introduced. Without the support of the major parties, they never got far. Irish MPs held differing views: John Dillon believed that women's suffrage would be the ruin of Western civilisation, while William Redmond and Tom Kettle supported women's right to vote. With Asquith vehemently opposed to giving women the vote, John Redmond and the Irish Parliamentary Party argued that women's suffrage would have to wait until after a Home Rule Bill was passed. Redmond's attitude lost him the support of the many influential women fighting not just for the vote but also for Home Rule.

Constance would argue that suffragists were fighting 'for the rights that every soul born into this world is entitled to – the right of taking up the responsibilities and duties of citizenship in the nation of which they form a part; and the right to their free share and portion of the advantages and privileges enjoyed by those who are already citizens.' In an article for *Bean na hÉireann,* she wrote that, while the vote had given men the opportunity to play their part in building up their nation, women were bracketed with 'criminals, soldiers and paupers, and robbed of the initial right of citizenship'. Getting the vote was not just a question of women gaining self-respect, 'but also a way of developing feelings of nationality'. Women must demand not only the vote but 'a Parliament to be represented in'.

The old notion that women could serve the nation only as wives and mothers was no longer valid and Constance rejected the idea that men and women, by nature, had separate spheres of influence. She believed that 'men would be the better for a little of women's unselfishness and spirituality' and that women would bring 'a lofter idealism and a purer atmosphere' to public and political life.

Irish women were looking for opportunities to regain their freedom and women in the past – like Queen Maeve – had been part of the military tradition. 'The men of our race, descended like us from a long line of martyrs in the cause of liberty, will not try to keep our rights and our duties from us, and the day that Ireland stands free before the world shall see our emancipation too.' Others were not quite as sanguine.

Men and women alike inherited from their ancestors the characteristics of courage, a striving for democracy and equality and an idealistic nature. Women should join 'the Movement', serve on committees and boards and manage money for committees: 'no one can help you but yourselves alone; you must make the world look upon you as citizens first, as women after'. She repeated her argument that, unlike most male politicians, women had 'an inner knowledge' of what was right in an article for *Sinn Féin*. Yet women had allowed the Irish situation to deteriorate when they abandoned their Dublin mansions to hire or buy houses in London. 'They followed the English court about and joined the English ranks of toadies and place-hunters, bringing up their daughters in English ways and teaching them to make English ideals their ideals and when possible marrying them to Englishmen.'

Constance echoed the views of James Connolly that women were doubly enslaved:

> As our country has had her freedom and her Nationhood taken from her by England, so also our sex is denied emancipation and citizenship by the same enemy. So therefore the first step on the road to freedom is to realise ourselves as Irishwomen – not only as Irish or merely as women, but as Irishwomen doubly enslaved, and with a double battle to fight.

Martyrdom in Christianity was linked to the fight for national freedom, and Constance compared the destiny of nationalists to that of Jesus Christ, whose death on the cross paved the way for a religious movement that would sweep the world. The reward for self-sacrificing nationalists would be greater than 'money or advancement, success or luxury, for they would be patriots and heroes'. The need for sacrifice emphasised by Constance was shared by Patrick Pearse, who increasingly believed that the only road to freedom was through a bloody fight, whatever the consequences. Pearse's ideal Irish hero was a man who combined the heroic virtues of Cú Chulainn with the self-abnegation, suffering, death and ultimate victory of Christ.

For Constance, Ireland's landscape was already steeped in blood:

> everywhere over Ireland had the soil been consecrated by the sacrifice of blood, the blood of our noblest and best ... every hillside, every potato patch, big town or lonely cottage has its own story to tell, stories of oppression and murder, tyranny and starvation, met with self-sacrifice and martyrdom.

Her aim was not to gain equal rights for women within the British Empire, but to strengthen Irish women's position in society so that their value as 'cultural carriers' and their pure vision would gain them equality in an independent state. Others argued that, without the vote, women would have no say in the formation of the new state anticipated under Home Rule.

Constance, aware of her own background, accused the British of conceding rights in a way that helped split the Irish. She believed that the Irish historically had allowed themselves to be drawn into faction fights, to the detriment of the national struggle. Education was critical; schools should teach a broader creed of nationalism, rather than encouraging sectarianism. She echoed the words of Wolfe Tone: Ireland should be one nation with the divisions between the Catholic masses, the Anglo-Irish and the Ulster unionists irrelevant. Irishness was unique and a product of environment: she believed in 'a nationality of the spirit as well as the letter'. Everyone should find their place in the newly independent nation. She advised women to join clubs that were open to everyone regardless of religious, class or political differences, such as Sinn Féin and the Irish Industrial Development Associations.

Constance continued to read widely and, in its first year at least, wrote regularly for *Bean na hÉireann*. Over the twenty years of her public life, her fundamental beliefs remained unchanged: freedom for Ireland, a fairer social and economic system decided on by the people, and equality for all men and women regardless of religion or class. She was a true egalitarian.

CHAPTER SIX

Na Fianna – Scouting for Ireland

Constance Markievicz's outstanding contribution to the fight for Irish freedom was the Fianna – a boy's brigade formed with the specific purpose of training boys to take up arms against the English. By the time of the Easter Rising, these boys were young men aged seventeen to twenty and, thanks to their years in Na Fianna, they formed a disciplined force, trained in the use of arms. Patrick Pearse was to say later that without the Fianna, there would have been no Volunteers in 1913 and no Rising in 1916.

In May 1909, Constance was objecting to the annual Army Bill, which contained a clause forcing households to billet British soldiers, in cases of danger, for six pennies a day in compensation and fulminating against the drift of young Irish men into the British army and against possible compulsory conscription. She declared, 'We have all known for some time that it was only the terror of arming and training the young patriots of Ireland in the science of war that has prevented conscription being adopted in the British Isles.' Ireland had been excluded from the Territorial Reserve Forces Act, which was passed despite strenuous opposition by Irish MPs in 1907, but it would be impossible to impose conscription on England, Scotland and Wales if Ireland was excluded.

Some, wrote Constance, suffered from 'scarlet fever', finding the red coats of the British troops glamorous. 'It is a terrible temptation to enlist or join the British army ... and the more our boys are brought into close quarter with the army, the more they will lose the horror of it unless a strong national feeling is created.'

The idea of a boys' army came to Constance when she read an account of the Lord Lieutenant reviewing a number of Boy Scout organisations.

The value of educating youth was recognised in a number of popular civic movements, among them the temperance movement. Aware of how impressionable a young mind can be, Constance foresaw young Irish boys:

> growing to manhood and gaily enlisting in the British army or police forces, and being used to batten their own class into submission into a class war at home, or giving their lives in an imperial war made to hold Ireland as a slave state within the British Empire, fighting always the battles of the international financier to hold in subjection India and Egypt and to fight other capitalist empires and states for the right to steal their valuable properties belonging to defenceless and undeveloped peoples.

She was aware that a war with Germany was looming.

> War with Germany must bring troubles in its train for England. The words, 'England's difficulty is Ireland's opportunity' kept beating in my brain, and the question ever arose, how are we going to profit by this opportunity: will it slip by as did the Boer War with no man ready to strike a blow for Ireland's freedom?

Markievicz made up her mind to start a Boy Scout organisation as quickly as possible, with the object of training boys mentally and physically to achieve Irish independence.

> Their minds were to be trained in the true principles of Nationality, and to understand the mistakes that had been made ... As Pearse put it: to vision an Ireland 'not free merely, but Gaelic as well; not Gaelic merely, but free as well.' They should be Irish in their knowledge of Ireland's history; Irish in their use of her language; Irish in their adoption of the fine code of honour of the old Fianna; and Irish in their prowess in arms and attitude of honourable soldiers waiting faithfully for the hour to come when they too should serve Ireland with all the passion of their glorious youth.

Her educational ideas reflected those promoted by the Irish Irelanders and by Patrick Pearse. Douglas Hyde argued that the English education system did not suit the Irish and made the reasonable point that Irish language and history should be taught to Irish children. Pearse, who claimed that the English system made Irish children into 'willing slaves', looked to the traditions of the ancient Fianna and especially Cú Chulainn for inspiration.

The first written suggestion for creating an Irish army by training young boys came in the May 1909 issue of *Bean na hÉireann*. Two months later, in the July issue, it was announced that a branch of the National Boy Scouts had been founded, called the Red Branch Knights. Promoters hoped to make it the nucleus of a national volunteer army. Constance had put the idea to Arthur Griffith, but he received it coolly, put off by her association with his old enemy Hobson and by his own opposition to physical force.

Over the summer, at open-air meetings held by Sinn Féin, she pushed her idea of a boys' organisation, getting a muted response and no offers of help. The Sinn Féin executive, to which she had been co-opted in August, argued that they could not sponsor such an organisation because they had no provision for raising any kind of army. Tom Clarke proved a rare ally. 'Many is the word of help and encouragement I got from him when we first started the Fianna, and the people were more inclined to laugh at than help the Boy Army.'

One difficulty she faced was in recruiting boys for the new organisation. She came up with the idea of approaching schools and asked a unionist teacher friend to give her the name of a Catholic teacher. He suggested Michael O'Neill, the headmaster of St Andrew's School in Great Brunswick Street, near Westland Row. Tom Clarke pointed out that, because she was Protestant, the teacher might suspect her of proselytising and suggested that she bring with her Seán McGarry, a future president of the Irish Republican Brotherhood's supreme council, who was impeccably Catholic and nationalist.

Around June 1909, Constance and McGarry spoke to the boys at St Andrew's. Although initially sceptical, O'Neill was impressed by Constance's commitment and introduced her to eight young prospects for the new organisation. He also told Eamon Martin, a past pupil who had only lately left the school, of her plans. With the approval of their parents, the boys needed little persuasion. Regular meetings to establish the organisation ensued, with Constance, Helena Molony, Seán McGarry and Pat McCartan making up an informal committee. They set to work learning about signalling, drilling and other aspects of scouting.

With her adventurous and boisterous spirit, Constance loved boys and they returned that affection. To the Fianna, she became known as 'Madame', following a trend among nationalist women – Maud Gonne MacBride was another 'Madame' – to eschew both the English 'Mrs' and aristocratic titles. Helena Molony proved her greatest ally and helped supervise a memorable first attempt at camping in the Dublin mountains.

Constance cheerfully admitted to knowing nothing about camping before their ramshackle expedition. She had bought a scout tent and borrowed a garden tent. The 'Fitzgerald boys' volunteered a pony and cart that were to see much use by the Fianna in the years to come. On to the cart were piled tents, rugs, cushions, food, saucepans and books. After what seemed like hours, they arrived at their location: a little valley with a stream running through it on the side of Three Rock Mountain.

After splashing their faces in the stream, they sank back on the 'soft green sward', dawdled over 'a most delicious tea' and drowsed away the evening, reading poetry and sketching. When the light started to fail, they set about pitching the tents, which turned into a comedy of errors. They had opted to pitch the tent on the slope leading down to the stream.

> It took a long, long time. Tents are very hard to pitch if you don't know how, especially at night. When you trip over a rope in the dark, the peg comes out, you probably fall on to the tent, and it collapses ... Next comes the task of trying to disentangle jam from the blankets ...

They finally made the tents serviceable, crawled into them and got some sleep. Next morning they woke early to a bright, sunny day. 'Early as we were, the boys were still earlier, and one was already improving his mind with W.B. Yeats's poems. The others were mostly blacking their boots, and quite ready for breakfast.'

After breakfast, the boys went to church nearby, while Constance and Helena Molony tidied up. It started to rain. 'We hastily grabbed all the blankets, coats, rugs and cushions that we had spread around in the sun to air. We piled them up into a snug nest, from which we defied the elements.' Not for long. A thunderstorm broke and because the tent was pitched on the side of a hill, it – and everything inside – was soon 'one soppy sponge'.

All ended happily. The sun came out and, with the aid of a primus stove, the blankets were dried out enough for a peaceful second night. After capturing their pony, which was enjoying its freedom, they returned to civilisation, a few short miles down the road.

Constance was convinced that a boys' organisation would be successful in Ireland, and she believed that the English Scouts' system of sections and patrols was too 'loose'. An Irish organisation would be run 'on the lines of a Boys' Republic' using an army-style system of leadership. Although some gave Bulmer Hobson the credit for forming the new organisation and the exact chronology of events varies from one account to another, it was Constance who came up with the idea, organised its structure, supervised meetings and paid rental for halls.

> I had been told that Bulmer Hobson had run an organisation for boys in Belfast some years before and that he liked and understood boys; so I told him I was willing to take a hall, and asked him to come along and help. At his request we named the organisation Na Fianna Éireann in memory of the organisation in Belfast.

In Hobson's organisation, the boys had played hurling and learnt the Irish language. They wore no uniforms and did not undertake drilling or military training of any kind.

Next step was finding a room and, for ten shillings a week, Constance booked the cold, draughty hall at 34 Lower Camden Street where, in previous years, she had attended National Theatre Society rehearsals. A notice advertising a meeting on Monday, 16 August 1909, to found a national brigade for 'boys willing to work for the independence of Ireland' appeared not just in the Sinn Féin newspaper but in other nationalist papers. To help identify the location, a lad holding a green flag stood outside the door.

About a hundred turned up, among them Eamon Martin, Paddy Ward and the Fitzgerald brothers. Hobson took the chair and Constance acted as secretary. Helena Molony was also present, as were Seán McGarry and Pat McCartan. There was a small hiccup when one of the older boys suggested that the two women in the hall should leave; this was, after all, a meeting of boys committed to an organisation offering training with a view to using 'physical force'. Hobson explained that one of those women had not only come up with the idea of the Fianna but was paying the rent for the room. Constance was elected joint secretary along with Patrick Walsh. In the main business of the meeting, the 'Red Branch Knights' – the group that had undertaken the infamous camping trip – were renamed Fianna na hÉireann.

Local branches of Sinn Féin and the Gaelic Leagues quickly distanced themselves from the new organisation. Not surprisingly, *Bean na hÉireann* came out in support. 'The boys of Ireland have got their own organisation' announced the September 1909 issue. 'They are the recruits for the future armies of Ireland and on them the future of Ireland must depend'. Within a month, the hall – dubbed 'the Fianna Hall' – was busy with activities every night of the week. On Mondays and Thursday, there was drill, on Tuesdays and Fridays games and on Wednesdays language and history classes.

Con Colbert, later to become one of the Easter week leaders, was elected to the committee and compiled a course of drill commands in Irish; Irish became the language for all commands. Outside the hall, members took turns standing in uniform beneath the large flag. Lecture topics included 'The Boy Heroes of '98', 'A Boy's National Duty' and 'Women of '98', a lecture given by Constance in November. The Fianna boys were organised into *sluagh*, the Irish word for multitude that gave rise to the English word 'slew', with Camden Hall becoming the *cead sluagh*. A *sluagh* was led by an O/C (officer commanding), backed up by an Adjutant, Intelligence Officer and Quartermaster – like an adult army. Each *sluagh* was a self-governing community.

> By working for Irish freedom, they are taught the lessons of self-sacrifice and service. By obedience to their officers and the discipline of their *sluagh*, they learn to obey and be self-controlled. By becoming officers they learn to command. By governing their organisation they gain experience and confidence, and learn to think for themselves.

Since ex-British army men were not trusted, it fell to Constance, an expert shot, to teach the boys how to handle guns. She had discovered a loophole in the law that allowed a householder to use a firearm 'inside his own compound'. Her rented cottage in the foothills of Three Rock Mountain, less than eight miles from Dublin's centre and about a mile from the tram terminus, was readily accessible. In front of the cottage was a large field where the boys camped, played games and learned how to shoot. Constance was a strict taskmaster and any boy pointing a gun at another got a clip around the ear.

Constance designed the Fianna uniform and a flag – a gold sunburst on a blue field, with 'Na Fianna Éireann' written across it. The badge had a full sun with a pike head superimposed and 'Na Fianna Éireann' around the top border. Around the bottom border was 'Remember Limerick and Saxon Treachery' a popular local slogan from the time of the Williamite War and the Treaty of Limerick in 1691. The fifteen points on the sunburst represented the twelve points of the code of honour and the three of the Fianna motto: 'Purity in our hearts, strength in our arms, truth on our lips.' Both Pearse and Constance believed in the civic education of the boys who as future citizens would transform society according to special Irish values.

In 1909, she and Casimir decided to move from St Mary's in Rathgar, where they had lived since they had come to Dublin, because it was expensive to run and the children were gone. They let it for a year and, with her husband on his annual trip to the Ukraine, Constance stayed at nearby Garville Avenue while exploring Bulmer Hobson's idea of establishing a co-operative community near Dublin.

Hobson had lent Constance a book written by E.T. Craig about Rahaline, the agricultural co-operative run by an Anglo-Irish landlord, Arthur Vandeleur, who then lost his fortune through gambling. Constance may also have read the writings of James Connolly on Rahaline, which he described in *Labour in Irish History* as a model for the future in an independent Ireland. She was fascinated by the story and assured Hobson and Helena Molony that her annual income of £350 was enough to establish such a co-operative commune, if they could find a suitable location. Molony's family had recently moved abroad and, although she lived a hand-to-mouth existence, she offered a small sum of money she was expecting.

After a brief search, Constance chanced upon Belcamp House, one of several eighteenth-century residences in the Raheny area of north Dublin. The house, designed in the 1770s by James Hoban, the Kilkenny-born architect of the White House, and containing the original Oval Office,· had been the residence of a young Henry Grattan for a brief period. It had twelve bedrooms, outhouses, stable yards and a neglected seven-acre garden. Constance secured the house on a three-year lease at £100 a year. The move took place in July.

Constance hoped that Belcamp would become a self-supporting farm and market gardening business, growing its own food and easing her family's financial worries. She and Molony lived at Belcamp from the start, cycling the five miles into Dublin every day for meetings and other activities. Donnachadh O'Hannigan was employed as gardener. His brother Donal also lived at Belcamp for a few months. Fianna boys camped there at weekends. Principal activities were the posting of anti-enlisting posters and the destruction of all British recruiting posters, usually outside Royal Irish Constabulary barracks.

> On many occasions all the RIC members of Santry and Raheny stations spent several hours nightly trying to catch us in the act of posting up the leaflets, leaving only one orderly in the barracks. They would return to find the windows and doors of the barracks plastered with our literature.

Constance's stepson Staskou, then at boarding school, returned to Belcamp for the holidays. He later wrote:

> Belcamp Park was a lovely old place with a beautiful old-world garden and park, all of which needed at least two thousand a year to keep up. We were installed there like gypsies with only a few of the rooms furnished and with one servant and a gardener. Helena Molony came to live and helped with the housekeeping. Bulmer Hobson also lived there for a few months; his room a mass of printing material, papers and the like.

There were unforeseen problems. The boys, born and bred in the teeming tenements of city centre Dublin, had little understanding of country life. They ran wild, robbing local farms of hens, eggs and vegetables. Staskou told of a lad who disappeared one day and returned with a bucket in his hand containing a dark grey liquid and something feathery. It proved to be milk and a dead hen. The boys thought everything in the country was 'wild' and free to take.

After the initial blips, large groups started coming to Belcamp for training. By the time Staskou arrived, the garden was looking tidier and the attitude of the Fianna had improved.

> Belcamp had about 40 acres of grazing land around it – ideal for camping and drilling. The only arms they had at first were an old army Mauser and two .22 bore rifles of mine ... with which the boys had their first shooting lessons. Plus my father's lovely Belgian shotguns which he used for hunting when at Lissadell and disappeared later, much to his chagrin.

Constance and Helena Molony dressed tailor's dummies in red coats and used them for rifle practise.

With Hobson often absent from meetings, the burden of administration fell on Constance and Helena Molony. Money was scarce and the large rooms were damp and draughty, and difficult to heat. With no electricity, candles provided the only light. The garden produced not vegetables but weeds, despite the best efforts of O'Hannigan.

When Casimir returned from Poland in the late autumn of 1909, he was less than pleased to find Molony and the gardener Donnachadh O'Hannigan living at Belcamp. Before seeking out his wife, he had spent a few hours in Davy Byrne's and Neary's pubs, hearing jokes about the *ménage à trois* in Belcamp. Suitably fortified, he hailed a horse-drawn cab to take him to the wilds of north Dublin. When he arrived, he walked up the long avenue to a dark and silent house. Only after he had banged the door several times and taken a tour around the back, did a window open. A 'dirty little ragamuffin' popped his head out and said: 'Who da?' Casimir informed him that he was Count Markievicz. After much scuffling, the door finally opened to reveal his wife. She apologised for the dark – the gardener was using their only lamp to read by.

An exasperated Casimir immediately returned to Dublin and found a bed at the United Arts Club. Later he was to write a series of articles about the Belcamp adventure and the 'sprouts' who ate his bacon and eggs, drank his whiskey and smoked his shag tobacco. He called them 'sprouts' because they appeared everywhere – beneath his bed, under chairs and in cupboards.

There was also a tale of a Belcamp 'ghost' who turned out to be a 'milkman' that a maid kept hidden in the house for five or six months because he was an army deserter. A puzzled Constance was awoken one night by footsteps in the house, and food was disappearing from the kitchen. When the source of these mysteries was discovered, Casimir wanted to turn him over to the authorities, but Constance insisted that the 'milkman' marry his maid and sent Casimir to Raheny by bicycle to find a priest. The pair were married in the dead of night and then packed off to Scotland where, later, the reluctant husband abandoned his wife even though she was pregnant. She found her way back to Belcamp, where Constance, with her usual charity, took her in.

Casimir had other Belcamp yarns. One day he arrived in town; he was hoarse, he claimed, after a night 'barking' at sheep to keep them out of the kitchen garden. The family celebrated Christmas at Belcamp with sausages and black pudding. For once, Staskou was glad to get back to school.

Constance had asked Staskou to join the Fianna, but he declined the offer – as an aspiring gentleman, he wanted no association with a scruffy bunch of ruffians. Yet, despite the chaos, Belcamp proved a valuable training ground for the young Fianna, who had happy memories of their time there. They were still around for St George's Day on 23 April 1910 when the Protestant church in Raheny displayed a Union Jack. With the help of the boys, Constance took it down and burned it down. Another activity was ambushing the police on the lanes around Belcamp using bicycle pumps, which the boys had realised could sound like rifle bolts.

With money leeching away, Casimir asked for detailed accounts of the commune's finances and enlisted the help of Æ, who had lived in a commune for seven years, in sorting out things. In Hobson's view, the crisis had occurred because they had got more young Fianna than expected. He returned to Belfast. Helena Molony found that she was responsible for half instead of a third of the liability, which included O'Hannigan's wages and the cost of moving Constance's furniture from Rathgar, but she remained loyal and Constance persuaded her to stay on. O'Hannigan left and Josslyn gave Constance some money to bail her out. The experiment had ended after only a few months, but the Markieviczs lived there for over a year and Constance continued to use the house for training her Fianna boys until 1911. Only then did she dispose of the rest of the lease, which still had a year left to run.

In October 1909, a few weeks after the Socialist Party of Ireland was launched in Dublin, Constance attended a lecture on 'Socialism and Nationalism' given by Frank Ryan, secretary of the new party, to Sinn Féin's Drumcondra branch. Socialism, Ryan argued, deepened the concept of true nationality. Constance was ready to hear his message and proposed the vote of thanks. However, unlike the more radical members of Sinn Féin, such as Bulmer Hobson, Constance was not ready to leave the party.

Meanwhile, the art exhibition for 1909 had to be postponed when Casimir developed pneumonia. The Markieviczs were still part of Dublin's artistic circle and, while at Belcamp, they visited Nathaniel Hone, who lived nearby in Raheny; he had little time for Casimir whom he described as a 'barbarian'. On 30 December 1909, they attended a meeting at the Mansion House to discuss the production of the first ever full-length Irish opera. It was called *Eithne* and was composed by Robert O'Dwyer who conducted the choir for the Gaelic League. After a small-scale performance in 1909, the first full staging took place at the Gaiety Theatre, Dublin, on 16 May 1910.

In 1909, a year after she joined Sinn Féin, Constance had been elected to the executive and she was soon mired in controversy. Irish history, as Constance had already pointed out, was littered with tales of disagreements and splits and Sinn Féin was no different. The executive was 'stultifying the useful work they might have been doing by splitting into two camps behind two jarring leaders' wrote Constance.

The row centred on the forthcoming general election. Throughout 1909, the Liberal government in England was wobbling over the 'People's Budget', which promised tax reform; it was finally rejected by the Lords in November. Redmond had modified his demands for Home Rule: he would now be happy with an Irish parliament working under the English parliament. The result was that William O'Brien, T.M. Healy and seven other members had split from Redmond and formed the 'All for Ireland Party'.

Just before Christmas 1909, a secret meeting of the Sinn Féin executive proposed a merger with the new organisation. Arthur Griffith saw it as a shrewd move that would extend Sinn Féin's power. Sinn Féin would run candidates in Dublin with funding from O'Brien; in return, Sinn Féin would support O'Brien candidates in the south and west. Hobson, P.T. Daly and Constance were dead set against working with any section of the Irish Parliamentary Party, which Constance saw as the party made up of 'men of position and power' happy to wait for the day when Home Rule would become a reality. Irish MPs in the House of Commons did not want 'disturbers' creating trouble; they preferred to fight 'on the floor of the House', which was safer and paid them well. The proposal was defeated and all attending the meeting were sworn to secrecy.

At the first Sinn Féin meeting she attended after the Christmas break, Constance was greeted frostily, suspected of leaking the details of the Sinn Féin secret. While others whispered, Jenny Wyse Power asked her directly whether she had leaked the detail of the pre-Christmas meeting to Mr Ryan of *The Peasant* in Tom Clarke's shop. She was dumbfounded: not only had she not spoken to any journalist, she barely knew the man concerned. An incomplete account of the meeting had been published in the *Sinn Féin* newspaper and Pat McCartan suspected the allegation was a crude attempt to persuade her to sign off on this account of the meeting. She refused to do so, winning the trust of men who may have suspected her motives before this. The lines were being drawn between the Home Rulers and the militants in Sinn Féin.

In January 1910, Constance travelled to England for the general election. Arthur Bulley was standing as an independent candidate on behalf of the industrial women suffragists of Lancashire, who had decided to pay the £500 it cost to put up a candidate. Constance, as well as Reginald, Esther Roper's brother, campaigned on behalf of Bulley. He got a mere 639 votes and finished bottom of the poll. Overall, Irish nationalists won eighty-two seats, with the Irish Parliamentary Party taking seventy-one of these. William O'Brien's All for Ireland Party won eight seats and independent nationalists a further three. Asquith and the Liberals formed a new government with the support of the Irish MPs and forty Labour members.

Casimir's play *The Memory of the Dead* received a rousing reception at the Abbey on 14 April 1910, and later played a full week at the Gaiety

Theatre. Telling the tale of 1798, it proved the most successful of his plays and was revived several times. Constance played the main role of Norah Doyle, the faithful wife of a patriot, in a play clearly written for her. 'If there are men in Ireland ready to die for their country, there are just as many women' was one notable line. Included in the drama was a fifteen-year-old boy, fighting for his native land: shades of Na Fianna. Also in the cast were Helena Molony and Seán Connolly, later to be killed during the Easter Rising.

After King Edward VII died in May of that year, a period of official mourning was announced; Constance defied convention by arriving at the theatre one night in a bright red dress. When the new King George V agreed to the creation of sufficient peers to allow a Liberal majority in the House of Lords, Redmond felt he could again push the case for Home Rule.

At the Fianna's first annual conference in Dublin's Mansion House on 21 August 1910, Constance was elected president, with councillor Paul Gregan and Bulmer Hobson as vice presidents, Padraic Ó Riain as secretary, Michael Lonergan as assistant secretary and James Gregan as treasurer. The organisation consisted of seven *sluaighte* or troops; five of them were based in Dublin, with one each in Waterford and Glasgow. Membership of the troops ranged from twenty to sixty. Holding on to members was proving a problem. Boys would join and disappear a week later when they discovered that they were not going out to fight the English in the next week.

While the Baden Powell Scouts did their daily good deed and learned how to tie knots, the Fianna boys were inflamed with talk of war. 'We have laid the foundation of a very important work – the raising of a disciplined army. We will go to fight praying to God for victory and we will fight, please God, with a right good will,' wrote Constance in *Bean na hÉireann*. She quoted the reply of Ossian to St Patrick: 'We, the Fenians, never used to tell an untruth; a lie was never attributed to us; by truth and the strength of our hands we used to come safe out of every danger.'

Despite initial scepticism, the founding of the Fianna renewed interest in educating children and youth within Sinn Féin, which was struggling to keep members. Early in 1910, an Irish Brigade was founded and a children's column appeared in the Sinn Féin newspaper.

Although Hobson left Sinn Féin in 1910, Constance decided to stay, perhaps because it was one of the few organisations admitting women members. She was also aware of the damage that quarrels and infighting had caused previous nationalist organisations.

Towards the end of 1910, Constance was involved with Maud Gonne in providing hot meals for children in Dublin's Liberties area. The Act of 1906 providing school lunches in Britain had never been extended to Ireland and Inghinidhe na hÉireann, along with Hanna Sheehy Skeffington, took up the cause. James Connolly, who had returned to Ireland during the year, proved a staunch ally and went with Gonne to meet the Irish Trades Council in November 1910; from that came a meeting with the Home Secretary in London. Placating the clergy, some of whom thought it was 'dangerous and subversive to feed starving children', as Gonne put it, was another challenge. By the end of the year, about 250 youngsters at St Audeon's School were getting a hot meal every day. Constance was one of the women doling out the stew and washing the greasy plates afterwards; helping out were the women who ran the Penny Dinners in Dublin's Meath Street. Soon the pupils of nearby St John's Lane were also being fed. Not until September 1914 was the scheme officially extended to Ireland.

In March 1911, James Connolly became district organiser of the Irish Transport and General Workers' Union for Ulster, moving with his family to Belfast. Women's suffrage was again taking centre stage in the House of Commons, with the Second Conciliation Bill debated as a Private Member's Bill; it was passed by a majority of 255–88. In August, Louie Bennett and Helen Chevenix founded the Irish Women's Suffrage Association; that same month, 3,000 women at Jacob's biscuit factory went on strike. It was the first major industrial dispute in Ireland involving women. In November, Asquith announced that he favoured a more general suffrage bill; suffragists could suggest and propose an amendment to give some women the vote. The bill for women's suffrage was dropped.

CHAPTER SEVEN

'The cause of labour is the cause of Ireland'

Constance first got to know James Connolly through the Fianna in 1911. Connolly's daughters, Nora and Ina, had helped organise the Betsy Gray *sluagh* – the only Fianna *sluagh* for girls in the country – in Belfast. 'And so it happened that when I was up in Belfast to lecture to the Fianna, the girls brought me to the Connolly house and we all became great friends,' Constance wrote in *The Nation* much later.

Her experiences with the Fianna had opened her eyes to the reality of life for low-paid workers eking out a living in Dublin's stinking and rat-infested tenements. She was ready to hear Connolly's message: that the fight for a just society and the battle for Irish independence must go hand in hand. Allied to that was the fight for women's rights; Connolly, unlike many nationalists of the time, was a thorough-going feminist who described women as the 'slaves of slaves'.

Constance quickly came to regard the Connolly's 'nice little house, high up on the Falls Road' as a home from home, where she would spend 'pleasant and interesting evenings ... listening to James Connolly and his friends talking'. The conversation was wide-ranging, covering history, politics, economics, social systems, class distinctions, culture and revolution: 'and everything discussed led back to the same question – how can we work out Ireland's freedom? Where can we find guidance in the past? What is at the back of the tyranny and sufferings of the present day, and where lies the inspiration to guide us as the future unrolls itself?' Keenly aware of her own ignorance, Constance listened and learned. She started reading the books Connolly and his friends recommended.

Connolly's syndicalism, absorbed during his stay in the United States, was based on the premise that workers should control the means of production. In his book *Labour in Irish History*, he added an Irish dimension: 'The Irish question is a social question ... who would own and control the land? The people or the invaders ...?'

As far as Constance was concerned, Connolly 'approached the question of Ireland's misery and subjugation from a broader standpoint than any man of his generation'. Social problems were caused principally by British imperialism. In Connolly's *Reconquest of Ireland*, the conquest was capitalist and the re-conquest would be socialist; for Constance, that meant a return to ancient Irish society and Gaelic ideals. Both Connolly and Larkin supported the Gaelic revival movement, admired Irish music and song, and read Irish history. With Sinn Féin policies not gaining the support Constance might have wished for, she looked to the labour movement as a new way to fight for Ireland's freedom.

Constance was not choosing Connolly's ideas from a belief in syndicalism, but because she agreed with his final goal: a revolution that would crush the British government and sever all links with it. She embraced his notion that the struggle for national independence was inseparable from the struggle for socialism: 'The cause of labour is the cause of Ireland, the cause of Ireland is the cause of labour. They cannot be dissevered.' Most labour activists were more moderate than Connolly; they favoured Home Rule and had no time for revolutionary socialism.

For Connolly, a visionary political thinker with a practical streak, Ireland was its people; he brushed off vague notions of Cathleen Ní Houlihan. Born in 1868 in Edinburgh, of Irish emigrant parents, he had left school at the age of eleven. After a stint as a compositor's assistant, which ignited his interest in the printing trade, he enlisted with the King's Liverpool Regiment, falsifying his age and his name. With the regiment, he spent seven years in Ireland, immersing himself in Irish politics and culture. When his father was injured in an accident, Connolly 'discharged himself' from the army and returned to Scotland as a deserter. There he met John Leslie, who introduced him to Marxism and socialist ideas. In April 1889, he married Lillie Reynolds, a young Wicklow woman he had met in Ireland.

By 1892, Connolly was secretary of the Scottish Socialist Federation and had begun contributing articles to *Justice*, the journal of the Social Democrat Federation. With a growing family, money was always tight and, when he was offered a paid job as organiser of the Dublin Socialist Club Society, he gratefully accepted. In April 1896, he moved to Dublin. Within days of his arrival, the Dublin Socialist Club had become the Irish Socialist Republican Party.

In August 1899, Connolly, along with Maud Gonne and Arthur Griffith, organised protests against the Boer War – a war 'enabling an unscrupulous gang of capitalists to get into their hands the immense riches of the diamond fields'. The first instalment of his finest work, *Labour in Irish History*, had been published in *Workers' Republic*, the pioneering labour newspaper he had founded in 1898. During 1901, he published *The New Evangel*, which attempted to persuade Catholics that socialism was compatible with their religious faith.

Still struggling to support his family, Connolly emigrated to the USA in 1903, where he found work as an insurance collector in Troy, New York. He joined various left-leaning organisations and unions, most notably the newly formed Industrial Workers of the World, or 'Wobblies'. He became organiser and secretary of the Building and Construction Workers Industrial Union in Newark and, in March 1907, he founded the Irish Socialist Federation in New York and launched a new journal called *The Harp*.

While Connolly was the first true Irish labour leader, the fiery James Larkin had organised dock workers in Belfast with spectacular success in 1907. Protestants and Catholics had united to fight for their rights, bringing the city to a standstill for two months. Larkin, originally from Liverpool, believed in 'one big union' and that 'an injury to one is the concern of all'. He used the 'sympathetic' strike as his main weapon. Employers came to loathe him.

Because Dublin had little industry, most men worked either as unskilled labourers or in the transport of goods. Larkin set up a branch of the British-based National Union of Dock Labourers (NUDL) for Dublin's dockers and, in November 1908, carters in Dublin and coal workers in Cork went on strike, defying orders from head office in

England. Larkin was expelled from the NUDL and, on 4 January 1909, he founded the Irish Transport and General Workers Union (ITGWU). In June 1910, the NUDL prosecuted Larkin on a dubious charge of diverting union funds to the fledgling ITGWU. He was convicted of embezzlement and sentenced to a year's imprisonment.

On his return to Ireland on 26 July 1910, Connolly launched a campaign to have Larkin released. With the support of the viceroy, Lord Aberdeen, Larkin's sentence was quashed and, on 1 October 1910, a mass meeting was held in Beresford Place to celebrate his release from prison. Constance cycled from Belcamp Park to hear him talk and gave a short speech herself. It was a scorching hot day and she was relieved to be rescued from the crowd by a friend and given a seat on the platform.

She described Larkin as 'some great primeval force'. He was 'a tornado, a storm-driven wave, the rush into life of spring, and the blasting breath of autumn'. His relationship with an audience was extraordinary. 'It seemed as if his personality caught up, assimilated, and threw back to the vast crowd ... every emotion that swayed them, every pain and joy that they had ever felt'. Larkin was an imposing figure and he 'forced his own self-reliance and self-respect' on the crowd, making them class-conscious and conscious of their nationality.

> Here was a man who had the brain and the courage to demonstrate by his actions that international socialism does not stand for the merging of our identity with that of England, does not demand the subjection of races, but stands for free nations or national units who, on a basis of absolute equality, associate together for the purpose of obtaining and holding for the people nationally, and for the nations internationally, a noble civilisation that should be based on national governments by the people and for the people, and the international union of these governments on the basis of humanity, to preserve peace, and to put an end to the control of world affairs by international financiers who foment wars between nations for their own profits, and who in their pursuit of wealth trick nations into policies which subject the majority of the human race to lives of misery and slavery culminating too often in the horrors of famine and war.

In the following weeks and months, Constance was to see Larkin frequently. A branch of the Fianna shared quarters with the ITGWU, first at 29–31 Beresford Place and later in the former hotel acquired by the union and named 'Liberty Hall'. Beresford Place, only one hundred metres from Sackville Street, had become the focus for political meetings; it was centrally positioned and easily accessible by train or tram.

In late 1910, Constance was not only lecturing to the Fianna's Belfast branches, but also organising an ambitious inter-*sluagh* scouting games at Mr Jolly's fields in Scholarstown, County Dublin, on a wet autumn Sunday. *An Chead Sluagh* and *Sluagh* Wolfe Tone combined to defend 'the citadel – an area of 400 square yards – from the attacking north Dublin *sluaighte*.' The outcome was inconclusive but the seventy young Fianna went home tired and happy.

After the British general election of 1910, with the Irish nationalist MPs holding the balance of power in Westminster, Home Rule looked inevitable as a trade-off for continuing Irish support. By 1911, Ulster Unionists who opposed Home Rule ('Rome Rule') were becoming increasingly vocal. In earlier years, they could rely on a Conservative government in Westminster to kill the idea. With the Liberals back in power, the spectre of rule from Dublin was all too real. They found their leader in Dublin-born Edward Carson, a Trinity College graduate and a member of the Irish bar.

Dominating public discussion at the time was Dublin Corporation's proposal to present the newly crowned King George V with an address on his forthcoming visit to the city. Not everyone supported this idea and some nationalists, including Constance, wanted to exploit the situation for propaganda purposes. Sinn Féin and the Irish Republican Brotherhood (IRB) felt it more advisable to lie low.

At the Robert Emmet birthday commemorative meeting in the Rotunda on 4 March 1911, Pat McCartan jumped up on the platform and, supported by Constance, proposed a resolution condemning Dublin Corporation's plan to present an address to the king. Tom Clarke, who had already told McCartan that the IRB was against any such resolution, reluctantly seconded him. For a short while, the resolution unified the various strands of nationalists. On 23 March, the national council of Sinn Féin formed the United National Societies Committee with Michael O'Rahilly, self-styled The O'Rahilly, as secretary. The committee called on Dublin Corporation to repeat its stand of 1903 when it declined to recognise Edward Vll as sovereign of Ireland. The resolution was supported by Constance, with members of the Irish labour movement joining nationalists on the issue.

It was during this campaign that Constance met Patrick Pearse. 'At this time he seemed like a man who was feeling his way, looking for a policy – not for a principle, for he was always quite sure of what he wanted, and was ready for anything he might have to sacrifice and suffer.' He would arrive at meetings with Thomas MacDonagh, both of them poets and teachers, both bursting with ideas. Another lively member of the committee was Eamonn Ceannt.

Four months of argument, debate and protests followed. Supported by Inghidhne na hÉireann, the Fianna's printing press cranked out thousands of handbills calling on Dubliners to rally in protest at the Corporation's plan to pay homage to the new king. Protests were planned for the king's visit. One proposal was to hold meetings at street corners in Dublin, with speakers standing on chairs or boxes. Arthur Griffith opposed the idea on the grounds that Sinn Féin should stand on its dignity. The O'Rahilly pointed out that if Sinn Féin went on standing on its dignity, it soon would have nothing left to stand on. Constance later remembered the influence of O'Rahilly: 'The O'Rahilly was one of the most active spirits among us. He had come back from America a short time previously and taken his old place on the executive of Sinn Féin at once. He was a most welcome reinforcement to the moribund society, for Sinn Féin was nearly dead.'

On 22 June 1911, the date of George V's coronation in Westminster Abbey, a monster nationalist rally attracted over 30,000 to Beresford Place and the surrounding streets. Speakers included James Connolly, Arthur Griffith, John MacBride and Cathal Brugha, as well as Constance, with two words ringing out: 'Republic' and 'Independence'. One of those listening was a young Éamon de Valera.

Protests against the forthcoming visit of the king continued and on 4 July, Constance, with Helena Molony, had her first brush with the law when she attempted to burn half of a large Union Jack she had 'captured' from the Leinster House lawn while attending a demonstration organised by the United National Societies at Foster Place. A policeman came hurtling in her direction and so she tied the flag around her waist. To the entertainment of the crowd, the policeman then started pulling at one end of the flag, while bystanders grabbed Constance, helping her to hold the other end. The flag began to slip out of her fingers and 'at last went with a bang', leaving the policeman to stagger back and fall.

'A mighty cheer went up from the crowd thinking that they had rescued me and for a moment there was a wild scrimmage'. When Jack McArdle was arrested, everyone sobered up. Constance still had half of the flag and gave a boy a few coins to buy some paraffin oil. By the time the boy had returned with the paraffin, the crowd was moving towards Queen Street. This time, protected by the crowd, Constance succeeded in making a blaze of the flag 'to wild shouts of applause'. The charred remains were cut into tiny bits at the meeting in Smithfield that followed. 'It made a fine show, and nobody was left in any doubt as to what we were doing. The police could not get at me, marching in the centre of a wild and excited crowd and the flag burnt itself out amidst wild shouts of applause'.

Supporting Constance all the way was Helena Molony. Remembering stories her brother had told her of smashing shop windows that displayed the Union Jack during the '98 celebrations, Molony had filled her handbag with stones from a building site. These she distributed to young men in the crowd, keeeping one for herself. After the Smithfield meeting, the crowd turned back to the city, following the speaker's horse-drawn wagon and singing nationalist songs. They were aiming for the Mansion House in Dawson Street, the official residence of Dublin's Lord Mayor. They got as far as College Green, where they met a police cordon stretched across Nassau Street.

On the corner was an optician's shop with a giant pair of spectacles in the window advertising its wares. Each lens displayed an image of George V. Molony could not resist. She took the remaining rock from her handbag and threw it, hitting the window's metal protection with a loud clatter. In the ensuing confusion, Constance grabbed the reins of the horses pulling the speaker's platform and turned up Grafton Street. When she was blocked again, she turned the horses into the police cordon, hoping the crowd would follow close behind and break through. They proved too slow and Helena Molony was arrested and escorted to College Street police station.

By the time Constance had succeeded in bailing her out (in general, police were unhappy about women posting bail), it was two o'clock in the morning and the two women were exhausted and hungry. When they approached a coffee stall in Beresford Place, they were initially refused because they were women. Fortunately someone recognised Molony and the women got their hot drinks. Disturbances continued the next day when protesters were refused entry to a City Hall meeting of Dublin Corporation. Constance scaled the wall and ran up the steps of City Hall before she was grabbed by several police officers and ejected. Helena Molony had followed her and received the same treatment. The meeting was adjourned with the result that no vote was taken on the presentation to King George; the protesters had won.

Four cases arising from the disturbances were heard that day. Seamus O'Duffy was charged with selling postcards without a peddler's licence. James McArdle got one month's hard labour for setting fire to a flag and assaulting the police. Constance testified that it was she who had set fire to the flag; the police argued that McArdle had helped and that he had resisted arrest. James Pike was given the choice of either a forty-shilling fine or one month in jail for disorderly conduct.

Helena Molony, the first woman of her generation to be jailed in the cause of Ireland, was convicted of throwing stones in Grafton Street and also given a choice of a forty-shilling fine or a month in jail. 'You will get no money from me, sir,' she defiantly told the judge. A group of friends attempted to provide her with a pot of tea from the nearby Four Courts Hotel but they were refused even after Constance offered to buy the pot. A friend stepped in and provided refreshments, after which the prisoner set off in a Black Maria to serve her sentence. Maud Gonne telegraphed her congratulations from Paris. After a night in jail, Molony was released when a well-wisher paid her fine. Molony found out later that it was Anna Parnell, who wanted her freed so that she could continue her work editing *The History of the Ladies Land League*.

King George and Queen Mary were due to arrive in Dublin for their five-day visit on 8 July. The O'Rahilly came up with the idea of making a large banner calculated for maximum embarrassment. On the banner was inscribed the well-known line 'Thou art not conquered yet, dear land' – a line from a song that Constance found 'haunting and beautiful, and just put into words what we all felt'. The National

Societies' Commission then applied to Dublin Corporation for permission to sink two poles at the end of Grafton Street to which they could attach the banner. Through the intervention of Eamonn Ceannt, then working for the Corporation, they not only got permission, but Corporation workmen lifted the pavements and made the necessary holes.

Meanwhile, work continued on the banner. 'We were busily engaged on the scroll: there was an immense amount of work in it. The O'Rahilly was one of the neatest and best-dressed men in Ireland, yet there he was down on his knees on a dusty floor, pencilling out the gigantic letters on the calico for us to fill in with printing ink.' At last it was ready and carried to a small whitewashed cottage in a yard near Westland Row, where the poles were prepared along with ropes and pulleys. At 11.30pm, the banner and poles were loaded onto a lorry. It was drizzling rain. 'There were very few people about; two or three policemen looked at the strange little convoy and then followed us, but they did not interfere. After some trouble, the man got the poles firmly planted and the scroll into position. It made a splendid show.'

By the time 'the enemy' had pulled it down late the next morning, thousands had seen it. Sinn Féin printed and circulated postcards captioned 'The Battle of the Poles' with a caricature of two well-fed policemen carrying away the poles, banner and all. At least one man was arrested for selling the postcards.

The king's visit proved relatively calm. With Griffith adamant that rioting must be avoided, the IRB held its annual trip to the grave of Wolfe Tone in Bodenstown that day, so removing several hundred firebrands from the city and boycotting the visit in a dignified manner. Much to Constance's disgust, Bulmer Hobson joined them.

> Mr Hobson had approved of this being done when it was first suggested, and had gone up to Belfast, leaving us under the impression that he would be with us. But on his return, he kept out of the way and joined the Bodenstown crowd. He was one of those who preferred the limelight and laurels to be won by a fierce speech at a rebel's graveside to the possibility of getting a hammering from the police or being arrested.

Constance, the Inghinidhe, the National Women's Committee and the Socialist Party did their best to make up for the absent republicans. They handed out handbills along the route of the procession, helped by Fianna boys who had stayed up half the night working their ancient printing press.

> Today another English Monarch visits Ireland. When will Ireland regain the Legislature which is by everyone granted to be her mere right? Never! As long as Irish men and women stand in the streets of Dublin to cheer the King of England and crawl to those who oppress and robe them. God save Ireland!

The more adventurous of the group were at Trinity College, a unionist stronghold. Constance stood on the corner of Nassau Street with a young man holding a black flag. She reported that most of the crowd held Union Jacks. When the procession with the king approached, she started handing out handbills and, as the first carriage came along, an irate old gentleman started whacking her on the head with the stick holding his Union Jack. The stick broke almost at once, though she reported that her back was 'pretty stiff'. It was one of a number of small disturbances along the route. The pro-unionists were tolerant and 'quite amused' at what was going on. 'Everything had been so quiet for so many years that they had come to believe that they had succeeded in pacifying Ireland.' Not so amused were her society friends from Dublin Castle and her family members. She was seen as a traitor to her class.

In spite of their efforts, the king and queen enjoyed their visit and sent a telegram of thanks to Lord Aberdeen from the Royal Yacht at Holyhead. In a letter to her brother Josslyn, Constance wrote that Dublin was back to 'its usual peaceful self' and hoped that King George would not return 'for many a long day' since kings' visits seemed to bring out 'the worst qualities of people'.

On Sunday, 6 August 1911, the Inghinidhe and the Socialist Party of Ireland held a demonstration in Beresford Place to welcome Molony and McArdle on their release from Mountjoy Gaol. While Molony had served only a day of her month's sentence, McArdle had done the full month. In the absence of the Socialist Party secretary, Walter Carpenter, himself in jail after a noisy public meeting at Beresford Place on 14 July, Constance presided. Around a thousand had turned up for the meeting, with about fifty policemen watching them warily. Constance made a forceful speech, arguing that, in future, physical force must be met by physical force.

Molony stood up to address the crowd. She mentioned the absent Carpenter and quoted his description of King George as 'one of the vilest scoundrels' ever to have visited Ireland. That was enough for the watching police. Two of them attempted to seize Molony and, in climbing onto the lorry, one of them was 'repelled by the Countess Markievicz by means of her foot' as a newspaper report put it. She and Molony were marched off to Store Street police station.

Constance told a different version of the story. She claimed that when one of the policemen took exception to Molony's words, she had stood up from her position on the platform to protect Molony and that a policeman standing in front of the lorry grabbed her ankles. Another seized her from behind, picked her up and threw her off the platform. She claimed never to have been so surprised in her life. She remembered only the flashing of batons and the stampeding of the crowd; she also recalled some girls who stood firm as she was dragged by two enormous policemen across Beresford Place to the police station. One Fianna boy followed the whole way, kicking at the legs of the police and shouting 'Ah you devils, ah you brutes'.

The charges brought against her were for resisting arrest and for throwing gravel at the police. Where she had found the gravel while standing on a platform was never explained. The two women spent a hot afternoon inside the police station, cheered by the voices of the crowd that remained outside. Seán Mac Diarmada sent in a bunch of grapes and Nancy Wyse Power contributed the absolute essential – a pot of tea. In the evening, they were released.

Their adventure was widely reported. Arthur Griffith had hoped to make it a test case for freedom of speech. 'If today a policeman can arrest a speaker because, as he alleges, the speaker is disrespectful to a monarch, tomorrow the same force will be empowered to attack a meeting and arrest a speaker because in their opinion he is disrespectful to a British Ministry,' he wrote in *Sinn* Féin. Constance did not agree with Griffith's insistence that they hire a counsel for their defence. She argued that, for propaganda purposes, it would have been better had she conducted her own defence, since lawyers had too much respect for the apparatus of the law.

She was found guilty of throwing dust and pebbles at the police, although she maintained that she had sat quietly throughout the excitement, writing notes. Molony, thrilled that she was to be charged with high treason like her hero, Wolfe Tone, was disappointed when the charge was reduced to one of 'degrading the king in speeches at Beresford Place'. No sentence was passed. Constance believed that a higher authority had intervened, belatedly realising that a prison sentence for the two women would have given them and their cause notoriety as well as publicity.

The *Sligo Champion* reported the case in full, to the great embarrassment of the Gore-Booth family. Over the next few years, the Sligo papers would ignore much of Constance's activities. As for Casimir, his chances of getting portrait commissions from the Castle set were dwindling and the family was struggling financially. That summer, he had hoped to travel to the Ukraine with Staskou, but he abandoned the plan when told that he would have to pay a fine of £4 for every year Staskou was out of Russia. Instead, Staskou was sent to Constance's sister, Mabel Foster, in Falmouth, Cornwall, for a holiday. Maeve now spent all her time with her grandmother, although she was later joined in the classroom by her cousin, Stella L'Estrange. She had a governess called Janet Clayton, referred to as 'the Sassenach' by Constance when they met first. Her parents were infrequent visitors; after one visit Maeve was reported to have remarked 'Well, that's over, she won't think of me for another year now.'

In those volatile and exciting times, suffragist societies had been springing up all over the country, not all of them agreeing with the radical tactics espoused by the Irish Women's Franchise League. In August 1911, the Irish Women's Suffrage Federation was founded in an attempt to provide a link between the various groups scattered around the country. Joint honorary secretaries were Louie Bennett and Helen Chevenix. Like Markievicz, Bennett had come to public life in middle age, in her case through membership of the Irish Women's Suffrage and Local Government Association. Unlike Markievicz, she was a pacifist and an internationalist, who believed in conciliation, not confrontation.

Constance, though always sympathetic, did not feel that the suffragists went far enough; 'for myself I demand and expect a great deal more'. Nationalists argued that suffragists were seeking a vote in a parliament that had no right to legislate for Ireland. In her earlier days as an activist, Constance had referred to the importance of getting women workers into parliament. A man with a vote had power to frame laws 'to protect his labour from the rapacious capitalist, who in return has the same weapon at his service for his defence'; women did not. In September 1911, at the foundation of the Irish Women's Workers' Union by Larkin and his sister Delia, Constance again highlighted the importance of votes for women:

> Without organisation you can do nothing and the purpose of this meeting is to form you into an army of fighters ... As you are all aware women have at present no vote, but a union such as has now been formed will not alone help you to obtain better wages, but will also be a great means of helping you to get votes ... and thus make men of you all.

In October, Constance was elected a vice-president of Inghinidhe na hÉireann. As part of the Sinn Féin executive, she attended the meeting that refused to accept the proposed third Home Rule bill. The Ulster Unionists were also unhappy with the bill but for different reasons. Constance made no comment on Ulster. She seemed to assume that the problems with Ulster could be solved by severing all links with the crown, believing, like many nationalists, that Ulster Protestant attitudes were the result of English duplicity and that alone.

After leaving Belcamp earlier in the year, she and Casimir lived temporarily with Helena Molony at 15 Lower Mount Street where most of their property remained in boxes. On a July visit that coincided with the Gaelic League's Oireachtas week, Rosamond Jacob, a suffragist nationalist from Waterford was struck by the bohemian atmosphere: no carpets on the floors, paintings by Casimir and Constance scattered everywhere, lots of books. There was also a human skull, 'very old and brown' and possibly of Asiatic origin, as well as a bronze bust of Robert Emmet on the chimney piece along with Russian icons, and a comfortable sofa covered in cushions. It was her first time meeting Constance: 'She is a good deal what I expected – very lively and talkative and intense – very intense – and with a very tony accent'. During the week, Casimir was showing his paintings, while Constance played a provincial queen in the Oireachtas pageant. She took one night out to entertain her mother, who was visiting from Sligo.

Constance had her own particular style of dressing and Jacob remembered her coming to breakfast wearing a white alpaca coat down to her knees, long pink stockings and high-heeled shoes. Even when dressed more soberly, she wore a pair of 'very swagger shoes'. Her speech was colourful, punctuated 'with damn and my God every now and then'. Jacob, a Quaker and vegetarian, was horrified by 'Madam's frightful callous talk about shooting birds, starlings included'. She was truly the product of her background in this regard – 'a bloodthirsty sportswoman'. She and Miss Molony argued all the time and their views on men differed. Emer – as Helena was known to Jacob – seemed to regard men 'more as a relaxation of an idle hour than in any more serious light'. She did not appear to believe in 'the one love of a lifetime' but rather in 'one minor flame after another'. She was not fond of the Count, finding his conversation 'a mixture of childishness and wickedness'. As Jacob put it, Molony 'prefers women and Madam prefers men'.

Not much changed when the Markieviczs rented Surrey House at 49B Leinster Road in Rathmines in early 1912. Surrey House (dubbed 'Scurry House' by some) was a tall, gabled, semi-detached house with a strip of garden to the front, located near the junction of Leinster Road and a smaller road leading to Grosvenor Square. It contained a riot of theatrical props, books, papers 'and a good deal of dust', according to Jacob. For Constance, it was less a home than a centre of activities, with an unceasing stream of visitors, among them fellow republicans and socialists, Fianna boys, and girls fired from their jobs in Jacob's factory. A window was left open at night so that any wandering friend in need could climb inside. Constance rolled up the rugs to make housekeeping simple, and a steady stream of handbills and posters emerged from the small printing press she owned. In the garden, a group of the Fianna known as 'the Surrey clique' might be found testing a Howth rifle, although Constance was not too keen on this.

The neighbours soon became aware of the eccentric behaviour of the new tenants. On one occasion, Casimir washed a collection of theatre wigs and left them to dry on the windowsill. Sometime later Constance noticed a gathering of passers-by outside the house talking loudly about human scalps scattered around the flowers and the lawn. Hanna Sheehy Skeffington, remembering this period later on, wrote of how Constance, who lived near her, would come 'flashing in' to invite her to an impromptu party or to meet Eva, 'pacifist, feminist poet', or Liam Mellows. As Constance became increasingly known to them, police were keeping a close watch on the comings and goings at Surrey House.

Constance's work with the Fianna continued, now monitored by the IRB, who saw it as a vehicle for recruits. In 1911, a separate IRB Circle for Fianna members, called the John Mitchel Literary and Debating Society for cover, had been formed with Con Colbert as Centre, which was the IRB term for commanding officer, and Padraig Ó Riain as secretary. From this time, the IRB controlled both the policy and administration of the Fianna, with Bulmer Hobson attending a meeting of the Circle before each Fianna *ard fheis* and instructing members on how the vote should go. The IRB was infiltrating any nationalist organisation it could, attempting to radicalise members by persuading them that the policies of the Irish Parliamentary Party were futile; the IRB believed that force 'was the only thing that got anything from Britain', according to Kathleen Clarke.

In December, the Independent Dramatic Company performed *Eleanor's Enterprise* by George Birmingham at the Gaiety Theatre before taking it to Belfast. Constance had met Canon Hannay (Birmingham's real name), when the Count's theatre group was playing in Westport and asked him to write a play for them. Although he professed no great interest in the theatre, he gave her the draft of a play he had written long before on certain conditions, most notably that, if she played the heroine, she would remain modestly dressed in a scene where she had to emerge from her bedroom in the middle of the night. Believing Constance to be 'brilliant but most erratic', Hannay wrote her several letters urging her to wear a dressing gown and slippers in this scene. These letters were discovered when Surrey House was searched after 1916.

In the play, the heroine Eleanor, just down from Girton College, Oxford, and played by Constance, sets herself the task of improving the lives of some Connacht peasants. Causing much innocent amusement amongst audiences was the donkey that appeared during the second act. 'Constance Markievicz can win hearts on the stage as she can off it,' said the *Irish Independent*. Alternating with *Eleanor's Enterprise* for the week was a new play written by the Count called *Rival Stars*, the story of an artist and his wife – played by Constance – gradually drifting apart through conflicting interests. After eleven years of marriage, it was obvious that Constance's energies were increasing devoted to revolutionary activities. Yet, although there were plenty of rumours about the Count's private life, the pair remained close.

In January 1912, Casimir directed and Constance played the lead in Edward Martyn's *Grangecolman*, a play about a well-born Irish suffragist, staged at the Abbey. The play was followed by *Unseen Kings*, a verse play in one act written by Eva Gore-Booth, who based it on the Cú Chulainn myths. In February, the company went to Cork with a production of *Memory of the Dead*, and in the spring Casimir helped Fred Morrow produce the Russian domestic tragedy *The Storm* by Alexander Ostrowski, designing and painting the scenery. He wrote an article for the *Freeman's Journal* castigating English critics for failing to appreciate Russian writers and for their preoccupation with sentimental melodrama and music hall freaks. 'London does not want reality and truth – she dubs it sordid realism,' he wrote.

In March 1912, the Irish Parliamentary Party had helped kill off the Parliamentary Franchise (Women) Bill, aimed at giving limited voting rights to propertied women; it was defeated 222–208 with not a single Irish MP voting for the Bill, although thirty one of the Irish members had supported it on its initial reading. English suffragists declared war on the Irish MPs, picketing the House of Commons with signs proclaiming 'No Votes for Women, no Home Rule'. On 31 March 1912, Sackville Street in Dublin was jammed for a Home Rule rally, where Redmond appealed for national unity on one of four platforms. Patrick Pearse preached a more radical message, though he was still in favour of Home Rule. Around the same time, small militias of unionists and Orange Order members began drilling in Ulster. At the time, James Connolly looked on Home Rule as a necessary first step to independence.

Constance continued her work for the Fianna and on Sinn Féin policy. Home Rule seemed a certainty, but Sinn Féin was not happy with the latest bill, introduced in April 1912, which gave the British parliament a veto in the proposed Irish parliament, as well as the rights to Irish minerals and the right to tax the Irish without the new Irish parliament's consent. Irish suffragists criticised the Home Rule Bill because it did not include votes for women who, for some time, had been eligible for election as Poor Law Guardians or county councillors.

On 1 June 1912, Constance attended a mass meeting of Irish women at the Antient Concert Rooms to demand the inclusion of women's suffrage in the bill. Copies of a resolution were sent to all Irish MPs. To a man, they ignored it. An exasperated Irish Women's Franchise League decided that direct militant action was the only option and took to lobbing stones and missiles at government buildings. When the women were arrested and fined, they refused to pay and ended up in jail, with some going on hunger strike. Although she did not support the fight for Home Rule, Constance supported Irish suffragists who wanted women's suffrage linked to the Home Rule Bill. She approved of the Irish Women's Franchise League's desire to work independently of the British organisations and respected its leader Hanna Sheehy Skeffington, who was a formidable political operator.

When the British prime minister, Herbert Asquith, visited Dublin on 18 July 1912, Sheehy Skeffington and other members of the Irish Women's Franchise League paraded with posters. A day later, Mary Leigh, an English suffragette – the newspapers' word for radical suffragists – threw a hatchet into the carriage in which Asquith and Redmond were travelling as it passed over O'Connell Bridge. The hatchet, which was wrapped in a text reading 'This symbol of the extinction of the Liberal Party for evermore', missed Asquith but struck John Redmond on the arm.

Later, Leigh and Gladys Evans 'made a spectacular show' at the Royal Theatre where Asquith was due to speak the following day. While the audience was dispersing, Leigh flung a flaming chair over the edge of the box into the orchestra, while Evans set fire to a carpet and then 'rushed to the cinema box, threw in a little handbag filled with gunpowder, struck matches, and dropped them in after it.' The fire was quickly extinguished. Their stunt, for which they were arrested, attracted widespread criticism. After Leigh and Evans were sentenced to five years' prison in Mountjoy Gaol on 7 August, suffrage prisoners went on hunger strike and a huge protest meeting took place in the

Phoenix Park, at which suffragists were attacked by a mob led by 'the Ancient order of Hooligans', as Francis Sheehy Skeffington called the reactionary Ancient Order of Hibernians, a Catholic version of the Freemasons. While most of the women prisoners were released, Leigh was force-fed for forty-six days until she was released on 21 September 1912 and Evans was force-fed for fifty-eight days until her release on 23 October 1912. The behaviour of the militant suffragettes was seen as an attack on Home Rule and the Irish Women's Franchise League disassociated itself from this behaviour.

At the Fianna *ard fheis* in August 1912, Constance, along with Nora and Ina Connolly, presented a motion arguing for the admission of girls. The Belfast girls' *sluagh* had never been officially affiliated to the Fianna. After a heated debate, the motion was carried by a single vote. While the right of girls to join the Fianna was reluctantly recognised, few ever took up the offer. The IRB, hostile as it was to women in its organisation, may have hindered the development of girls' branches.

Constance continued as chief scout for the rest of her life, despite her strong disapproval of secret societies. Officially she had been told nothing of the IRB takeover, but she was aware of what had happened and expressed her disquiet whenever she could. To the younger boys, she was still the chief, and even the IRB acknowledged that the Fianna would never have happened without her considerable organisational ability, energy and money.

When Casimir returned to Ireland in the autumn, the Independent Theatre Company went on tour with *Eleanor's Enterprise*, visiting Tralee in County Kerry, Cork city and Liverpool, as well as playing another week in Dublin. At the end of the year, the Count dissolved the company and, with Evelyn Ashley, formed the Dublin Repertory Theatre. Its aim was to bring the best of European drama to Dublin.

Anti-Home Rule rumblings continued in the north east of the island. Ulster had begun preparations for a giant 'Ulster Day' in September, built around a covenant based on the Scottish Solemn League and Covenant of 1643. Those who signed the covenant pledged to defend their cherished position as equal citizens of the United Kingdom. At Belfast City Hall, on 28 September, Carson was the first of 218,206 men and 228,991 women to sign. Ulster was saying no.

CHAPTER EIGHT

Locked Out

By 1913, Constance was increasingly involved in the labour movement, estranging herself further from her family and from her class. While support for Home Rule or even Sinn Féin was just about respectable, talk of the class war and association with Larkin's 'Rabble' emphatically was not. Yeats's sister Lily gave what was a common view: 'Her followers are said to have been either small boys or drunken dock workers out of work, called the Citizen Army.' Labour unrest was affecting all classes in Irish society; in Sligo, the shirt factory run by her brother Josslyn got into trouble for receiving goods carried by a non-union carter.

In early 1913, James Larkin achieved some notable successes in industrial disputes in Dublin by using sympathetic strikes and boycotting of goods as tactics. Larkin's aim was to unionise the unskilled workers, who typically worked ten hours and more a day, lifting between 100 and 200 tons of cargo; these men were paid in pubs where part of the deal was that they bought drink – a custom that promoted drunkenness and alcoholism. He coined the slogan 'A fair day's work for a fair day's pay'. Guinness and the Dublin United Tramway Company were the main targets for Larkin's organising ambitions, although workers at the Guinness brewery – one of the biggest employers in the city – remained non-union because they were well treated.

The year 1913 proved pivotal on a number of fronts. It was the year of the lock-out, when months of bitter labour strife ended with the formation of the Irish Citizen Army and helped create the conditions that would lead to the 1916 Rising. On the Home Rule issue, the Ulster Volunteers and later the Irish Volunteers were taking up arms, marching through the streets and giving every appearance of being prepared to fight. Women were still agitating for the vote and Hanna Sheehy Skeffington, Louie Bennett and Lady Margaret Dockrell represented Ireland at the seventh conference of the International Woman Suffrage Alliance in Budapest.

For Constance, life was not all politics. In April 1913, the Dublin Repertory Theatre was launched with a production of François Coppée's *For the Crown*, a drama of political greed and family tensions set in the fifteenth-century Balkans, previously staged in Dublin fifteen years earlier by Eric Forbes-Robertson, a friend from the Markieviczs' Paris days. Constance played a minor role. It was an ambitious enterprise for a company of limited means and received a lukewarm reception.

In mid-May came George Bernard Shaw's *The Devil's Disciple*; this was Casimir's most ambitious production on the Dublin stage and his most successful. As well as the main cast, fifty extras were employed for the fight scenes. Casimir had astutely chosen Trinity students to act as British soldiers and Fianna boys and nationalists for the mob. Critics praised the scenes for their realism and the production played to packed houses. Constance, in her final appearance on the Dublin stage, played Judith Anderson.

After the show, the Markieviczs gave an extravagant party with Constance producing a tiered cake topped by an effigy of Mephistopheles and 'Long Live the Devil' written in chocolate icing. Casimir supplied the champagne and Constance the beer and food. Casimir, who was leaving on his summer visit to the Ukraine, was presented with a gold match box. In the midst of the revels, one guest, Tommy Furlong, announced that he would sing 'God Save the King'. Do that, said Constance, and I'll empty the tea urn over your head. Furlong went home, changed into a bathing suit and, after his return, began to sing. He was promptly soaked in tea. At five in the morning, the revels ended when the survivors took taxis to another house. As late as 1913, Constance's life was not all serious, with Casimir providing much of the fun.

In the summer of 1913, with suffragette protests at their peak, the Prisoners (Temporary Discharge for Ill-Health) Act, popularly known as the 'Cat and Mouse Act', was extended to Ireland. After the Act was introduced, suffragettes were no longer force-fed in prison. When they became extremely weak, they were released to recover. Any wrongdoing would see them jailed again. The largest protest against introducing the act into Ireland came at a meeting at the Mansion House in June 1913. Constance was on the panel of speakers, along with Louie Bennett, Tom Kettle, Kathleen Lynn and Mary Hayden. She signed a petition against the Act, which she described as barbarous and unworthy of any civilised country. In her speech, she said that the actions of the suffragettes showed that the spirit of martyrdom had not died in Ireland. She was proud to be a woman and asked how many men would undergo a hunger strike for a principle.

Constance was inspired by heroic women who, like her, believed in the value of sacrifice for a greater good. She saw Joan of Arc as an appropriate icon for women in the early twentieth century. Unlike Cathleen Ní Houlihan or Dark Rosaleen, urging their sons to fight for their honour, Joan of Arc was a Catholic soldier, taking up arms herself, unafraid of dying for her beliefs. She saw women as makers of their own destiny and argued that Irish women should free themselves from the last vestiges of the harem.

On 3 August, the Irish Transport and General Workers' Union opened its new recreation centre at Croydon Park in Fairview with a 'Grand Temperance Fete and Children's Carnival'. James Larkin planned to use the leased house and its garden to promote the growing of vegetables and flowers and as a focus for social activities. At the same time, the union bought its own premises at Beresford Place. The Northumberland Buildings, renamed Liberty Hall, cost the union £5,000.

Thanks to the efforts of Larkin, and to the dismay of employers, most of Dublin's unskilled labour was unionised by the summer of 1913. The flashpoint came with the Dublin United Tramway Company (DUTC), whose chairman William Martin Murphy was described by Larkin as 'the most foul and vicious blackguard that ever polluted any country'. For his part, Murphy loathed James Larkin and all he stood for, and membership of the ITGWU meant instant dismissal for any of his employees. First to strike on 15 August were dispatch boys employed by the *Irish Independent* newspaper, owned by Murphy, who locked out all workers who had joined the union. A strike at Eason's, which carried the Murphy newspapers, was then called. Dockers joined in, refusing to handle any goods coming to or from Eason's.

On the morning of Tuesday 26 August, the opening day of Horse Show week, tram drivers and conductors donned their union badges and walked away from their trams, leaving bewildered passengers standing on the footpaths around Nelson's Pillar on Sackville Street. The Dublin Trades Council gave them unanimous support. In all, 700 men came out on strike that day, with a hundred staying in.

Two days later, detectives raided the homes of Larkin, P.T. Daly, Thomas Lawlor, William Partridge and William O'Brien, all union officials who had addressed a rally outside Liberty Hall. They were charged with incitement before the city's chief police magistrate, E.G. Swifte, who was a substantial shareholder in the DUTC. After they were released on bail, Larkin spoke to their supporters from a window of Liberty Hall on the right to hold public meetings. He announced that he would speak in Sackville Street on the Sunday.

On Friday 29 August, Murphy called a meeting of the Employers' Federation, formed in 1911 at the first threat of strikes. Over four hundred employers decided to lock out all employees who were members of the ITGWU. They were joined by the Coal Merchants' Association and the Master Builders' Association when 3,000 men refused to sign a pledge never to join the union. Next to be locked out were a thousand farm workers and the employees of timber and cement merchants. Soon 25,000 were out of work. In court, E.G. Swifte banned the Sunday meeting. Larkin burnt a copy of the proclamation at a rally outside Liberty Hall and promised to speak at Sackville Street on Sunday 'dead or alive'.

A day later, James Connolly, who had arrived from Belfast, was arrested and charged with incitement. In court, before E.G. Swifte, he said that he did not recognise 'the English government in Ireland at all'; this resulted in a three-month jail sentence for 'treason'. In Dublin's inner city, riots broke out. On the evening of Saturday 30 August, James Nolan, on his way to Liberty Hall to pay his subscription, was fatally injured when a group of police officers baton-charged a crowd of strikers on Eden Quay. He died on Sunday morning in Jervis Street Hospital. Also beaten senseless, near Butt Bridge, was John Byrne, a fifty-year-old labourer; he died at home five days later.

With tension mounting, the authorities issued another warrant for Larkin's arrest; he was in Liberty Hall when he heard the news and they would clearly come looking for him there. His supporters decided that the safest place for him that evening was Surrey House, although smuggling him into the house might pose a problem. By a stroke of luck, Casimir had returned that very evening from the Ukraine. He was met at the train station by his friends from the theatre world and, after visiting a few hostelries in the city, they carried on to Surrey House to continue the party, distracting the watching detectives, who failed to spot the arrival of Larkin. That night, Gussie McGrath, a young College of Science student, booked a front room for a 'Reverend Donnelly' and his 'niece' at the Imperial Hotel, owned by William Martin Murphy. The hotel, at 22–24 Sackville Street, had four floors, with four windows on each facing Sackville Street.

The next morning, Larkin was transformed into 'Reverend Donnelly', an aged clergyman, who would be escorted into the hotel by his 'niece'. She would do all the talking, since Larkin's scouse accent was a giveaway. Taking on the role of the 'niece' was Nellie Gifford who had been working in Meath and was unknown to the police. Casimir reluctantly lent his frock coat and top hat to the cause. It fitted Larkin perfectly. By Sunday, union officials had decided to cancel the Sackville Street meeting and William O'Brien organised a march from Beresford Place to Croydon Park. Despite this, a substantial crowd had gathered in Sackville Street hoping that Larkin would appear and the street was lined with policemen. Swelling the numbers were worshippers leaving the twelve o'clock mass in the nearby Pro-Cathedral.

At 12.45pm, a taxi pulled up at the Imperial Hotel and two passengers emerged. A well-dressed young lady helped a stooped gentleman into the hotel. Once inside, the gentleman walked slowly upstairs to the dining room. When he saw that flowerpots were blocking the window, he stood up straight and raced to another room. Stepping out onto the balcony he found there, he pulled off the false beard, threw back his shoulders and shouted to the crowd. When the crowd surged forward and began cheering, more than a dozen policemen stormed into the hotel and pulled him away from the window. A few minutes later, Larkin, still with a remnant of his false beard stuck to his face, emerged from the hotel's front door, escorted by the police.

The Markieviczs, along with Sidney Gifford and Helena Molony, had arrived by car in time to see Larkin appear at the balcony. Constance reached the hotel door as Larkin was emerging with his police escort, and when she was recognised by the crowd, she called for three cheers. When she shook Larkin's hand and wished him good luck, the inspector leading him punched her in the face. She fell back against another policeman, who 'pulled her about', tearing all the buttons off her blouse, and then threw her on to the ground, where other policemen kicked her. One of the policemen who hit her smelled strongly of drink. By now, the police, lined up in a long cordon from the GPO to the O'Connell monument, had charged the crowd, including women and children.

Nora Connolly described the fracas:

> A lad beside me yelled 'Hey, the peelers have drawn their batons'. The next thing I knew the peelers were upon us. All you could hear was the thud, thump, crack of the baton as they fell on the heads of the crowd ... the peelers came steadily like mowing machines and behind, the street was like a battlefield dotted with bodies.

Constance attempted to get out of the way and was hit again on the face, this time by a police baton. Another policeman seized her by the throat and let go only when Casimir pretended the pipe in his pocket was a revolver and said 'another step and you are a dead man'. She was rescued by passers-by who took her into a house, where she stopped the blood flowing from her mouth and nose and tidied her clothes.

The apolitical Casimir, an unbiased observer, was so shocked by what had happened that he wrote a strongly worded letter to the *Freeman's Journal*. 'There was no sign of excitement, no attempt at Larkin's rescue and no attempt at a breach of the peace, when a savage and cruel order for a baton charge was given to the police.' He had witnessed scores of police pursuing a handful of men, women and children running for their lives. One young man was felled by a baton stroke and then kicked and hit with batons while on the ground. Everywhere ordinary citizens lay on the ground senseless and bleeding. Terror-stricken passers-by who had taken refuge in doorways were batoned by the rampaging police. 'It was, indeed, a bloody Sunday for Ireland' said the Count.

Baton charges were not new to Dublin, but the Sackville Street charge of 1913 proved particularly savage, with 433 treated in hospital and countless more injured. One who made a safe getaway was Nellie

Gifford. After resolutely refusing to give the police her name or any information, she picked up her bags and set off for Surrey House.

Two days later, two tenements on Church Street, occupied by sixteen families, collapsed. Fifteen people were trapped in the rubble; seven died and at least another seven were seriously injured. One of the dead was seventeen-year-old Eugene Salmon, who had saved six members of his family before losing his life in an attempt to reach the last child. Salmon was a union member locked out of Jacob's.

A day later, an enormous crowd of 11,000, many with visible wounds, walked behind the coffin of James Nolan to Glasnevin cemetery. Leading them was the Lord Mayor of Dublin, Lorcan Sherlock, along with British labour leader Keir Hardie, Constance, and Helena Molony. Both Larkin and Connolly were in jail. The Trades Union Council, then meeting in Manchester, sent a committee, led by Arthur Henderson. They decided that the locked-out men must be supported.

Liberty Hall was draped in black with a large placard on the front of the building proclaiming 'In Memory of Our Murdered Brothers'. An inquiry was held but nothing much would change in the teeming back streets of Dublin's city centre. James Connolly, still in jail, went on hunger strike on Sunday 7 September and, on the seventh day, he was visited by his wife Lily and daughter Ina, who were worried about his health and appealed to the Viceroy, the Earl of Aberdeen. Connolly was released under the terms of the 'Cat and Mouse Act' and driven to Surrey House in the vice-regal car, where Constance and Kathleen Lynn nursed him back to health until he was strong enough to return to Belfast.

A day later, the poem 'September 1913' by W.B. Yeats was published in the *Irish Times*. It was one of his most emotional works, excoriating Murphy and his ilk, fumbling in the greasy till, adding the halfpence to the pence:

> For men were born to pray and save,
> Romantic Ireland's dead and gone,
> It's with O'Leary in the grave.

On 12 September, Larkin was released from jail on bail and left immediately for England in an attempt to raise funds. Connolly returned to Dublin to manage the union in his absence, staying at Surrey House and paying Constance ten shillings a week for his lodgings. Later that month, Constance spoke at an Irish Women's Franchise League meeting, emphasising the moral and educational value of giving women the vote. She described the nationalist, women's suffrage and labour movements as 'all really the same movement in essence, for they were fighting the same fight, for the extension of human liberty'.

For seven more months, the lock-out inflicted untold misery on tens of thousands of Dublin's workers and employers, with Larkin portrayed as the villain by Murphy's three main newspapers, the *Irish Independent*, *Sunday Independent* and *Evening Herald*. For its part, *The Irish Worker* published the names and addresses of strike breakers. Yet Larkin never resorted to violence. He knew that he could not build support for the trade union movement by wrecking the firms where his members worked.

Cultural activities in Dublin stuttered on during the lock-out, with an exhibition of paintings by Constance, Æ and Frances Baker going ahead while, at the height of the agitation that followed the Sackville Street riots, John Galsworthy's *Strife*, the story of a strike by workers at a tin factory, produced by Casimir, played in Dublin's Gaiety Theatre. In search of realism, Casimir hired real labourers for the big scene, at 1/6d a night.

Casimir had planned to revive *Eleanor's Enterprise* in the autumn but, as a result of his outspokenness and his wife's activism, the Markieviczs found themselves frozen out of the Dublin Repertory Theatre. David Telford, chairman of the Gaiety Theatre, had written to Evelyn Ashley expressing his view that, owing to 'the high feeling' in Dublin at the time, the appearance of Constance on stage could do the repertory company 'irreparable injury'. Casimir left the company, finding Ashley's view 'insulting to the people of this city'. The company's productions were boycotted by labour activists for victimising 'our good friend the Countess' who had dared to identify herself with the cause of the locked-out workers of Dublin. The situation made earning a living almost impossible for either of them.

As the lock-out continued and it became apparent that workers and their families would starve, Constance and Delia Larkin were put in charge of the union members' welfare. Constance supervised the collection of food and, with the help of Patrick Lennon, Seán

O'Casey and Hanna Sheehy Skeffington, soon had kitchens going in Liberty Hall, a building that was well suited to their needs. In the 1830s, it had seen service as the Northumberland Coffee Rooms, later the Northumberland Hotel. In the basement were kitchens and space enough to set up dining rooms. The women prepared and served the food, helped by the men, who stoked the fires and undertook the heavy labour.

'Madame had a personal contact and real sympathy for the poor that removed all taint of Lady Bountiful and made her a comrade among comrades,' said Hanna Sheehy Skeffington, who considered this to be Constance's finest moment. Louie Bennett remembered creeping 'like a culprit' into Liberty Hall to see Madame Markievicz 'in a big overall, with sleeves rolled up, presiding over a cauldron of stew, surrounded by a crowd of gaunt women and children carrying bowls and cans.' William Orpen came to sketch. The labour movement would not forget the support given them by suffragists during the lock-out.

Food packages were made up and handed over when the men arrived to collect their strike pay, and when Constance discovered that the women were taking away their dinners to give to their families and did not eat themselves, a special dining room was set up for mothers. Tons of potatoes and carrots and other vegetables were peeled and thousands of bones scraped. Many of those helping out were women strikers from Jacob's factory, who sang rebel songs to keep up their spirits. The work, in sweltering heat, was gruelling and thankless.

Every day, queues armed with mugs, tin cans and other containers formed; no one was turned away. Hanna Sheehy Skeffington remembered an incident. 'One day a youngster came along, a boy of about ten, with his little soup-can only to be recognised and pushed aside scornfully by the others with a taunt "Go away, your father is a scab".' Constance, seeing the hurt look on the child's face, called him back. 'No child is going to be called a scab. He can't help his father. When he grows up, he'll be all right himself, won't you sonny? And now have some soup.'

Through the long months of the lock-out, Constance was a familiar early morning sight, cycling to Liberty Hall from her home in Rathmines and staying in the kitchens until late at night. Harry Gosling, a union leader, remembered her working all day long, sleeves rolled up, wearing an apron made of sack and usually smoking a cigarette. After she had used up all her money, she took out loans to buy food. No detail was too small for her – she found a number of large copper pans and begged bones for stock. Her exotic name, her accent and even her beauty and her height all added to her appeal.

After the British Trades Union Congress pledged to supply food to the striking Dublin workers, the *SS Hare* arrived in Dublin from Manchester on 26 September, carrying £5,000 worth of food bought through the Manchester-based Wholesale Co-operative Society. Potatoes, bread, butter, sugar and tea were distributed to the workers. Food that might use up the workers' meagre fuel supply was sent to Liberty Hall for cooking. Traditional Sinn Féin members were unhappy – they believed that the £5,000 should have been spent in Ireland and not all Sinn Féiners supported the lock-out. Arthur Griffith believed the workers should be 'bayoneted', while Bulmer Hobson offered no assistance, becoming further estranged from Constance for this reason. With a few notable exceptions, nationalists remained silent. The arch-conservative Catholic hierarchy was ambivalent at best and downright hostile in many cases. However, the brutality of Bloody Sunday and the extension of the lock-out to thirty-seven unions had aroused the sympathy of Dublin's citizens.

With winter closing in, there seemed no end to the lock-out in sight, with both sides entrenched in their views and Dublin Castle, the police, the military, the press and some clergy continuing to denounce the striking workers. A clothing centre was set up in Liberty Hall to distribute donations of warm clothing, and unemployed seamstresses went to work altering the clothing to fit.

On 7 October, Æ's open letter to the Dublin employers was published in the *Irish Times*. In stirring terms, he denounced the 'masters of Dublin' and their 'devilish policy of starvation' after refusing to accept the recommendations of a Board of Trade Inquiry. 'You refused to meet them further ... and are determined deliberately in cold anger to starve out one-third of the population of this city, to break the manhood of the men by the sight of the suffering of their wives and hunger of their children.' He described them as four hundred masters 'deciding openly upon starving one hundred thousand people'.

A public inquiry under Sir George Askwith was held in October, with Larkin making a two-hour speech. In its report, presented on 6

October, employers were criticised for banning their workers from joining the ITGWU. The employers refused to accept the report and said that they would accept the union only if its officials met with their approval.

By the end of October, the supply of food for the workers was running out. In that month, an English philanthropist, Dora Montefiore, made a call for the children of strikers to be sent to English homes where they could be cared for. Howls of outrage from the Catholic clergy, led by the parish priest at Westland Row and an organisation called the Leo Guild, followed. What Catholic mother would send their children to an environment where they might be cared for by non-Catholics fulminated Dr Walsh, the Archbishop of Dublin, in a letter to the *Freeman's Journal?* Pure farce followed when a party of priests swooped on the Corporation baths, where fifty children were being washed before they set off. They physically removed all but nineteen. Ten more were grabbed before they reached the boat at Kingstown and the remaining nine were persuaded to leave the vessel before it sailed. Montefiore and her assistant, Lucille Rand, an American, were arrested on kidnapping charges. Delia Larkin took over their work, but her attempts to get more children away were prevented by priests who picketed the quays and caused such a disturbance at Amiens Street station that the children, heading for Belfast, were brought back to Liberty Hall. The scheme was abandoned.

By now, even the comfortable middle classes could see that the situation in working-class areas of Dublin was desperate. In the hard-hit inner city parishes of Marlborough Street, Westland Row and City Quay, free breakfasts were given to children as well as some free dinners. Countess Plunkett opened a large house in Sandymount for poor children in need.

On 27 October, Larkin was sentenced to seven months' imprisonment for sedition. In London's Royal Albert Hall on Sunday 1 November, a mass meeting organised by the *Daily Herald*, a socialist newspaper, demanded the release of Larkin. From the stage, Æ again denounced the businessmen of Dublin: 'If the courts of justice were courts of humanity, the masters of Dublin would be in the dock charged with criminal conspiracy. Their crime was that they tried to starve out one-third of the people of Dublin.' George Bernard Shaw pointed out that citizens might resort to violence to get justice: 'If you put a policeman on the footing of a mad dog, it can only end in one way, and that is that all respectable men will have to arm themselves.' The men remained locked out.

Constance wrote a fiery article for the *Irish Worker*:

> Jim Larkin is in jail. In jail for fighting the workers' cause. In jail for championing the poor against the rich, the oppressed against the oppressor. For daring to speak straight and fight straight, he is sentenced to seven months for 'using seditious language'. He dared attack 'Capitalism'. Under the flag of 'Capitalism' you find the British Crown with all its minions, its judges, magistrates, inspectors, spies, police, the Ancient Order of Hibernians – even some of the clergy – all the worshipers of Mammon, all these were ranged against Jim Larkin.

She saw Larkin first and foremost as a martyr following in the steps of Emmet and fighting the British, rather than as a socialist championing the cause of the workers. In her opinion, it was British rule that had provoked the crisis and not the clash between employers and workers.

On 1 November, an article called 'The North Began', written by Eoin MacNeill, the scholar and founder of the Gaelic League, appeared in the *Claidheamh Soluis*, the magazine of the Gaelic League. The O'Rahilly had been appointed as unpaid manager of the publication and was determined to bring it back to life. He had asked MacNeill to write an article on the topic of forming a volunteer army to support Home Rule. Because he was laid up with flu and had time on his hands, MacNeill agreed. In the article, MacNeill pointed out that the Orangemen in Ulster were fighting for their own version of Home Rule and had set up a citizen army to support their struggle. There was nothing now to prevent the rest of Ireland organising a 'citizen force' to establish self-government and prosperity for the Irish people. He called for a national army that would not rest until the Irish national flag flew over Dublin Castle.

MacNeill's call was received enthusiastically by the Irish Republican Brotherhood, which had long awaited a figurehead who could be used as a front for their plans to raise just such an Irish republican army.

Bulmer Hobson, the man in charge of the Dublin 'centres', made an approach to MacNeill. James Connolly again hinted at the need for a citizens' army when he spoke at a suffragist meeting attended by Constance in Dublin on 11 November. Connolly said that women, like workers, had been tricked at every turn and had learned not to trust any of the political parties. That same night, a smaller meeting organised by the IRB discussed the formation of the Irish Volunteers. Among the eleven invited were Bulmer Hobson, Eoin MacNeill, Patrick Pearse, Seán Mac Diarmada, Eamonn Ceannt and The O'Rahilly.

One night later, on 12 November, the Civic League was formed at a small meeting held in the rooms of Reverend R.M. Gwynn at Trinity College. Captain Jack White, a former British army officer whose father, Sir George White VC, had defended Ladysmith against the Boers in South Africa, proposed a drilling scheme for the strikers. So it was that the first practical plan for a citizen army came from a Protestant British army man at a meeting held in Trinity College, the stronghold of the unionist establishment.

The news came through a day later that Larkin had been released, seventeen days into his seven-month prison sentence. Connolly had appealed to the labour movement in Britain to fight the Liberals until Larkin was free, even if it threatened Home Rule. As a result, the Liberals lost a by-election in Reading and only scraped in at another by-election in Linlithgow. With Larkin free, Dublin was treated to a fireworks display from the roof of Liberty Hall celebrating the union's first significant victory. A marching band led a noisy procession of around 10,000 along the quays to Sackville Street.

When the procession returned to Beresford Place, James Connolly spoke, outlining plans for a citizen army:

> Listen to me. I am going to talk sedition. The next time we are out for a march, I want to be accompanied by four battalions of trained men. I want them to come with their corporals, sergeants and people to form fours. Why should we not drill and train our men as they are doing in Ulster?

He asked able-bodied men to sign up for the army when next they came to claim their strike pay. When they needed arms, he said, they would know where to find them. Sitting behind him on the platform, Constance applauded Connolly's every word and was one of the first to sign up for the Citizen Army. Connolly promised the citizens of Dublin that the Citizen Army would become a well-drilled, disciplined body that would resist police brutality.

Later that night, the Civic League held its first open meeting at the Antient Concert Rooms where the formation of a citizen army was again announced. Constance went on to the meeting after she left Liberty Hall; on the platform were Reverend Gwynn, Professor Collingwood, Francis Sheehy Skeffington and Darrell Figgis. Missing was Hanna Sheehy Skeffington. She was in nearby Mountjoy Gaol after her arrest for allegedly assaulting an officer while attempting to hand suffragist literature to the Conservative leader, Andrew Bonar Law, on the doorstep of Lord Iveagh's residence on St Stephen's Green.

A week later, the Civic League met again, with the audience swelled by a hundred Trinity students, most of them attending because the provost had forbidden them to do so. The main topic for discussion was the postponed inquiry into police conduct. Captain White again outlined his plans for training a citizen army and read a message of support from Sir Roger Casement, who had been knighted for his *exposés* of worker exploitation in Africa and South America. Constance spoke strongly in favour of the police inquiry.

On Sunday 23 November 1913, enough men to form two companies signed up with Captain White at Croydon Park. The name Transport Union Citizen Army was first used, soon shortened to Citizen Army and later expanded to the Irish Citizen Army. The Citizen Army promised that when their men were trained and drilled, there would be no more baton charges by police in Dublin. Their philosophy was simple: 'The ownership of Ireland, moral and material, is vested of right in the people of Ireland.'

Two days later, a meeting to organise the Irish Volunteers attracted such large numbers that it took over not only the Rotunda itself, but also the Rotunda Rink, a cavernous shed outside the building used to accommodate roller skaters. Even Sinn Féin now supported an armed volunteer force and, from the start, the Irish Volunteers attracted men from all classes. By contrast, members of the Citizen Army were mostly working-class, mobilised because of the lock-out and the recurring arrests of their leaders. While the Citizen Army welcomed women as equals, the Volunteers did not. Freeing Ireland from British rule was top priority for both organisations.

By December, the Citizen Army had between 500 and 600 recruits, while the Irish Volunteers had 3,500, many of them young. For the general population, nationalism was more appealing than class warfare and the Volunteers always attracted bigger numbers and was better funded. An alarmed Dublin Castle responded to the increased militancy in the country by declaring an arms embargo in December 1913; this was ignored.

Although Constance was working long hours in the Liberty Hall kitchens, she found time to plan a Christmas party for some 20,000 children at Croydon Park. The Manchester Co-operative Wholesale Society had provided small gifts and sweets for the children, and Constance and some of the Liberty Hall helpers prepared individual packets for each child. She had her critics, most notably Seán O'Casey who was never going to forgive her for her background and described her as a shrill-voiced and 'scintillating harlequin', whirling through the Liberty Hall kitchen, sampling a bit of stew here and there and rushing for a ladle whenever a photographer chanced by. His views were at odds with the general opinion. James Connolly was one of many who appreciated Constance's ability to muster up food for thousands of locked-out strikers every day and to keep the Volunteers happy. Throughout the strike, Casimir supported his wife, although with his theatre work drying up, their financial situation was precarious. In December, he left to work as a war correspondent in Albania, where the German prince, William of Wied, was a reluctant sovereign, shored up by the European Great Powers.

After a winter so cold that the ponds of Dublin froze over, the first breach in the strikers' solidarity occurred on 10 December when the London and Northwestern Railway Company workers announced they would abandon their sympathetic strike. At a special Trades Union Congress in London, Larkin and Connolly's hopes for sympathetic strikes in Britain were quashed. Instead, a resolution to negotiate with the employers in Dublin was proposed. An amendment by Larkin supporter Jack Jones that transport unions should not handle Dublin traffic after a certain date and that a monthly levy be collected to support the Dublin workers was beaten by over two million to two hundred votes. Dublin port reopened after fourteen weeks.

By February 1914, the Dublin Relief Fund, sponsored by the Trades Union Council, had shut down and the kitchens at Liberty Hall had been forced to close. The lock-out petered out. Men and women slowly drifted back to work, ground down by starvation and the bitter cold. Workers signed a pledge not to join the union, but kept up their membership anyway. Many smaller businesses went bankrupt.

The report of the Dublin Disturbances Commission was published on 9 February 1914. It noted that because the police had done their job so effectively, in only one case had it been necessary to call in military reinforcements against the unarmed workers. In spite of continued protests from Constance and others, the month-long hearings were closed to the public and to labour representatives.

The lock-out firmly established the principle of union action and workers' solidarity in Ireland. Perhaps more importantly, Larkin's rhetoric, condemning poverty and injustice and inspiring the oppressed to stand up for themselves, made a lasting impression. Louie Bennett believed that the shameful treatment of the workers during the lock-out made Connolly, previously a Home Rule supporter, a bitter man. From this point on, he was committed to fighting for Irish independence through physical force.

CHAPTER NINE

Two Cathleen Ní Houlihans

In early 1914, Arthur Griffith was confidently proclaiming that Home Rule would become law before the summer. Constance, with the encouragement of James Connolly, visited Belfast for three days in February, addressing several meetings on the need for co-operation between workers in all parts of Ireland. She struck a positive note, stressing the advantages of solid organisation and dialogue in a workers' republic. Ever the idealist, she was blind to the selfish and petty motives of others. She urged the women to organise and agitate. James Connolly added that if Belfast workers opposed the division of Ireland, they could help prevent the exclusion of Ulster under the Home Rule Act.

In March 1914 came the so-called 'Curragh Mutiny'. British prime minister Herbert Asquith had warned the cabinet that the Ulster Volunteers might attempt to commandeer barracks and police stations if Home Rule was enforced. Sir Arthur Paget, commander-in-chief of the British Forces in Ireland, was an Ulster Unionist supporter, as was Major-General Henry Wilson, Director of Military Operations in the War Office. On 20 March, when told by the government that they might have to take action against the Ulster Volunteers, Brigadier-General Hubert Gough and sixty-one officers of the 3rd Cavalry Brigade made it clear that they would rather resign than do so.

Gough and his colonels were called to Whitehall, where they requested a written assurance that they would not be ordered to enforce Home Rule in Ulster. The Secretary of State for War, J.E.B. Seely, agreed to their demands, but Asquith demurred. After a lengthy Commons debate on 23 and 25 March, Seely, along with the Chief of the Imperial General Staff, John French, and Adjutant General to the Forces, John

Spencer Ewart, resigned. It was another setback for Home Rule, with the faith of nationalists in the politicians' ability to bring even limited independence to Ireland severely shaken. Only a month later, the Larne gun-running would further shake their composure.

At a Sinn Féin conference in Dublin, Constance, along with Hanna Sheehy Skeffington and Jennie Wyse Power, proposed that the women of Ulster be allowed to vote on Home Rule. Arthur Griffith ruled it out of order, though many in the room approved the sentiment. Within five months, Europe was at war and the Home Rule question was shelved.

In 1914, top priorities for Constance were the labour movement and the Citizen Army, although she continued her work with the Fianna, kept up with friends in the Irish Volunteers and was active in the battle for women's rights. She provided a vital link between the various organisations. The dispiriting end to the 1913 strike had affected the Citizen Army. Activists were exhausted and depressed after a long struggle that had ended in failure, and numbers attending drill were falling.

In March 1914, with unemployment rampant and thousands on the poverty line, Captain White organised a hunger march from Liberty Hall to the Mansion House. With Constance among them, the marchers had barely begun before they were stopped by the police at Eden Quay. Despite his skill with a blackthorn stick, White was beaten badly and arrested. Constance defied the police to come to his aid and, at the police station, forced her way in and demanded that a doctor be sent for at once. The first time they flung her out, 'but she ducked between policemen's legs and got back again somehow' using a solution of Jeyes fluid to bathe White's head wounds.

On 22 March, a public meeting was held in Liberty Hall to reorganise the Citizen Army. Seán O'Casey had set the agenda and drafted a constitution. This affirmed that 'The first and last principle is the avowal that the ownership of Ireland is vested of right in the people of Ireland; that the Citizen Army shall stand for the absolute unity of Irish nationhood, and shall support the rights and liberties of the democracies of all nations; that the Citizen Army shall be open to all who accept the principle of equal rights and opportunities for the people of Ireland; that one of its objects shall be to sink all differences of birth, property and creed under the common name of the Irish people.'

Larkin suggested that every applicant must be a member of a trades union recognised by the Irish Trades Union Council. Constance proposed that the clause be inserted in the constitution, and her proposal was seconded by Tom Healy. Captain White was named chairman; Larkin and Francis Sheehy Skeffington were among the five vice-chairmen, with Seán O'Casey as honorary secretary, and Richard Brannigan and Constance as treasurers. Connolly, based in Belfast, was not on the committee, set up to serve for six months.

O'Casey, a divisive figure in the Citizen Army, argued that the more popular Irish Volunteers were bourgeois and anti-labour. He described the situation in *Drums Under the Windows*: 'Now there were two Cathleen Ní Houlihans running around Dublin: one ... in green dress, shamrocks in her hair ... the other Cathleen coarsely dressed, hair a little tousled ... at ease with the smell of sweat and the sound of bad language'. O'Casey's refusal to compromise, along with a poor response to his drilling and training sessions, saw an exasperated Captain White leaving the Citizen Army in May. Larkin took his place.

While Larkin and O'Casey were hostile to the Volunteers, Connolly, White and Constance believed in co-operation. Tensions between the sides flared in an argument about the Citizen Army uniform. Constance suggested a brassard of St Patrick's blue for the men and red for the officers. Captain White, as an army man, agreed. Larkin went further, arguing that nothing short of a uniform would give the men the *esprit de corps* they needed. O'Casey disagreed; he maintained that it would be far more useful for members to use guerrilla tactics, wearing civilian clothing that would allow them to blend into the citizenry and 'to strike and dodge'. The argument was settled when Captain White revealed that he had already ordered fifty uniforms from Arnotts.

There were efforts at recruitment. One fine Sunday in April 1914, Captain White, P.T. Daly, Constance and Seán O'Casey drove to Lucan and Clondalkin villages on the west side of Dublin in an attempt to recruit new members. After a pleasant tea in a local restaurant, they moved on to the meeting place, where about five hundred had assembled. The three men spoke first but it was Constance's rousing rhetoric that resulted in twenty new members signing up. In Clondalkin, the locals were more apathetic, although the Captain's car inspired awe. The Citizen Army decided to stick to its heartland in Dublin city.

In the 4 April issue of the *Irish Worker*, a note announced that fifty men would receive the first set of Citizen Army uniforms at a special meeting. The uniforms were dark green with a wide-brimmed hat that many turned up on one side and fastened with a Transport Union badge. Those who did not have uniforms wore armlets of blue, with officers wearing red, as Constance had suggested. The men paid for their own uniforms – a big expense in those destitute times. Later, when an indoor firing range was set up in Liberty Hall, many could not afford the one penny charge for three shots.

The 'Starry Plough' made its first appearance at that same meeting – a flag of deep blue poplin embroidered by the Dun Emer guild, a women's craft studio. The plough represented the turning over of the soil and the planting of seeds for the future; the stars stood for the dreams and ideals of the workers' movement. O'Casey remembered his strong emotions when he first saw it:

> There it was – the most beautiful flag of the world's nations: a rich, deep poplin field of blue; across its whole length and breadth stretched the formalised shape of a plough, a golden-brown colour, seamed with a rusty red, while through all glittered the gorgeous group of stars enriching and ennobling the northern skies.

Constance, he reported, glanced at it and resumed oiling her gun, saying the design had no republican significance.

Constance continued urging women to fight for Irish independence. On 2 April, the first official meeting of what would become Cumann na mBan, an organisation of women in support of the Irish Volunteers, attracted about a hundred to Wynn's Hotel, Dublin. Presiding was Agnes O'Farrelly, a stalwart of the Gaelic League. The role of Cumann na mBan would be 'to assist in arming and equipping a body of Irishmen for the defence of Ireland'.

Constance supported Cumann na mBan, although it cautiously defined the role of women as 'different from that of men and rightly so'. In her inaugural address, O'Farrelly made plain its aims. 'Our first duty is to give our allegiance and support to the men who are fighting the cause of Ireland ... We women are not politicians, but we know what we want ... we pledge ourselves ... to give support morally, financially, and in every way we can'. Constance gave many practical suggestions and helped raise funds.

Tensions moved up a notch after the night of 24 April 1914 when 20,000 German-bought rifles, along with ammunition, were landed at Larne by Ulster loyalists, who were supported by the British Conservative Party, led by Andrew Bonar Law. Although Asquith assured the Commons that the law was upheld, destroyers off the Ulster coast did nothing to stop what was an illegal activity. In the USA, Roger Casement hailed Carson as a great Irishman because he had shown nationalists that they must arm themselves also.

Molesworth Hall was the venue for the Great Daffodil Fete, a fundraiser organised by the Irish Women's Franchise League that same weekend. The centrepiece was a one-act play specially written for the occasion by Francis Sheehy Skeffington called *The Prodigal Daughter*. The cast included Máire Nic Shiubhlaigh and Marie Perolz, with the action centred on the youngest daughter of a prominent local family who is returning to her small town by train after a spell in Mountjoy Gaol for suffragist activities.

There were also thirteen 'Suffrage Tableaux' featuring famous women from history, among them Florence Nightingale, Queen Maeve, St Brigid, Anne Devlin and two versions of Joan of Arc. Kathleen Houston, newly released after six months in Mountjoy Gaol, played Joan at the stake; Constance was the fighting Joan in full armour, who came as a vision to Houston. She had flung herself into the role with typical zest, taking great trouble to make her cardboard armour look suitably fifteenth-century.

In May, Constance presided over a meeting of Inghinidhe na hÉireann at Sinn Féin headquarters where thirty women signed up for an Inghinidhe *craobh* (branch) of Cumann na mBan. Other branches were formed in Cork, Limerick, Killarney, Tralee, Dingle, Enniscorthy, Wexford and London, where the committee was headed by the historian Alice Stopford Green. First task was a Defence of Ireland fund for arming and equipping the Volunteers.

Not everyone was a supporter of the new organisation; Hanna Sheehy Skeffington described it as 'an animated collecting box for men'. Cumann na mBan and the Irish Volunteers reflected the norms of the time, which dictated that women had no legal status and a 'person' was defined as a male person. It had no position on votes for women, although many members were active suffragists. Although Constance did not criticise Cumann na mBan in public, she was more forthcoming when addressing a private audience. 'Today the women attached to national movements are there chiefly to collect funds for the men to spend. These Ladies' Auxiliaries demoralise women, set them up in separate camps, and deprive them of all initiative and independence,' she told a meeting of the Irish Women's Franchise League.

Her sympathies lay squarely with the labour movement and the suffragists. Although she would later call Cumann na mBan 'her organisation', she was more at home in the Citizen Army, where women were treated as equals and where she was honorary treasurer. Before 1916, her involvement with Cumann na mBan, through the Inghinidhe branch, was confined to an occasional speech.

As the Irish Volunteers grew to an estimated membership of almost 200,000, John Redmond worried that the authority of the Irish Parliamentary Party was under threat. Knowing that most Irish Volunteers members were Home Rule supporters, he and Eoin MacNeill began negotiations to clarify the relationship between the two organisations. On 9 June, after the talks had dragged on for a few weeks, Redmond issued an ultimatum through the press, demanding that the Provisional Committee of the Volunteers co-opt twenty-five Irish Parliamentary Party nominees. With several Irish Parliamentary Party members and supporters already on the committee, this would guarantee them a majority. The Irish Republican Brotherhood (IRB) was completely opposed to Redmond's demands, while the Irish Women's Franchise League urged Cumann na mBan to oppose the move since Redmond did not support women's suffrage.

On 16 June, the inclusion of Redmond's nominees on the Volunteers committee was reluctantly agreed to on the advice of Bulmer Hobson, who wanted to avoid another split among nationalists, especially since he was aware of secret plans to bring guns into the country. Unfortunately, he did not take the time to explain his position to the IRB's inner circle. A minority of eight, most of them hardline IRB members, protested that Redmond's proposal violated the Volunteers' basic principles. Among them were Eamonn Ceannt, Con Colbert, Eamon Martin,

Patrick Pearse, Seán Mac Diarmada and Piaras Beaslai. Hobson was ostracised from the inner circles of the IRB and his influence waned, although he remained active in the Dublin Centres Board. Despite the change to the structure of the Volunteers' committee, Eoin MacNeill remained chairman and The O'Rahilly continued as treasurer, with the IRB faction, which included Patrick Pearse, Joseph Plunkett, Eamonn Ceannt, Seán Mac Diarmada, Thomas MacDonagh and Tom Clarke, still largely in control.

At the 1914 Wolfe Tone commemoration in Bodenstown, Jim Larkin headed two companies of the Citizen Army while Constance led the Fianna boys. Thanks to the influence of Tom Clarke, the Citizen Army was invited and headed the procession. The Irish Volunteers were there in number, as were members of Cumann na mBan. The honour guard around the grave was formed by equal numbers of Volunteer and Citizen Army members. Tom Clarke gave the oration.

By June 1914, the Irish Trades Union Council had become the Irish TUC and Labour Party, giving labour a political voice. At an open meeting in Dublin's Phoenix Park, which was to be addressed by Larkin and Connolly from two platforms simultaneously, Larkin began too early and annoyed Connolly. Later that year, the mercurial Larkin resigned from the ITGWU, suffering from nervous exhaustion. His friends persuaded him to withdraw his resignation and to undertake a fundraising tour of the United States as a break.

On Sunday 26 July, the Volunteers successfully stage-managed a gun-running operation into Howth harbour just north of Dublin. In charge were IRB members of the Volunteers, led by Thomas MacDonagh and Bulmer Hobson. John Redmond knew nothing of it, despite his recent endorsement of the Volunteers. Erskine Childers, his wife Mary Spring-Rice, Alice Stopford Green, Sir Roger Casement and Darrell Figgis had planned the move from London as a response to the Larne gun-running organised by the Ulster Volunteers. Figgis and Childers spent three months in Germany acquiring the rifles. They planned to ship them to Ireland in three yachts, with the main consignment arriving on Childers' yacht the *Asgard* at Howth – a location picked because it was close to Dublin, but not too close.

That day, the Volunteers set off on routine marches in at least two directions. One group headed for Howth, accompanied by Fianna boys pulling a trek cart they thought was packed with 'minerals and refreshments' but which, in reality, was filled with 200 handmade oak batons for the protection of the gun-runners. Off the coast, Childers was cruising in the *Asgard*. In its hold were 900 second-hand Mauser rifles and 29,000 rounds of ammunition picked up from a tug in the North Sea on 10 July. Cathal Brugha was commanding the men at the pier and Liam Mellows leading the Fianna.

Hobson had not told Constance what was going on. On Sunday morning, members of the Fianna camping at her cottage left for Dublin, telling Constance that they were invited to 'something' and that no girls were welcome. This was unusual, since Constance was usually in the thick of everything. The women who remained, including Nora and Ina Connolly, were quite pleased to have Constance to themselves for once. Usually, wrote Ina later, she was 'surrounded by a group of people making demands on her in some shape or form'.

Although the Volunteers and Fianna initially thought they were heading for a parade in the Father Mathew Park at Fairview, they passed through Fairview and then Clontarf and continued on to Howth. As they marched, the rumours that they would be picking up rifles began to spread. In the harbour, the *Asgard* docked and was welcomed by The O'Rahilly and others. Amid big cheers, the unloading began, with the Fianna clubs handed over to a chosen group of men who would act as guards if the police interfered. The remaining men carried away what rifles they could, while the rest were loaded into cars.

By the time the coast guards at Howth realised something was up, it was too late – the guns were unloaded and the march back to Dublin was underway. When the Volunteers got to Clontarf, they were stopped at a police road block. Soon after, the King's Own Scottish Borders, with guns loaded and bayonets fixed, arrived as support. William Harrell, the Assistant Commissioner of Police, made the order to seize the rifles. According to Bulmer Hobson,

> While we were facing the soldiers at Howth Road, several of our men who had small arms fired at the soldiers and would have precipitated a catastrophe for us had the officer in charge of the soldiers not thought that the shots came from a hostile crowd assembled in a side street.

After this brief skirmish, Darrell Figgis stepped between the two groups. While he spoke to Harrell, all but the front company slipped away and hid their guns in hedges, ditches and outhouses. Showing considerable presence of mind, a number of the Fianna boys swung down the Malahide Road and pretended to be camping in a small wood after asking permission from the owners of the adjoining big house. They buried the 'treasure' and, as soon as it was dark, moved it all to a safe place by taxi.

On the way back to Dublin, a growing number of spectators lined the streets, shouting slogans and pelting the British soldiers with rocks. By the time they turned into Bachelor's Walk, just off Sackville Street, many of the soldiers were injured and emotions were running high. The troops halted, and when they heard a shot, they fired into the crowd. Three died immediately: Mrs Mary Duffy, whose son was a British soldier, and James Brennan and Patrick Quinn. A further thirty-five were wounded and a fourth man, John Connolly, died of his wounds a few weeks later. The King's Own Scottish Borders were transferred from Dublin immediately and Harrell resigned.

Later in the day, a group of elated Fianna boys arrived at Constance's cottage full of their day's adventures. The women were aggrieved to have missed out. All that changed the next morning when, soon after Constance had left for town to find out what was happening, Joe Robinson arrived at the cottage with twenty rifles in three cars. A neighbour spotted the men unloading the rifles and warned Nora Connolly that a retired police sergeant lived up the road. She set off for the Volunteers office in Dublin immediately where Liam Mellows arranged to send out a taxi to collect the rifles. A long day followed during which Nora and her sister Ina performed shuttle runs with the taxi, sitting on the rifles in an effort to conceal them. After all the rifles from the cottage had been taken away, the women helped Mellows move other consignments of guns around the city. Their reward was a rifle each, while Ina got the job of carrying guns to Belfast. Constance sent her on her way: 'You are the first woman to run guns up to the North. Show Eddie Carson what you can do!'

The Howth gun-running improved Volunteer morale and new companies were formed. Yet the venture had been a minor affair compared to Larne, where the Ulster Volunteers had landed £60,000-worth of new guns without interference. At Howth, the Volunteers landed £1,500 worth of second-hand guns, most of which proved at best unreliable and at worst dangerous.

On the day after the gun-running, Constance was kept busy at Surrey House making wreaths for the victims of the Bachelor's Walk massacre. Volunteers, Citizen Army, Fianna and Cumann na mBan marched together in a show of solidarity at the funeral for the victims, held on the evening of 29 July so that workers could attend. At the graves, a salute was fired by the Volunteers, using Howth rifles. All British soldiers were confined to quarters for the evening.

Less than a week after the funeral, on 4 August, the United Kingdom of Great Britain and Ireland declared war on Germany. On 18 September, the Home Rule Act was passed, although suspended until after the war. Two days later, John Redmond made a speech in Woodenbridge, County Wicklow, pledging the support of the Irish Parliamentary Party and the Irish Volunteers to the cause of Britain in the war. He believed that if Ulster and Irish Volunteers fought together, they might find common cause and support Home Rule. While the majority of Irish men and women had some sympathy for Redmond's position, his views were utterly at variance with those held by the more extreme members of the Volunteers, as well as by ordinary people disappointed by the decision to suspend Home Rule. It caused a bitter split.

Constance was increasingly coming to the attention of Dublin Castle, who saw her as a dangerous firebrand and kept Surrey House under close surveillance. Staying with her at the time was Staskou, who was studying French and Russian at the Berlitz School of Languages in Grafton Street. Constance made time to help him with his studies, reading the *Echo de Paris* with him and correcting his accent. There was talk of him finding work with the family solicitors or even of studying at Trinity College, although Constance feared that in Trinity he might be tempted to join the Officers' Training Corps.

In September, Harold Asquith came to Dublin to address a giant recruitment meeting. A plan to invade the Mansion House with a combined Irish Volunteers and Citizen Army force was abandoned in favour of a protest by the Citizen Army. A brake set out from Liberty Hall, carrying Larkin, Connolly, Constance and P.T. Daly; Constance was the only Sinn Féin member involved. Following behind were a hundred

Citizen Army members armed with fixed bayonets. They marched down Sackville Street, around College Green and into Grafton Street, which was the nearest they could get to the Mansion House since the nearby streets were cordoned off. So loud were the cheers of their supporters that they succeeded in drowning out Asquith. The meeting produced a miserly six recruits.

That same month, the IRB's supreme council called a meeting at the Gaelic League headquarters. Tom Clarke, Arthur Griffith, Patrick Pearse and Seán Mac Diarmada all attended, along with James Connolly. The possibility of an armed insurrection against the British was discussed and all agreed that it must take place before the world war ended. Only the timing was left undecided. At their October convention, the Irish Volunteers repeated their pledge to resist conscription for the British armed forces in Ireland. Cumann na mBan issued a pamphlet calling on all Irish men to remain in their country and join the army of the Irish Volunteers.

In the Irish Citizen Army, Seán O'Casey was continuing to attack Constance. Because of her background, he assumed she would support the Redmondites, ignoring her strong anti-British bias, her enduring sympathy for the underdog and her popularity among Citizen Army members. As honorary secretary of the Citizen Army, he called a meeting of the council to discuss whether members should continue to have an 'active and sympathetic connection' with the Volunteer movement, which he saw as anti-labour. Since Constance was a member of Cumann na mBan, in his view she was linked to the Volunteers.

His ploy failed – Tom Foran, president of the ITGWU, who rarely attended meetings, came specially to support Constance. A vote of confidence was passed by seven votes to six. O'Casey was called on to apologise, which he refused to do. He remained bitter: 'had she refrained from voting for herself, as Sean did, like a fool, the vote would have been an even one'. O'Casey's was the only published account of the meeting, but Frank Robbins, who was present, wrote down what he remembered.

According to him, O'Casey argued that Constance, because of her bourgeois background, as well as her links with the Irish Volunteers and Cumann na mBan, was not fit to be a member of the Irish Citizen

Army. He accused her of being a spy for the Volunteers and requested her expulsion. He pointed dramatically at James Larkin and proclaimed that he was afraid of no man – 'not even him'. Larkin protested strenuously and called on O'Casey to withdraw anything he had said about Constance for the sake of peace. O'Casey had lost his audience. He left the Citizen Army for good.

In early October, Seán T. O'Kelly and Seán Milroy wrote a circular announcing the foundation of the Irish Neutrality League 'for the purpose of defining Ireland's present attitude towards the Anglo-German War as one of neutrality, preventing employers from coercing men to enlist, and taking steps to preserve the food supplies of Ireland for the people of Ireland'. James Connolly presided at the inaugural meeting, held at Antient Concert Rooms on 12 October, with Arthur Griffith, Francis Sheehy Skeffington and William O'Brien also present; the plan was to bring all strands of nationalism together, although the IRB was not represented. Officers elected included Connolly as president and Constance on the committee. In its brief existence, the league organised lectures by, among others, Thomas Ashe and Jenny Wyse Power and, on the suggestion of Connolly, popularised the wearing of green, white and orange colours. On 18 October, Constance gave a lecture under the auspices of the Irish Labour Party at the Trades Hall in Capel Street. Its theme was neutrality: 'The present duty of every Irishman is to stay at home and fight, if at all, for the welfare of his own country.'

On 24 October 1914, James Larkin at last set off for the USA. He ended up imprisoned in Sing-Sing, keeping him away from Ireland at the time of the 1916 Rising and for a further six years. James Connolly became the acting general secretary of the ITGWU and the editor of the *Irish Worker*, despite Larkin's efforts to install P.T. Daly. 'We serve neither King nor Kaiser, but Ireland' proclaimed its masthead on the 24 October issue. A linen banner bearing the same message was draped across the front of Liberty Hall.

Connolly instilled much-needed discipline in the flagging Citizen Army. Practical drills and rifle practise were introduced, along with route marches and outdoor exercises. Punctuality was paramount. Connolly continued his efforts to promote co-operation between all nationalists and included Cumann na mBan and Irish Volunteer notes in the *Irish Worker*.

On 25 October, at a Volunteers' convention, which had been summoned to repudiate Redmond's undertaking to support Britain in the war, a manifesto signed by, among others, Eoin MacNeill, Bulmer Hobson, The O'Rahilly, Patrick Pearse, Thomas MacDonagh and Joseph Plunkett expelled Redmond's nominees from the Volunteers' committee. In response, Redmond set up the National Volunteers and took with him 168,000 members, with 12,000 of the more zealous nationalists sticking with MacNeill. IRB leaders were pleased that Redmond's speech had separated the sheep from the lions. Also split was Cumann na mBan, which was revealed in its full militaristic fervour, with a quasi-military structure and much emphasis on training, signalling and gun-cleaning. Although most Cumann women shrank from carrying guns, some branches organised rifle practice, with members of the Belfast branch, led by the Connolly sisters, proving particularly good shots. The Inghinidhe branch held rifle practice on its premises.

The Fianna continued to post anti-enlistment bills, printed in Surrey House, keeping them high and away from the reach of passing policemen by using bicycles as stepladders. The Fianna boys were assigned to reconnoitre certain areas in preparation for a future revolution; they might walk, for instance, Sackville Street, taking in details of its length and breadth, the location of shops and other useful information. Their first aid skills came in useful. When a fire broke out at a pavilion during the St Enda's Fete, the Fianna joined hands and formed a line to control the crowd while others guided people to the gates of the park. On another occasion, when camping at Constance's cottage, word arrived that a local lad had drowned in an abandoned quarry at nearby Barnacullia. Four Fianna boys took two hours to bring the boy's body back to land, winning the respect of local residents, who awarded them with special medals.

In 1914, the first Fianna handbook was issued, with some fifty pages of drill and rifle exercises as well as instructive articles on first aid, knot-tying, signalling, swimming, camping and observation. Constance provided the drawing for the cover, showing Ireland as a Gaelic goddess, standing on a hill with a sunrise behind her. She also wrote the introduction and persuaded Sir Roger Casement and Patrick Pearse to provide articles.

In her article, Constance made an emotional appeal: 'This year has felt the spirit of Cathleen Ní Houlihan moving once more through the land. It will take the best and the noblest of Ireland's children to win freedom for the price of freedom is suffering and pain.' She evoked the spirit of the Manchester Martyrs, Robert Emmet, Wolfe Tone, Joan of Arc, Indian revolutionary Madan Lal Dhingra, and nameless heroes of the South African veldt.

Sir Roger Casement wrote on chivalry: 'The inheritance of chivalry is with us still – a motherland to serve, a fair country to feed.' In his essay, Patrick Pearse pointed out that the ideals of the original Fianna were lost when brother turned against brother. He warned that 'no strength of hand or valour of heart will hold a league or an army or a nation together unless there be peace and gentle brotherhood between all'.

The handbook became one of the most widely read pieces of nationalist literature and, following its success, the Fianna decided to issue a Christmas paper, financed by advertising. Some of the few surviving pre-1916 letters from Constance concerned this venture. In one, she begs a short story from Robert Brennan and tells him about the paper: 'We are going to try and make it bright and funny and not too political.' Æ supplied a poem – 'To a Statesman' – and James Connolly wrote an article on 'Boys and Parents'. Constance wrote of 'How the Fianna was Started' and Padraig Ó Riain, under the pen name 'Corporal Willie Nelson', gave an account of the Howth gun-running. Staskou supplied a gruesome tale of grave-robbing on an Arctic expedition, possibly inspired by tales of his step-grandfather in Lissadell.

Constance's life was a whirl of activity. Although her theatre days were over, she liked to recite patriotic poems, such as Æ's 'Gods of War', or her own 'Battle Hymn', published in 1915.

> Armed for the battle, kneel we before thee
> Bless thou our banners, God of the brave.
> 'Ireland is living!' shout we exultant;
> Ireland is waking, grasp we the sword.
> Who fights for Ireland, God guide his blows home;
> Who dies for Ireland, God give him peace.

Not great poetry, but effective propaganda.

On 13 November, the Citizen Army and the Volunteers attended a public meeting in front of the memorial arch at St Stephen's Green to protest against the treatment of Captain Robert Monteith, ex-British army and the Volunteers' best instructor. When Monteith refused to re-enlist as head of recruitment for the British army in Ireland, he was dismissed from his job at the Ordnance Depot in Islandsbridge so swiftly that he was forced to leave his coat and pipe behind. Presiding over the St Stephen's Green meeting was William O'Brien. Constance, along with James Connolly, William Partridge, The O'Rahilly, P.T. Daly and Seán Milroy all spoke, with a large force of police standing by. Constance announced that members of Cumann na mBan were learning to shoot so that they could resist conscription. The meeting ended with the singing of 'A Nation Once Again' and the firing of a number of shots by the Volunteers.

In December 1914, Cumann na mBan held its first convention, with members described as auxiliaries to the Volunteers. Although Cumann na mBan made its own decisions, it had no control over how the money it collected was spent. Nor could it express its views on political matters, although this would change. With anti-recruiting propaganda continuing, the chief secretary, Augustine Birrell, threatened to seize the presses of the more radical newspapers, including *Sinn Féin*, the *Irish Worker* and the *Irish Volunteer*. At a protest meeting in Beresford Place, Connolly declared that Dublin was under 'martial law', while Constance announced that any Irishman who joined the British army would be regarded as 'a traitor to his country'.

Just before Christmas, Nora Connolly was summoned to Dublin by her father. In the presence of Constance, he told her that she was to make a trip to the USA with a message so secret and dangerous that it could only be given verbally and that five people including herself would be hanged for treason if it were discovered. The other four were Tom Clarke, Seán Mac Diarmada, Constance and himself. In New York, she was to contact the German envoy and tell him that the British were building Q-boats, designed to lure the lethal U-boat submarines into surfacing, in Queenstown.

Nora stayed at Surrey House until she sailed to New York via Liverpool; Constance lent her a fur coat for the journey. In New York, she was met by Jim Larkin and Sidney Gifford, who knew nothing of her mission. She stayed with Padraic and Mary Colum for several weeks before her father decided it was safe for her to return to Ireland. After meeting the veteran Fenian John Devoy, a staunch supporter of physical force nationalism, she brought back with her some money as well as letters from Sir Roger Casement to a variety of people in Ireland including his sister; Casement was in Germany seeking arms and ammunition for the Irish cause and attempting to raise an Irish Brigade from prisoners in German camps. He was in constant contact with John Devoy.

Sir Roger Casement remained one of the more enigmatic supporters of the Irish cause. Born in 1864 of a Protestant father and Catholic mother and brought up in Antrim, he was knighted for exposing Belgian atrocities in the Congo and, later, the slaughter of the indigenous populations of South America during the Amazon rubber boom. After he retired in 1913, he stayed in touch with his nationalist friends, seeing much of Arthur Griffith on visits home and making friends with Constance and her sister Eva. In July 1913, he wrote an article for the *Irish Review* under the pen name 'Shan Van Vocht', arguing that Ireland could benefit if Britain was defeated in any forthcoming conflict.

In February 1915, the Irish Citizen Army and the ITGWU held a ceremony at Croydon Park to honour Constance's services during the 1913 lock-out and to make her an honorary member of the union. The 'address', or scroll, was a customary means of expressing loyalty and gratitude in Irish life. A few, presented by grateful tenants, hung in Lissadell. Constance was presented with an elaborately illuminated address bordered with Celtic knots and illustrated with sketches of Lissadell, Liberty Hall and a photograph of herself. It was signed by ten men, among them Thomas Foran and James Connolly. Constance was immensely proud of the honour and, until 1916, the address hung in Surrey House alongside Casimir's *Bread Triptych*, her own *The Conscript* and other favourite paintings.

Around the same time, the Aberdeens were replaced in the Viceregal Lodge by Lord Wimborne, who was determined to be more than a figurehead and would head up the new Department of Recruiting for Ireland.

In April, Constance received a letter from Casimir. When war broke out, he left the Balkans, where he had been working as a newspaper correspondent, and travelled 700 miles to join an Imperial Hussar regiment. After he was wounded in the winter campaign in the Carpathians, his brother Jan brought him home to convalesce. It was decided that Staskou should go to the Ukraine and join his father. Constance, deeply in debt because of her husband's extravagances and the after-effects of the lock-out, was forced to ask Josslyn for the price of Staskou's fare, promising she would live more frugally once her stepson was gone. On 15 June, she and Æ's son Brian Russell, saw Staskou off. When he arrived at Zywotowka, he discovered that the war had been good for the Markievicz estate, yet in Dublin, Constance was left to deal with Casimir's considerable debts.

Life had its lighter moments. Nearly every Sunday, concerts or plays took place in Liberty Hall, with members of the Fianna often taking parts, and Michael Mallin organising a small orchestra. James Connolly loved to sing and the Citizen Army sang rousing rebel songs like 'O'Donnell Abu', and 'Wrap the Green Flag Around Me' on its route marches, along with 'The Germans are Winning the War Me Boys' and 'Armed for the Battle', both written by Constance.

At the annual Wolfe Tone commemoration at Bodenstown, Constance led the Fianna, and Cumann na mBan was well represented, as were both the Volunteers and the Citizen Army. Tom Clarke gave the graveside address and, in his eyes, Constance fancied she could see 'the vision of freedom ... a glimpse of the promised land'. Around this time, the Fianna was reorganised under strictly military lines; the IRB thought it was time to acknowledge its control. Eamon Martin, proposing the change, said that since the movement was essentially military, having a president instead of a military chief as its head was ludicrous. Both Bulmer Hobson and Con Colbert opposed the change and said that character-building and training boys in citizenship was more important than drills and musketry. Constance did nothing to oppose the change. Although all other honorary offices were abolished, she retained the title of president.

The Volunteers and the Citizen Army united for the funeral of O'Donovan Rossa, the long exiled Fenian, who died on 1 August in the USA. His funeral, masterminded by the IRB, who brought his body home, became a significant propaganda coup, with tens of thousands of nationalists turning out to pay homage. The police and army stayed away, leaving the Irish Volunteers and Citizen Army to supervise traffic and guide the procession as well as forming a guard of honour. Conspicuous by their absence were the National Volunteers.

Patrick Pearse's stirring graveside oration turned into a battle cry: 'They think they have foreseen everything, but the fools, the fools, the fools! – they have left us our Fenian dead and while Ireland holds these graves Ireland unfree shall never be at peace.' A volley was fired over the grave by the Volunteers. For Constance, it was the day to 'renew our baptismal vows and rededicate our lives to Ireland'. Yet Eva Gore-Booth, present with her friend Esther Roper, noticed that, despite the solemnity of the occasion, numbers from the two republican armies were relatively few. 'Well thank goodness, they can't be planning a rising now, not with such a tiny force,' she said to Roper.

While the British were continuing their recruitment campaign in Ireland, they did not help their cause by patronising any Irish attempting to enlist. Lord Kitchener, the Minister for War, refused commissions to educated young Irishmen simply because he distrusted their nationalism. When a flag, specially made by Lady Mayo and her school of embroidery for John Redmond's proposed Irish Division, was dismissed, Irish pride was hurt. A further setback to recruiting in Ireland occurred when Sir Edward Carson was given the position of Attorney General in a coalition government. John Redmond was offered a place in the cabinet but refused it. David Lloyd George, then Chancellor of the Exchequer, was one of the few to recognise that the British attitude was serving only to stoke nationalist fervour.

Nearly every Sunday and bank holiday, the Citizen Army held drills and parades and, occasionally, mock attacks on various buildings around Dublin – a 'Wolf Wolf!' strategy that James Connolly hoped would cause confusion. Dublin Castle was the focus of one manoeuvre in October 1915. With a heavy fog enveloping the city, the entire Citizen Army, men and women, set off from Liberty Hall, heading for the Castle by different routes. The detectives of the G-division did their best to follow the muffled tramping of the various units, divided into attackers and defenders. Two hours later, the 'attack' was over and everyone marched to Emmet Hall in Inchicore for tea and songs. The police had mixed views; Colonel Edgeworth-Johnstone, its chief commander, reported only that a 'large portion' of the Sinn Féin army marched by Ship Street, close to the Castle. Superintendent Dunne was more concerned: 'It is a serious state of affairs to have the peace of the city endangered by a gang of roughs with rifles and bayonets at large at that time of night, with a female like the Countess Markievicz in charge.'

During the summer, Delia Larkin had resigned from the Women's Workers' Union after a disagreement over financial matters including the purchase of a piano and, in November, the union was reorganised with Helena Molony as the driving force and secretary. Constance and James Connolly were elected vice-presidents with Miss Mulhall the treasurer. James Larkin, although in the USA, was made president. Molony set up the Irish Workers' Co-Operative Society, a sewing shop for women who had lost jobs during the lock-out. A dozen sewing machines churned out shirts and underclothing that were then sold, alongside nationalist publications, in the shop at Eden Quay beside Liberty Hall. This forged closer links between the men and women in Liberty Hall. While the prominent women of the Citizen Army, like Constance, were middle class, the rank and file were mainly young women who had lost jobs because of their union membership.

At Christmas, a young woman from Glasgow called Margaret Skinnider arrived at Surrey House with a supply of detonators. She had crossed the Irish Sea with the detonators in her hat and the wires wrapped around her body under her coat. Fearing that any form of heat would set off the detonators, she spent a long, cold night on deck. Surrey House she remembered as being so full of books 'you could not walk about without stumbling over them'; she noted that it occasionally resembled the wardrobe of a theatre with people in all manner of costumes coming downstairs.

Constance took Skinnider to the Dublin Mountains, where they succeeded in blowing up a wall with one of the detonators. Earlier they had acquired a few birds after Poppet, Constance's Irish cocker spaniel, decided to go hunting with two men they bumped into. During the visit, Constance told Skinnider of plans for a shipload of arms and ammunition to arrive in Ireland around Easter Sunday. The information had possibly come through Roger Casement.

Skinnider remembered the kindness of Constance towards the Fianna boys who came and went in Surrey House. In the house was a boy who was slowly going blind. Constance was encouraging him to sing, determined that he must have a livelihood. She spent hours teaching him the words and music of patriotic songs and ballads.

In Dublin, hundreds of men, blacklisted from their jobs after the lock-out, found themselves forced to join the British army in order to feed their families. Constance took Skinnider to see the hidden Dublin of crumbling tenements and overcrowded slums: 'She took me to Ash Street. I do not believe there is a worse street in the world than Ash Street. It lies in a hollow where sewage runs and refuse falls; it is not paved and is full of holes.'

James Connolly told Skinnider that when the police were called out for strike duty or a riot, they were given permission to drink as much as they liked from big barrels of porter at every station. That the half-drunk police then used their batons like shillelaghs was no surprise. To disperse a crowd, they assembled on four sides, pushing even innocent bystanders into the middle of the crowd.

Ireland was clearly on the brink.

CHAPTER TEN

'Ireland is waking'

In January 1916, conscription was made law in Britain, although no decision was made about Ireland. A few weeks later, British officials decided that Constance, born of an Irish family, bred in Ireland and living in Ireland, was Russian by virtue of her marriage to the Count, who came from a part of Poland annexed by Russia. They ordered her to register as an alien. She was incensed, and her speeches around that time were more intemperate than usual. In Cork, she spoke on 'The Sacrifices of Robert Emmet' but brought the subject around to the topic of conscription, saying that the British government did not dare introduce conscription to Ireland because the Volunteers had guns and were prepared to use them.

At every possible opportunity, Constance made appeals for action – for instance, when Francis Sheehy Skeffington spoke to the Irish Women's Franchise League on his return from the USA. Presiding at the meeting was James Connolly, who was continuing to press for an uprising, although he praised Sheehy Skeffington for his resolute pacifism. Speaking of the women he had met in the USA, Sheehy Skeffington said that they were not as advanced politically as Irish or English women, despite their energy and enterprise. He approved the work of Henry Ford's Ford Peace Crusaders, who had arrived in Oslo by ship on 18 December 1915 and would carry out their anti-war work until February 1917, winning respect for their idealism. Constance dissented; although pacifism was a noble ideal, in a letter to the *Workers' Republic* on 22 January 1916, she wrote that she did not want the war stopped until the British Empire was smashed. Sheehy Skeffington, who was appalled by the carnage in Europe, challenged Constance to a public debate.

The notion of war as noble was hard to dislodge. Canon Sheehan in his novel *The Graves of Kilmorna* wrote:

> The country is sinking unto the sleep of death and nothing can wake it but the crack of the rifle. As the blood of martyrs was the seed of saints so the patriots will be the sacred seed from which alone can spring new forces and fresh life to a nation that is drifting into the putrescence of decay.

His view was typical.

Through the *Irish Worker*, Connolly was preparing the ground for a rising, writing pointed articles about the lessons nationalist movements could draw from previous uprisings in Moscow, the Tyrol, Paris, Belgium and even the Alamo, where the battle was lost but the war won. He gave lectures on street fighting and urged the Citizen Army to study and prepare.

Since 1907, the Irish Chief Secretary had been Augustine Birrell, a literary man, liberal and benign, who spent a lot of his time either in London or fishing in the west of Ireland. Wary of provoking trouble, he refused to arrest nationalist leaders, to seize arms or to proscribe organisations. He knew nothing of the Irish Republican Brotherhood's influence over the Irish Volunteers. Nor was he aware that Joseph Plunkett had travelled to Germany seeking arms and men. Like Birrell, Dublin Castle believed that the radical nationalists were all talk. Madame Markievicz, drilling a handful of men with ancient rifles, was clearly mad. Birrell's advisers were John Redmond, who thought the chances of insurrection were negligible, and John Dillon, who believed there was a danger but advised against intervening.

Dublin Castle was moving cautiously. Under the 1914 Defence of the Realm Act, it had issued deportation orders to the Volunteer organisers, Ernest Blythe, Liam Mellows and Alfred Monaghan. When these were ignored, the trio was interned in Mountjoy Gaol. A huge rally against the deportations had taken place in the Mansion House on 30 March 1916, but the British policy had some effect, silencing all but the most militant nationalists.

Earlier in the year, Connolly had been co-opted on to the IRB's Military Council, a move shrouded in mystery at the time. Only a few years earlier, Connolly had supported Home Rule, but the 1913 lock-out and the failure of international socialism had changed his viewpoint. He was ready for a fight. Since the IRB feared that he might attempt an Irish Citizen Army rebellion in an effort to goad the Volunteers into action, negotiation was vital, but attempts to arrange a meeting were proving fruitless. At lunchtime on Wednesday 19 January, Connolly was stopped by IRB members Frank Daly and Eamonn Dore as he left Liberty Hall and was asked to step into their car. After telling him that Pearse, Mac Diarmada and Joseph Plunkett wished to speak to him, they drove to a brickworks in Dolphin's Barn. The purpose of the meeting was to thrash out their differences once and for all. Connolly, disillusioned by the lack of support from nationalists for the 1913 lock-out, had little sympathy for the young bourgeois members of the Irish Volunteers. For their part, the Volunteers saw Connolly as awkward, quarrelsome and dangerously obsessed with the naïve idea that a small Citizen Army could lead an all-Ireland insurrection. Three days of intense discussion on the IRB plans for a rising ensued. Plunkett, who had drawn up the plan, later said that he had never enjoyed anything so much as this wordy 'duel' with an 'extraordinary man'. The Rising was officially fixed for Easter Sunday.

As far as his family and friends were concerned, Connolly had 'disappeared'. He had left no message with Thomas Foran, the ITGWU president, of his whereabouts, nor had he spoken to Michael Mallin, the vice-commandant of the Irish Citizen Army, although he had, apparently, sent a brief message to his wife in Belfast. When he failed to show up either at Liberty Hall or Surrey House that night, his friends became alarmed. The next day, William O'Brien, his brother Daniel O'Brien, Thomas Foran, Eamonn Ceannt and Michael Mallin, along with Constance, gathered to discuss possible actions. Some believed that Connolly had been taken by force and that his body would be found in a ditch; others guessed that he was attending a secret meeting. Constance demanded that the Citizen Army rise immediately, as Connolly had suggested they do should he ever disappear. The more moderate Mallin suggested that they speak first to the IRB Military Council. Nothing happened.

On the evening of Saturday 22 January, Surrey House was raided by forty G-men with a District Inspector. Constance arrived home in time to see the small printing press being carried out through the door. In the house were a few Fianna boys who entertained the searchers with spirited renditions of rebel songs. As well as the printing press, a number of American magazines, a miniature rifle, a few ballads, a few teaspoons and a bar of carbolic soap were seized. As the G-men left the building the boys and girls sang 'Will ye no come back again?' Around this time, Constance's housekeeper had the foresight to hide her study of Emmet's plans for the 1803 rising, identifying four points of attack – the Pigeon House, Dublin Castle, the Artillery Barracks at Islandbridge and Cork Street Barracks – as well as checkpoints at the old Custom House, Mary Street Barracks and the Corner House on Capel Street. It noted two lines of defence along Beresford Street North and Merchant's Quay South. While it may have been nothing more than notes for a lecture to the Fianna, the study showed that the rebels were making a close study of previous rebellions in Dublin.

Three hours after the raid, at around eleven o'clock, Constance and a group of Fianna boys were drinking tea when Connolly walked into the room and stood calmly by the fire. The boys were immediately banished. When an astonished Helena Molony asked him where he had been, Connolly replied that he had been to hell, 'but I conquered my conquerors'. He refused to speak further on the matter.

The debate on 'Shall We Make Peace Now?' between Constance and Francis Sheehy Skeffington took place on 15 February. Louie Bennett, a pacifist, was not impressed: 'Madame Markievicz has no powers of debate. She reiterated the same few points in various wild, flowery phrases, and talked much of dying for Ireland.' Still, she had the hall on her side and Bennett felt that her supporters spoke in a 'bitter and sinister vein'. By contrast, Hanna Sheehy Skeffington described a warmly contested word-duel, with a speech from Connolly at the end swinging the vote in favour of Constance.

What few knew – including the moderate arm of the Volunteers led by Hobson and MacNeill – was that plans for a rising were already far advanced. Tom Clarke had picked a group of single-minded IRB members to make up a Military Council – Pearse, Ceannt, Seán Mac Diarmada, Thomas MacDonagh and the exotic Joseph Plunkett who, despite his many rings and bracelets, was considered an expert military tactician. They would make up a clique within a clique within a clique. Supporting their efforts was the ferociously militaristic Clann na Gael in the USA.

In February 1916, the veteran Fenian John Devoy of Clan na Gael got a coded message: the IRB's Supreme Council had decided on the date of Easter Sunday 23 April for the insurrection. For Patrick Pearse a rebellion would have a mystic quality; it was the duty of each generation to rededicate itself to Ireland, even if such a rebellion became a blood sacrifice. Connolly believed that a bold military action – even if it failed – was necessary in order to spark a social revolution. Eoin MacNeill, chief of staff of the Volunteers, thought differently. He did not want to sacrifice a single Volunteer's life if there was no hope of a military victory. He laid down three conditions for an insurrection: an attack by the British, an attempt to enforce conscription or a German invasion. A third group of nationalists, including Robert Monteith, believed that guerrilla warfare using the element of surprise and local knowledge was the best method of dealing with a more powerful oppressor with access to a military machine. They were in the minority.

Those who wanted an immediate rebellion had to work together. While the IRB had some influence over the Volunteers, it did not have complete control. As for the Citizen Army, few in the union had any interest in armed rebellion. On St Patrick's Day 1916, 1,600 Volunteers lined up in College Green, armed with new bayonets. Nearby, in Beresford Place, the Irish Citizen Army stood by in case of trouble before setting off on a seventeen-mile march, taking in Dundrum and Booterstown. A fully armed Constance, aged forty-eight, was among them.

A week later, on 24 March, Constance was shopping in the Liffey Street area when she saw that the police had raided the pro-republican Gaelic Press, allegedly in a routine search for a newspaper called the *Gael*. Fearing that they would move next on Liberty Hall, which by now contained a formidable arsenal of weapons and ammunition, she rushed there looking for Connolly. When she arrived, several policemen were about to leave the Workers' Co-Operative Society shop on Eden Quay, from which a door led to the printing room. Behind the printing room were stored the weapons. When the policemen claimed that they wished to seize the latest issue of the *Gael*, Connolly demanded to see a search warrant, although this was not necessary under the terms of the Defence of the Realm Act. This was not forthcoming and Connolly drew a gun; the police backed off.

Constance reported what she had witnessed in Liffey Street, which suggested that the authorities were planning a general suppression of the press, as had happened in 1914. With the police expected to return any minute, Connolly ordered the Citizen Army men present to mobilise members on the railways, docks and building sites. Nora Connolly immediately began printing off Citizen Army mobilisation forms.

By the time the police returned, Connolly, Constance and Helena Molony, all armed, were waiting, along with a number of Citizen Army members; Nora Connolly had delivered mobilisation orders to Mallin and others and they were on their way. Connolly again demanded a warrant. With both Connolly and Constance armed and Citizen Army reinforcements arriving, the sergeant ordered a retreat. No one had any idea what had caused the raids and so Constance and the women searched for copies of the latest *Gael*. It had not arrived.

Soon, a third group of policemen led by Inspector Bannon appeared at the Eden Quay shop and, this time, a warrant to search the premises was produced. Connolly told them to go ahead with the search but warned them against setting foot in Liberty Hall. After turning over the shop, the police left. By now, around 150 Citizen Army members had downed tools and arrived at Liberty Hall, some dripping wet after swimming across the Grand Canal. Although still in their working clothes, many were armed and both Dublin Castle and the Viceregal Lodge received hundreds of calls from alarmed citizens.

For the rest of the day, with the level of excitement boosted by wild rumours of an attack, guards were posted at the Liberty Hall doors. All day, a stream of Fianna and Women's Ambulance Corps, as well as Citizen Army men, came and went. Constance had returned to Surrey House in the late afternoon and Connolly sent his daughter, Nora, after her to collect a carbine and bandolier. When she told Constance that her father expected that 'anything may happen at any time', Constance replied that she would return to Liberty Hall immediately and take her turn at standing guard. She was wearing a dark green woollen tunic with brass buttons, dark green tweed knee breeches, black stockings and heavy boots. The jacket had come from Michael Mallin; the shirt and breeches she had bought herself. Around her waist was a cartridge belt with an automatic pistol on one side and a Mauser pistol on the other. Over her shoulder was a bandolier and, on her back, she carried a haversack. 'What do I look like?' she asked Nora. Nora replied that she looked like a real soldier. Her own outfit was much the same, although she wore puttees instead of boots. There followed a brief discussion about the most appropriate hat to wear, with Constance opting for her best hat, made of black velour with a plume of feathers.

As they were about to leave, there was a knock at the door. Two detectives stood outside with an order prohibiting Constance from entering 'that part of Ireland called Kerry'. An exchange of views followed, with the policemen taking careful note of Constance's pistol. 'Remember I am quite prepared to shoot and be shot at,' she said as she shut the door. Constance was scheduled to give a lecture on 'The Fenian Rising of '67' to Fianna boys in Tralee, County Kerry the following Sunday. Connolly advised her not to go; she would risk arrest at a time when there was important work to do in Dublin. She was still in the process of making large-scale maps of Dublin city for use in the rebellion – the perfect job for a trained artist. Marie Perolz went in her place, delivered the speech written by Constance and enjoyed herself thoroughly, especially when she was questioned about her Russian nationality. 'Those were great days and I would crawl on my knees to do it all again,' Marie was to say later.

Although the Gaelic Press printing machines were confiscated, some frames of type escaped attention. With the help of the owner, Joseph Stanley, these were rescued from the Liffey Street printing shop by a group of Irish Citizen Army men wearing working clothes and using a hand cart. Watched by the police, they loaded up the cart and took the frames of type back to Liberty Hall. The *Spark*, owned by Perolz and edited by Constance, and another newspaper called *Honesty* came out as usual that week. Later, this type was used for printing the Proclamation of the Irish Republic.

With four weeks to go until Easter, Liberty Hall was guarded night and day, with Constance regularly taking her turn as sentry and bringing cakes for tea. Some of the Irish Citizen Army men slept there and, when not on guard duty, occupied their time by making bombs. Although members of the secretive Military Council were the only ones who knew the date set for the Rising, it was obvious to any close observer that something was imminent. Three weeks before Easter, Connolly asked Thomas O'Donoghue what he knew about street fighting; O'Donoghue went off to research the topic at the National Library. He was told that when they were given three-day ration packs they would know for sure that the Rising was happening.

A poem by Constance called 'The Call' was published in the *Workers' Republic* of 15 April:

> Do you hear the call in the whispering wind?
> The call to our race today
> The call for self-sacrifice, courage and faith
> The call that brooks no delay.

On Sunday 26 March, the Union Dramatic Society staged a play written by James Connolly called *Under Which Flag?* The hero, played by Seán Connolly, is torn between enlisting with the British army and joining the IRB. The play ended – prophetically – with the hero raising a green flag and uttering the words 'Under this flag only will I serve. Under this flag, if need be, will I die.'

Connolly used pageantry to boost morale in the tense weeks leading up to Easter. On Palm Sunday, 16 April, the Irish Citizen Army assembled outside Liberty Hall making three sides of a square. Inside the formation, the women's section, the Irish Citizen Army boy scouts under Captain Carpenter, the Fianna, and the Fintan Lalor Pipers' Band lined out. A colour guard of sixteen uniformed men escorted a young girl called Molly Reilly as she placed a green flag on a pile of drums in the centre of the square. After inspecting the troops, Connolly, wearing a uniform for the first time, took up his position as commander in front of the drums, flanked by Michael Mallin and Constance.

Only then did the young flag bearer climb to the roof of Liberty Hall and unfurl the flag – a gold harp on the green background. That night, *Under Which Flag?* played again in Liberty Hall. Constance, in the thick of it all, wrote that she was proud to be accepted by Tom Clarke and the members of the provisional government as the second of Connolly's 'ghosts'; those given enough information about the plans for the Rising to take over if anything happened to him. While the leaders of the Rising held out little hope of success, the Military Council hoped that, by proclaiming an Irish Republic and remaining in control for a period of time, they would win Ireland a place at the peace conference that would follow the ending of the world war.

The strategy for the Rising, worked out mainly by Joseph Plunkett, was to take and hold several public buildings in the centre of Dublin, controlling the railway stations and main entrances to the city, and leaving the military barracks outside the defence line. Detailed plans were made for cutting the telephone and telegraph wires. The General Post Office (GPO) on Sackville Street was chosen as headquarters. Patrick Pearse was named Commander-in-Chief of the Army of the Irish Republic and President of the Provisional Government. James Connolly was to command the Dublin division. Also assigned to the GPO were three more members of the provisional government: Clarke, Mac Diarmada and Plunkett. These five were to sign the Proclamation of Independence, with Tom Clarke, as the elder statesman of the rebellion, first on the list. Also signing the Proclamation were Thomas MacDonagh, commanding the Irish Volunteers at Jacob's biscuit factory, and Eamonn Ceannt, commander of the South Dublin Union located at what is now the site of St James' Hospital.

The ring around Dublin's city centre stretched from the GPO to the Four Courts, the South Dublin Union, Jacob's factory, St Stephen's Green and Bolands Mills. From these, smaller groups would be deployed: for instance, the North Dublin Union, which controlled Broadstone Station, would be occupied by a force operating from the Four Courts. Thanks to Mac Diarmada and Clarke's obsession with secrecy, no one had any idea of the plan. Although they were aware of the manoeuvres scheduled for Sunday, few knew a Rising was imminent, although Cumann na mBan members were kept busy assembling first aid kits and Liberty Hall had turned into a munitions factory, with a stockpile of home-made bombs, grenades and bayonets.

The plan did not assume public support, since the citizens of Dublin were, by and large, indifferent, if not downright hostile, to politics and patriotism. Most felt that their duty was to help Britain in the war, especially with Home Rule on the way as soon as it all ended. The war had improved the standard of living for many, with factories and dockyards busy and the families of the 150,000 fighting with the King's army getting dependants' allowances. For many 'separation women', it was the first time they had ever enjoyed a regular income.

To rouse the Volunteers, the IRB made use of a document that had come into their hands from Dublin Castle. On the surface, it was innocuous enough: a contingency plan to arrest key nationalists in the event of serious unrest. At the meeting of the Dublin Corporation on Thursday 20 April, Alderman Tom Kelly had read aloud the document, so ensuring it came into the public domain. The document, written in code, revealed, when it was deciphered, the authorities' plans to seize key buildings used by the Volunteers and the Irish Citizen Army and to arrest all Sinn Féin members and Volunteers. The British denied they had written the so-called 'Castle document' and there were rumours that it was a forgery concocted by Joseph Plunkett. Years later, it was revealed that the document was genuine; it had been smuggled out of Dublin Castle by a nationalist member of staff.

With the Rising only days away, the exposure of the document succeeded in its task of rousing indignation among Volunteers and Citizen Army members. On Wednesday, Connolly had rounded up the Citizen Army officers and told them that the Rising was planned for Sunday at 6.30pm in Dublin and 7pm in the provinces. On Thursday, Constance made a rousing speech when a presentation was made to Kathleen Lynn in Liberty Hall, also giving Dr Lynn a poem she had written.

Another of Constance's poems, called 'Our Faith' was printed in the last edition of the *Workers' Republic*, published on Easter Saturday, 22 April. It ends:

> So we're waiting til 'Somebody' gives us the word
> That sends us to Freedom or death.

To keep herself occupied, Constance set to work preparing a flag; many shops were closed for Easter Week and she was forced to improvise, starting with a green bedspread and using gold pan and mustard to paint the words 'Irish Republic' on it. Máire O'Neill, Delia Brennan, Laurence Ginnell and his wife Alice were all at Surrey House. No sooner had Margaret Skinnider arrived from Scotland than she was

1. Lissadell House in Co. Sligo where Constance Markievicz grew up. (Photograph by the author)

2. Eva and Constance Gore-Booth dressed as Drumcliff Co-Operative dairy maids for a fund-raising fancy dress ball in 1895. (Reproduced courtesy of the National Library of Ireland)

3. Portrait of Constance Markievicz from about 1908. (Reproduced courtesy of the National Library of Ireland)

4. Constance Markievicz with a group of Fianna boys (undated). (Reproduced courtesy of the National Library of Ireland)

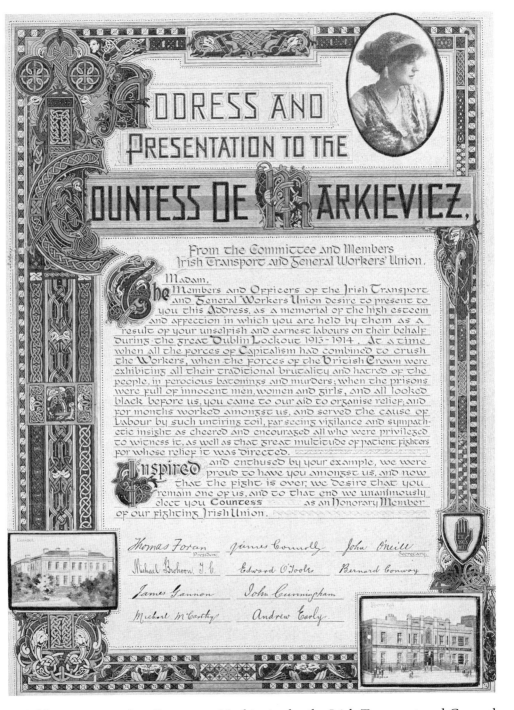

5. Address presented to Constance Markievicz by the Irish Transport and General Workers' Union for her work during the 1913 lock-out. (Reproduced courtesy of the National Library of Ireland)

6. Constance Markievicz as Joan Arc appearing to a woman politi prisoner played by Kathleen Houst in a *tableau vivant*, 1914. (Reproduc courtesy of the National Library Ireland)

7. Seated studio portrait of Constance Markievicz, around 1915. (Reproduced courtesy of the National Library of Ireland)

8. Surrey House on Leinster Road in Rathmines, Dublin (on left), where Constance Markievicz was living in 1916. Next door is Dorset House. (Photograph by the author)

9. Constance Markievicz in military uniform, around 1915. (Reproduced courtesy of the National Library of Ireland)

10. Royal Fusiliers' Arch (also known as Traitors' Arch), St Stephen's Green, Dublin, through which the Irish Citizen Army marched on Easter Monday 1916. (Photograph by the author)

11. The Royal College of Surgeons in Ireland on St Stephen's Green, Dublin. Note the bullets marks on the facade. (Photograph by the author)

12. Poem by Dora Sigerson Shorter, which was illustrated by Constance Markievicz while in Aylebsury Prison in 1917 and given to Gerard Crofts as a belated wedding gift. (Reproduced courtesy of the National Library of Ireland)

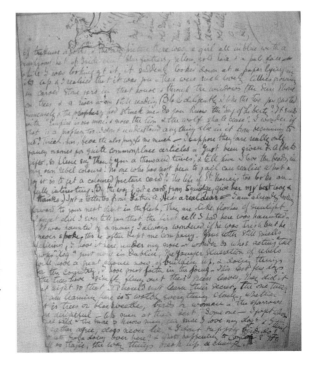

One of Constance Markievicz's ...rs to her sister Eva from ...esbury Prison, dated 14 May 1917, ...d by Esther Roper. (Reproduced ...rtesy of the National Library of ...and from MS5673)

14. Watercolour of a horse leaping over the prison walls from one of Constance Markievicz's letters from Aylesbury Prison in the spring of 1917. (Reproduced courtesy of the National Library of Ireland from MS5673)

15. Peace meeting at Mansion House, Dublin, 1921. Left to right: Kathleen Clarke, Constance Markievicz, Kate O'Callaghan and Margaret Pearse. (Reproduced courtesy of the National Library of Ireland)

16. Éamon de Valera and Constance Markievicz standing in a garden (undated). (Reproduced courtesy of the National Library of Ireland)

Caricature by Constance ▪kievicz of William T. Cosgrave ▪ted in *The Fenian – Daily War ▪etin*, which was published from ▪ to October 1922. (Courtesy ▪a O'Keeffe)

18. Statue of Constance Markievicz by Seamus Murphy (1954) in St Stephen's Green, Dublin. (Photograph by the author)

sent to Belfast; she returned with Lillie Connolly. The Connolly family was to stay at Constance's cottage during the Rising. With them they brought all their possessions, leaving for ever their home of five years.

Bad luck and the IRB's addiction to secrecy bedevilled preparations for the Rising in the final few days. Although MacNeill was technically head of the Volunteers, he had not been told the date of the Rising by the Military Council. Bulmer Hobson, still a member of the IRB, was likewise unaware of plans. Wild stories were circulating in the provinces and, on Thursday, Commandant Liam Manahan arrived from Limerick at the Volunteers' headquarters in Dawson Street seeking information. The contents of the 'Castle document' had made him and many other Volunteer commandants uneasily aware that they had little information to go on. Bulmer Hobson, who knew no better, assured him that nothing exceptional was planned.

Later that evening, Hobson and J.J. O'Connell, a Volunteer officer, overheard enough of a conversation to make them suspect that a rising was indeed planned for the Sunday. They immediately set off for MacNeill's house, where they reported the conversation. The three then headed for St Enda's to confront Patrick Pearse. It was after midnight when they arrived. When Pearse confirmed their assumptions, MacNeill was furious both about the secrecy surrounding the plans and what he saw as the folly of calling out a poorly prepared army at a strategically bad time. He warned Pearse that he would do everything he could to stop the Rising, short of informing the Castle. Supported by The O'Rahilly, MacNeill's first step was to send out an order cancelling 'all orders issued by Commandant Pearse or by any other person heretofore'.

Pearse summoned Seán Mac Diarmada and Thomas MacDonagh for an urgent meeting and, early on Friday morning, the trio arrived at MacNeill's house. They told him that Roger Casement was bringing a shipload of arms from Germany and that the Rising must begin on Easter Sunday. The arrival of arms removed one of MacNeill's objections. He accepted that the Rising was inevitable and sent out a second round of dispatches, this time confirming that the announced manoeuvres would take place as originally planned. The result was utter confusion, not helped when the German arms failed to arrive. One Munster commandant remembered getting five separate orders.

On Thursday, off the coast of Kerry, the *Aud*, a German ship disguised as a Norwegian trawler, lay off Fenit pier waiting for a signal from the shore. In a disastrous failure of communication, the local Volunteer officer did not expect the boat until the weekend. Indeed, the entire adventure was doomed to failure when the schedule was changed after a submarine along with the *Aud* had set sail from the German naval base of Heligoland. On board the submarine were Roger Casement, Robert Monteith and a member of the Irish Brigade called Sergeant Beverly (under the name 'Daniel Bailey'). Unknown to them, the British Secret Service had cracked German radio codes and, for some time, had known of Casement's machinations and of the planned Rising. They had asked Augustine Birrell to arrest the prominent Sinn Féin leaders but, since they could not tell him why, he was not convinced.

While Pearse and MacNeill were meeting in Dublin in the early hours of Friday morning, Robert Monteith, with Casement and 'Daniel Bailey', had gone ashore to supervise the landing of arms and ammunition from the *Aud*. A local farmer walking along Banna Strand noticed the three strangers and alerted the Royal Irish Constabulary. 'Bailey' was arrested along with Austin Stack and Con Collins, who were the local contacts.

A second attempt to collect the shipment also failed. Five men had left Dublin for Killarney by train on Friday morning. They drove away in two cars and, in the pitch black night, one of the cars took a wrong turning and drove off a pier at Ballykissane. Three of the men drowned. The other car waited for three hours past rendezvous time and, when no one showed up, returned to Dublin. At sea, the *Aud* was seized by the watching British naval forces and brought to Cork.

Monteith was still at large and his main concern was to get a message to MacNeill that the arms had not arrived and that it might be wise to call off the planned insurrection. The message was delivered not to MacNeill or Bulmer Hobson as Monteith had ordered but to James Connolly at Liberty Hall. Connolly called an emergency meeting with Pearse and others and gave them Monteith's message. After much discussion, the Military Council decided to go ahead with the Rising. Pearse and Mac Diarmada saw MacNeill on Saturday morning and told him of Casement's arrest.

In Cork, the *Aud* and her British escort had arrived in Queenstown harbour. Lifeboats were lowered and the crew members in their German uniforms jumped in. No sooner were they safe than the ship exploded, with 20,000 rifles, ten machine guns and one million rounds of ammunition lost. The news quickly arrived in Dublin and decided MacNeill's next move. On Saturday afternoon, he met a number of activists including Arthur Griffith, Joseph Plunkett and Thomas MacDonagh; he told them that he planned to cancel all orders for Sunday.

Plunkett and MacDonagh, both members of the Military Council, objected strenuously, but MacNeill was adamant that it was his duty to save the Volunteers from useless slaughter. Among the messengers who set out for the provinces was The O'Rahilly, who left his all-too recognisable De Dion Bouton car at home and took a taxi to deliver cancellation orders in six counties before ending up in Limerick the following morning. Late on Monday, news would reach him of the Rising. He was driven back to Dublin and joined in the fighting. His reason was simple: 'Well, I've helped to wind up the clock – I might as well hear it strike!' To Constance he commented, 'It is madness, but it is glorious madness.' He fought in the GPO and would die during the retreat.

On Saturday evening, Eoin MacNeill made a mad dash by bicycle to the offices of the *Sunday Independent* with a copy of the order rescinding Sunday manoeuvres. He arrived just in time to make the morning paper.

Those in Liberty Hall were continuing with their plans. The women cooked hams and sliced bread to make hundreds of sandwiches for the 'ration packs'. William O'Brien, Winifred Carney and Constance prepared mobilisation orders and officers' commissions. Constance's own commission as a lieutenant was typed out by Winifred Carney and signed by Connolly. A friend came to the hall and, noticing the general bustle, assumed the Liberty Players were getting ready for a production. 'Rehearsing I suppose?' she said to Constance.

'Yes,' replied Constance.
'Is it for children?' asked her friend.
'No,' said Constance; 'for grown-ups.'

The mobilisation orders for the Citizen Army were sent out: they were to meet at Liberty Hall at 3.30pm on Sunday, with full equipment. With most of the Citizen Army living in Dublin, assembling them was relatively easy. Meanwhile, Volunteer messengers were spreading out around the country by train, tram and bicycle since cars were rare in those days. The messages had to be delivered in secrecy to someone known. It took time, and those who felt the Volunteers were not ready to fight had some reason on their side.

Others believed in the words of Fintan Lalor to Young Ireland before the 1848 Rebellion: 'Somewhere and somehow and by someone, a beginning must be made, and the first act of armed resistance is always premature, imprudent and foolish.'

CHAPTER ELEVEN

Easter Week 1916 – Year One of Irish History

Sunday newspapers in Ireland traditionally made most of their sales outside churches, with posters on railings proclaiming the big stories of the day.

On Sunday, 23 April 1916, the men, women and children attending Easter services could not fail to notice the placards announcing that Volunteer manoeuvres planned for later in the day had been cancelled. The headlines took up much of the space on the front page of the *Sunday Independent*, and for those who knew what was afoot, this was devastating news. Few associated the move with two other items on the page: one concerned the seizure of arms in County Kerry and the other a tragic accident, also in Kerry, in which three men drowned after their car took a wrong turning. The day was to pass in 'doubts, grumblings and rumours', as one Volunteer put it.

When Constance saw the front page, she raced to Liberty Hall 'heart-broken' and found James Connolly and Seán Mac Diarmada sitting with Tom Clarke at a table in the small bedroom Connolly used at the back of the building. She believed that 'Professor Eoin MacNeill and Mr B. Hobson had treacherously acted a coward's part, secretly through the Irish Republican Brotherhood (IRB), and publicly through the daily papers'. She got that wrong – Hobson had been placed under house arrest by the IRB Military Council, fearing his influence over MacNeill.

Markievicz, as well as Clarke and Connolly, knew that MacNeill's action had ended what little chance the rebels had of holding out long enough to influence public opinion and save the lives of the leaders. That MacNeill's move was intended to save lives meant nothing. 'There is only one sort of responsibility I am afraid of and that is preventing the men and women of Ireland fighting and dying for Ireland if they are so minded' was how Connolly put it.

The day that followed was the 'busiest I have ever lived through', wrote Constance later. 'Messengers came and went, and the Provisional Government of the Republic sat the whole day in Connolly's little room.' By one o'clock, it was settled. Although MacNeill had 'cut the ground from under their feet', they would carry on as planned, although a day later, knowing that the decision would mean certain death for the leaders. Despite the knowledge that, after years of meticulous preparation, much would be left to chance, the mood was one of euphoria: 'the cloud had passed' said Constance.

After Dublin Castle heard that Roger Casement was in custody, orders were prepared to arrest other rebel leaders. These had to be signed, but with senior officials away for the holiday weekend, this was not possible. When under-secretary Matthew Nathan and army officers read the notice in the newspapers cancelling 'manoeuvres', they relaxed their guard.

Since the Citizen Army had been mobilised for the Sunday, the planned drill went ahead to give the impression that all was normal. Shortly after 4pm, the men were on their usual march with Connolly and his second-in-command Michael Mallin at the head; Constance marched not far behind. From Liberty Hall they made their way to St Stephen's Green, then on to Dublin Castle, where they were observed by the guard on duty, before returning to Liberty Hall via the quays. In Beresford Place, Connolly made what would be his final public speech. Referring to the question of England brokering a peace deal with Germany, he said that, at such negotiations, Ireland should be represented. 'You are now under arms. You will not lay down your arms until your have struck a blow for Ireland!' he said in conclusion. The men cheered and shots were fired into the air; the watching police made no move.

During the day, the Proclamation of the Irish Republic was printed in Liberty Hall by a group including the trade unionist Rosie Hackett; she remembered the men resenting the presence of women in the room. After the 'Proclamation' rolled off the press, one story has Constance picking up a copy and reading it out to a small crowd that had assembled in Beresford Place. All the signatories to the Proclamation were men but, if this story is true, it was Constance, a woman, who was first to read the Proclamation in public. All but one of the seven signatories had agreed to its theme of equal rights for men and women, and Hanna Sheehy Skeffington had been chosen as a member of a civil provisional government should the Rising succeed.

To explain the large numbers congregating around Liberty Hall, the usual Sunday night concert went ahead. Nerves were on edge: 'The day dragged through somehow, the night passed with little rest for anyone, and next morning we were all at our posts at cockcrow, everybody in the highest spirits.'

Along with Winifred Carney, who was Connolly's secretary, Constance was spending the night at the William O'Brien household in Belvedere Place. After the family had gone to bed, they heard a shot. While unloading her automatic, an exhausted Constance had fired a shot through the door of the O'Brien's bedroom. Fortunately, no one was hurt. The next morning, she arose and put on the uniform that Nora Connolly had already seen – the tunic that had belonged to Seamus Mallin, which fitted her well although the sleeves were short, along with jodhpurs, boots and her favourite hat with its plume of feathers. She and Margaret Skinnider were the only women to wear military uniform that week.

At 10am on Easter Monday, the four city Volunteer battalions were to parade with full arms and equipment, each commandant announcing the plans for his men. Every man was armed with a rifle and a pike. From Larkfield in Kimmage came fifty-six men from England and Scotland, who travelled into town by tram.

Constance remembered seeing Tom Clarke in those last few moments.

> Happy proud and gay was Tom Clarke on that day. His life's work had borne fruit at last ... we met for a few minutes just before the time fixed to march out. It seems queer, looking back on it, how no-one spoke of death or fear or defeat. I remember saying goodbye to Tom Clarke just at the door of Dr Kathleen Lynn's little surgery ... We then went downstairs, and each man joined up with his little band.

Pearse, provisional president of the Irish Republic, was there with a group of Irish Volunteers from St Enda's; so too was Thomas MacDonagh. Connolly, as Commandant-General of all the insurgent forces in Dublin, told the troops that there was no longer a Citizen Army and a Volunteer force but an Irish Republican Army that included the female members of the Citizen Army ambulance corps. He made it clear that they were to fire their guns only as a last resort, for defensive purposes. No one counted the little band; it numbered about a thousand, far short of the 5,000 originally expected. When William O'Brien asked Connolly whether there was any chance of success, he replied 'None whatever'.

At 11.45am, bugler William Oman sounded the fall-in and Connolly and his men set off along Abbey Street towards Sackville Street and the GPO. It was a motley army; some were in full uniform, others in hats, leggings and militaristic tunics. Many wore only armbands. 'Each man had a different kind of kit. No two had it affixed in the same way and probably no-one could have put it on in the same way twice,' remembered John Gallogly. A group of men pulled two drays loaded with pistols, shot guns, rifles, explosives and home-made bombs assembled with tin cans and gelignite.

At the end of Abbey Street, Connolly gave the order: 'Right turn – the GPO. Charge!' In Kathleen Clarke's account, Tom Clarke, as president and first signatory of the Proclamation, was the man to lead the rebels into the GPO, followed by Mac Diarmada, Plunkett, Connolly and Pearse. Clarke and Mac Diarmada, one elderly, the other lame, had driven to Sackville Street. In the GPO, a few customers buying stamps were bustled out of the building. A Royal Fusiliers lieutenant who was sending a telegram was taken prisoner, along with the sentries guarding the telegram room. Those still at Liberty Hall could hear the distant sound of breaking glass as windows were smashed to clear the line of fire. Within minutes, both the tricolour and Constance's home-made flag were fluttering above the building. The rebels in the street below raised a cheer.

It was now Constance's turn.

> I stood on the steps and watched the little bodies of men and
> women march off, Pearse and Connolly to the GPO, Seán Connolly

to the City Hall, all marching proudly, confident that they were doing right, sure at last that they had made the subjection of Ireland impossible for generations to come. I went off then with the Doctor [Lynn] in her car. We carried a large store of First Aid necessities and drove off through quiet dusty streets and across the river, reaching the City Hall just at the very moment that Commandant Seán Connolly and his little troop of men and women swung around the corner and he raised his gun and shot the policeman who barred the way. A wild excitement ensued, people running from every side to see what was up. The Doctor got out, and I remember Mrs Barrett and others helping to carry in the Doctor's bundles.

Constable James O'Brien from Kilfergus, County Limerick – unarmed – had fallen victim to the first shot of the Rebellion; an ugly start. In the delirium that followed, the rebels did not appear to realise that the half-empty Castle was theirs for the taking; only six soldiers were on guard that day, backed up by a garrison of less than twenty-five in the Ship Street Barracks beside it. At the GPO, Patrick Pearse had stepped out of the building and read the Proclamation of the new Irish Republic, claiming 'the allegiance of every Irishman and Irishwoman', to a handful of bemused Dubliners.

After Constance had left Beresford Place, it was the turn of Captain Richard McCormick and his group, who marched up Eden Quay making for Harcourt Street Station. The St Stephen's Green group moved off soon after. The original plan for the south side of the city was to capture the Green and surrounding buildings and make it the base for an army of 5,000 rebels after the nearby barracks were captured. Surrounding the twenty acres of the Green were at least two hotels and numerous private clubs and houses, where soldiers and prisoners could be billeted. On the east side was St Vincent's Hospital, with the Meath and Adelaide hospitals also close by; the wounded would be well looked after. Inside was a lake that would guarantee a water supply.

The outpost at nearby Jacob's would control access to Dublin Castle from Portobello Barracks, as would the two small outposts at Davy's pub on Portobello Bridge and at Harcourt Street station. Bolands

Mills on Ringsend Road would control the roads from the ferry at Kingstown, about ten miles from the GPO; to stop trains arriving from Dublin's southern suburbs, the garrison quickly ripped up a section of the railway line.

The actress and Cumann na mBan member Máire Nic Shiublaigh, had cycled to her post at Jacob's biscuit factory. After she arrived, she looked out of a window on the Peter Street side of the building and saw an open two-seater car swaying from side to side. As it drew alongside Jacob's, a figure in Citizen Army uniform stood up in the front seat and waved a hat. With Kathleen Lynn remaining at City Hall, Constance was on her way to St Stephen's Green with the rest of the first aid supplies. 'Go at it boys!' she yelled. 'The Citizen Army are taking the Green! Dublin Castle is falling!' Dublin Castle never fell; the Green held out for only a day.

Dr Lynn's car was one of the few available to the insurgents and was manned by a Volunteer called Mark Cummins, who was described by Lynn as 'a most reckless driver'. His job was to transport Constance between the rebel posts, but the car ended up as part of a barricade on St Stephen's Green and it was months before Dr Lynn saw it again. For the rebels, the bicycle would prove a far more effective means of moving around the city.

When they arrived at the top of Grafton Street, the main body of rebels marched through the Dublin Fusiliers' Arch into the Green. Thomas O'Donoghue and his group wheeled left, marched to the Shelbourne Hotel corner and entered the Green through the gate there.

Constance arrived at St Stephen's Green between one o'clock and two o'clock, according to the pageboy at the University Club at her trial following the Rising. By the time she arrived, the Green was occupied by a hundred Irish Citizen Army soldiers. When the Irish Citizen Army troops arrived, they had seen Thomas MacDonagh's troops parading on the west side of the Green in front of the Royal College of Surgeons before marching off towards Cuffe Street to take over the Jacob's building. MacDonagh's second-in-command was Maud Gonne's ex-husband, John MacBride, who had come to Dublin to meet his brother and could not resist joining the fight. It would cost him his life.

Margaret Skinnider, sent off as an advance scout by Mallin, had arrived at the Green on her bicycle. There were no soldiers in sight; all she could see was a single unarmed policeman, who paid no attention to her. He was probably Constable Michael Lahiff who, at around noon, was shot, allegedly by Constance. After he fell, Constance had run triumphantly into the Green crying 'I got him' according to an account, typewritten a year after the event, by Geraldene [*sic*] Fitzgerald, a nurse at the St Patrick's Nursing Home on the south-west corner of St Stephen's Green. Yet when Lahiff was shot, within five minutes of the Green's occupation, Constance was still on her way from City Hall, as witnessed by Máire Nic Shiublaigh. At her court martial, no mention is made of her killing an unarmed policeman, or indeed of killing anyone. Later, Father Sherwin of the Catholic University church on St Stephen's Green wrote to Josslyn to assure him that 'it was not your sister who fired the shot. She has given me leave to state that this is a fact.'

Several months later, Constance told Eva that she had held a revolver at a policeman's chest but could not pull the trigger to shoot him because she realised that she knew him. She admitted that she shot another in the arm 'as he jumped'. Lahiff was sent to the Meath Hospital and died half an hour after he was admitted. The death certificate described the cause as 'a bullet through both lungs and left arm'. If she had shot him, Constance may not have been aware that he later died.

Was there anyone else who could have shot Constable Lahiff? The available facts are that he was at St Stephen's Green, that he was unarmed and that he was shot at around noon. When Margaret Skinnider arrived at the south side of the Green, she reported that she saw only a single policeman in the area that day. A few minutes later, when the Irish Citizen Army arrived, James O'Shea remarked in his witness statement that a policeman passed a comment about them playing at soldiers. He decided to get his revenge. 'We had orders not to fire until we heard firing from Harcourt Street, so when firing was on for a minute or two, I went to the gate to fire at the policeman, who had passed the remarks earlier. He was at Noblett's Corner at the time so I had a shot at him.' What is not recorded is whether O'Shea's shot hit or even killed the policeman.

Noblett's Corner was at the junction of Grafton Street and South King Street, facing St Stephen's Green; O'Shea's immediate orders were to dig trenches inside the Dawson Street entrance to the Green. While digging the trench, a man stumbled up, pretending to be drunk. O'Shea decided he was a spy and, by his own account, shot him dead at close quarters. Although Connolly had given orders to members of the Irish Citizen Army that no unarmed soldier or policeman was to be shot, the police were held in contempt by many Dubliners because of their behaviour during the 1913 lock-out. Certainly O'Shea had no qualms about killing a perceived enemy. Three unarmed Dublin policemen were killed in the opening hours of the Rising, which caused them to be withdrawn from the streets, to the serious detriment of public order.

After Commandant Mallin arrived at St Stephen's Green and seized the keys to the park, he had ordered his men to start digging deep trenches beside the hedges just inside the railings. Others were ordered to make barricades on the roads ringing the Green and commandeered a large laundry van, a side car, a dray and two private cars. These battle techniques had worked well in countries, such as India, where Mallin had served during his British army days. Whether they were suitable for the wide streets of a Georgian city like Dublin is open to argument. No effort was made to seize the buildings around the Green. With fewer men than he had hoped, Mallin had asked Constance to remain with his group, leaving her in charge of the trenches and barricades and then nominating her as his second-in-command. Guests staying in the Shelbourne Hotel, many of them in Dublin for the Fairyhouse races, gathered at the windows to observe the strange goings-on. They caught little more than the occasional glint of a rifle or a glimpse of a uniformed figure among the bushes.

They had something to talk about when Constance, with a rifle on her shoulder, began marching up and down in front of the hotel. A woman in uniform was an unusual sight, to say the least. When some British officers in the Shelbourne Hotel and the United Services Club began shooting at the Green, Constance quietened them by returning their fire. She wrote later: 'This work was very exciting when the fighting began. I continued round and round the Green, reporting back if anything was wanted, or tackling any sniper who was particularly objectionable.'

Later that day, the writer James Stephens, puzzled by groups of people standing near his office on Merrion Row, asked a 'kindly-looking lad' armed with a gun what was going on. He was told that the city had been 'taken' by republican rebels and that they held the GPO and had seized Dublin Castle. Many of the rebels were teenagers; the youngest was twelve-year-old Tommy Keenan, who fought alongside Constance at the Royal College of Surgeons, hiding his Fianna shirt under a jumper when he left the building with messages or to find food. Because he was so small, no one paid him any attention.

The curious crowd that had gathered at Merrion Row, which leads on to the Green, was initially unconcerned about the danger they put themselves in. All that changed when an elderly man, who had been warned several times not to remove his lorry from a barricade, was shot dead by a young rebel near the Shelbourne Hotel. At the sound of the gunfire, women began crying and shrieking and falling to their knees.

As soon as the small troop was established in the Green, Margaret Skinnider cycled down Leeson Street towards the Grand Canal to see if there was any sign of British soldiers leaving Beggar's Bush or Portobello Barracks. Everything remained quiet. She was then sent to the Harcourt Street train station, where she found that Captain McCormick and his men had managed to cut the telegraph and telephone wires, a priority for all the battalions at their posts. Because one telephone wire was missed, word of the Rising reached London sooner than expected.

Back at the Green, the men were busy digging themselves in, using shrubbery as protection. Two British officers were taken prisoner. Afterwards, they complimented the rebels on how well they had been treated. According to Skinnider, soldiers from Portobello Barracks were sent out twice on Monday to clear the Green. The first time they were stopped at Portobello bridge when they were fired on by three snipers from the roof of Davy's pub. They backed off, not realising that the pub was held by only eight men. Then, at dusk, Skinnider was on her way back from the GPO when she saw two people hurrying from the Green. They were William Partridge and Constance. At the same time, she saw British soldiers advancing up Harcourt Street.

> The countess stood motionless waiting for them to come near ... At length she raised her gun to her shoulder – it was an 'automatic' over a foot long, which she had converted into a short rifle by taking out the wooden holster and using it as a stock – and took aim. Neither she nor Partridge noticed me as I came up behind

them. I was quite close when they fired. The shots rang out at the same moment and I saw the two officers leading the column drop to the street. As the countess was taking aim again, the soldiers, without firing a shot, turned and ran in great confusion for their barracks. The whole company fled as fast as they could from two people, one of them a woman!

This episode may have been what the nurse Geraldene Fitzgerald witnessed.

The plans to establish outposts that would give the rebels in the Green time to dig themselves in before troops arrived from Portobello Barracks did not work out. When Sergeant Joe Doyle and his seven men realised that they were facing 650 men led by twenty-one officers of the 3rd Irish Rifles who were assembling at Portobello Barracks, they swiftly retreated from their post in Davy's pub.

Lack of manpower meant that moves to secure the Harcourt Street train station were also a failure. Captain McCormick had ordered Sergeant Frank Robbins and three men to barricade both ends of Hatch Street for a day and so cut off one means of access to the Green. To build the barricade, they commandeered a White Heather Laundry van and also raided a garage on Earlsfort Terrace for motor cars, despite the protests of the staff. At the station, the train to Wexford was delayed for four hours until Constance issued a permit for it to run. The rebels then moved back to the Green and ordered a man driving a dairy cart to back up against the gates facing Leeson Street. An attempt to take over a tram backfired when the driver went into reverse and escaped.

At the Green, many of the women initially assigned to first-aid stations and to the commissary were pressed into service. They patrolled the Green and found a few stragglers, including a clergyman and a young woman who became quite hysterical. Mary Hyland and Kathleen Cleary had taken over the summer house and had laid out sandwiches, ham, cheeses and cakes to feed the insurgents. To the casual onlooker, it was a bizarre sight – the men in uniform swinging their pickaxes and spades to make trenches and the women laying out food for a picnic. During the afternoon, members of the Volunteers arrived, looking to join the fight. Three Cumann na mBan women – Nora O'Daly, Bridget

Murtagh and May Moore – had arrived at the Green on their way to Jacob's factory. Not quite knowing what to do, they met Constance, who brought them to the summer house where Madeleine ffrench-Mullen was in charge of first aid. They decided to stay. Also arriving during the afternoon was Nellie Gifford and Liam Ó Briain, a 2nd Battalion man, who joined the St Stephen's Green force and spent the day digging a three-foot deep trench at the Leeson Street gate. It was soon pretty clear that taking the Green without securing at least one of the surrounding buildings had been a mistake.

Standing on the west side of St Stephen's Green was the Royal College of Surgeons in Ireland – a granite fortress of a building that was closed for the holiday weekend. A few hours after the Green was occupied, Mallin ordered Constance, Frank Robbins and ten others to search the college for rifles and ammunition belonging to the Officers' Training Corps. As Mallin unlocked a gate opposite the college, he noticed that the caretaker of the college was at the front door, attempting to get rid of Dr John Knott, an elderly fellow of the college who liked to spend his days in the library and, according to Robbins, 'was looking the worse for drink'. Mallin had told Constance and her group to veer left as if they were going to York Street so that the caretaker would not suspect their plan. As they passed it, Robbins sprinted for the main door, ordering the others to follow him. When Robbins reached the top step, a shot rang out, whizzing past his ear and hitting the top right-hand corner of the door, which the caretaker was attempting to slam shut. Robbins threw his full weight against the door and it gave a few inches. He jammed his foot in the gap and put the muzzle of a gun to the caretaker's throat.

When the caretaker professed no knowledge of the officers' corps or where they might find guns, Robbins was all for roughing him up until Constance took control. She ordered the caretaker, with wife and child, to be locked in their own bedroom. They protested mightily and banged on the door for some time, but finally went quiet. The rebels set about searching the building, with no success. When a supply of bombs arrived from Mallin, Constance and her group went to the roof of the building and awaited further orders. From the roof, they could see a woman on a bicycle waving to them. It was Margaret Skinnider, who brought them a tricolour that, despite a struggle with the rotting runners of the flagpole, was soon flying proudly over the college. On the street, the rebels were kept busy with a number of local women, mostly wives and relatives of Irishmen serving in the British army, who attacked them at every opportunity.

Constance found that she was too tired and excited to sleep that first night. She walked about looking for shelter and tried lying in one of the trenches. Because it was a cold, damp night, the ground was chilly, so she resumed walking until she noticed Dr Lynn's car, by then part of a barricade. She climbed in, found a rug and went to sleep in comparative comfort. Other members of the small force huddled under trees or stretched out on benches inside the Green, while the first aid and dispatch women slept on the floor of the summer house, a building that had no walls but did have a roof. When morning came, Constance could not forgive herself for having slept in comfort all night. She had intended to sleep only for an hour or so before giving up her place to someone else, but she woke only at 4am when a hail of machine-gun bullets hit the roof of the car.

On the second day, Hanna Sheehy Skeffington and members of the Irish Women's Franchise League arrived at the Royal College of Surgeons laden with food. Despite her husband's pacifism, Hanna was broadly supportive of the Rising. The couple had walked into Dublin's city centre where Hanna had stopped at the GPO to offer her assistance as a messenger. One of the first people she met was her priest uncle, Father Eugene Sheehy, an old-style Fenian and believer in physical force. After speaking to Connolly, Hanna was sent to St Stephen's Green. Constance remembered noticing some women approaching:

> Just then the leading figure approached and asked for Commandant Mallin. Some of us recognised the voice. It came from the lips of Hanna Sheehy Skeffington, who was struggling under the weight of a huge sack bulging out in queer shapes and completely concealing her. She was followed by more laden figures. They proved to be members of the IWFL ... and had collected a store of all manner of eatables from their friends ... to bring them to us though the bullet-swept streets. We had great fun unpacking the parcels and hearing who had contributed this ham or that tin of salmon or soup before we sat down and had a glorious meal.

Securing the overlooked spaces of St Stephen's Green was always going to be a problem. In all, there were 138 men and women in the Green, of whom about 103 men and fifteen women were members of the Irish Citizen Army. The remaining twenty or so were Volunteers. On Monday night, while the small rebel force huddled together to stay warm, British troops made their way up Kildare Street and into the Shelbourne Hotel by a side entrance, unheard and unobserved. Soon the front door to the hotel was barricaded with mattresses and soldiers were stationed at every window facing the Green, where the trees offered little in the way of protection.

At daybreak on Tuesday 25 April, it was not only Constance who was awoken by the sharp rattle of machine-gun fire from the roof of the hotel. Mallin and his troops, along with the women in the summer house, were forced to run for safety from the trench opposite the Shelbourne Hotel to the south-west corner of the Green, where the shrubs, trees and an embankment offered some protection. Mallin then sent Skinnider to the GPO with a dispatch; he realised at once that they would have to evacuate the Green. When Skinnider returned from the GPO, she was sent to bring in the sixteen men guarding the Leeson Street bridge before they were cut off, although the post could have proved its worth when British troops started marching into Dublin from the ferry in Kingstown. She cycled as fast as she could with bullets rattling the metal rim and the spokes of her wheels and puncturing a tyre.

All the rebels were, by then, retreating in twos and threes to the Royal College of Surgeons. In St Vincent's Hospital, Dr Louis A.D. Courtney later recalled hearing the faint sounds of 'A Soldier's Song' as it floated across the Green in the early morning. One young Citizen Army soldier was killed while retreating and, contrary to all humanitarian rules, the first aid women in their white frocks with big red crosses were fired on, with bullets tearing through one woman's skirt and knocking the heel off another's shoe. Five bodies were left in the Green, along with food, provisions and equipment. That more were not killed was a miracle. While Skinnider was reporting back to Mallin, a bullet whizzed through his hat: 'He took it off, looked at it without comment, and put it on again.' On the roof of the college, Michael Doherty lay slumped over the parapet, his blood staining the stonework. He was rescued by

Joseph Connolly, a brother of Seán Connolly. The two prisoners held in the Green were taken to the Royal College of Surgeons. One of them, W. Hopkins Ashmore, later reported that Constance was profuse in her apologies to the prisoners, explaining that their detention was for the cause of Ireland. She was not so calm when one officer they had released reported back to his superiors on everything he had seen, despite a promise that he would not do so.

By 7am, everyone was safely inside the Royal College of Surgeons. They rolled themselves up in rugs and slept. Later that day, with no police on the streets to stop anyone, looting broke out in the city, particularly in Sackville Street, where the Dublin poor climbed through the smashed windows of shops such as the branch of Noblett's confectionary shop, Saxone shoes and Lawrence's toy shop to scoop up armloads of sweets, toys and shoes. Excited children ran around playing 'rebels' and firing imaginary guns; an improvised game of golf took place in Sackville Street.

By now, 20,000 British soldiers had arrived in Dublin and martial law was proclaimed by Sir Matthew Nathan. Inside the college, the insurgents were well protected by the thick walls of the three-storey building. On the ground floor were lecture rooms and a museum; the classrooms and laboratories, as well as the library and boardroom were one storey up. On the third floor were the caretaker's quarters and a kitchen; Mallin and Constance used the caretaker's two rooms as offices. One end of a classroom on the second floor was curtained off and used as a first-aid room. Windows were barricaded with furniture and books. In all parts of the college, the smell of chemicals was all-pervasive and the presence of glass bottles containing unspecified parts of the human body were unnerving.

Nellie Gifford was put in charge of cooking, but could produce nothing in the way of hot food until she acquired a bag of oatmeal. Keeping the rebels fed was a problem at all the outposts, although those in Bolands had a plentiful supply of bread, flour and fruit cake and the Jacob's battalion gorged themselves on biscuits and cream crackers. At the GPO, bacon and eggs were available at the Pillar Café for anyone brave enough to make a break for it.

Constance was a whirlwind of activity, searching for anything that might be of use and offering advice and encouragement. She acted as a strict chaperone for the 150 men and twenty women who were living under the same roof, making regular inspections. There was intermittent firing on the college during the week and sniping from the rebels installed on the roof – except at midday, when a brief truce allowed the St Stephen's Green park keeper to feed the ducks.

On the north side of the Green, the United Services Club and other buildings were occupied by the British forces. Mallin organised groups to break through the walls from house to house on both the north and west sides of the Green. The original plan was to set fire to the buildings on the north side in an attempt to shift the British troops, but just before 10pm, when the fires were to be started, Constance crawled through the walls with an order from Mallin to stop.

Food was running out. Early in the week, Mary Hyland had left the park and, finding a milkman on his rounds, ordered him to hand over a can of milk. In similar fashion, Lily Kempson held up a bread cart with a revolver and Nellie Gifford acquired sacks of flour. When these provisions ran out, they began looting nearby houses and shops, finding bread, cheese and Oxo cubes. Mary McLoughlin made the hazardous journey to the GPO to explain to Connolly that the garrison was short of food and ammunition. He gave her £80 to bring to Michael Mallin, who refused it. They needed food and ammunition, not cash.

The garrison's only female casualty was Margaret Skinnider, who had spent Wednesday on the college roof. Seeing the damage at the Shelbourne Hotel that had been caused by the machine gun, she suggested cycling over to the hotel and lobbing a bomb attached to an eight-second fuse through one of its bow windows. The time lapse would allow her to escape before the bomb exploded; or so she argued. Mallin deflected her from this plan with an alternative job. On the roof of the University Church, on the Green's south side, was another machine-gun post and, to cut off the British soldiers in that post, Mallin wanted to burn out two buildings situated behind the Russell Hotel on the corner of Harcourt Street. He delegated Skinnider, William Partridge and three men to deal with one building. When they reached the building, Partridge smashed open its glass door with his rifle butt. The British opened fire, hitting Skinnider on her right side with three bullets. Partridge lifted her up and carried her to the street, where she saw Fred Ryan, aged only seventeen, lying in a pool of blood.

With help, she managed to walk to the corner and then Partridge and another man carried her back to the Royal College of Surgeons.

They laid her out on a large table, where she burst into tears not from the pain but because they had to cut away her fine uniform, supplied by Constance. When she refused to be evacuated to hospital, Madeleine ffrench-Mullen removed the bullets, with Constance standing by holding her hand. She was bandaged up and given a cot to sleep in. Later, Liam Ó Briain gave her a nightdress he had found in a nearby flat.

Soon after, Constance and William Partridge disappeared. When they returned, Constance quietly said: 'You are avenged my dear.' They had gone to where Fred Daly lay, and to attract the fire of the soldiers across the street, Partridge had stooped over the dead boy to lift him. There were only two soldiers and they both fired, giving Constance a chance to sight them. She fired twice and hit both. Or so she told Skinnider, who was soon in a delirious state, moaning and talking incoherently.

To keep fear at bay, many of the Catholic rebels turned to prayer. Constance was particularly impressed by the humility and gentle nature of William Partridge, who led the prayers of the rosary each night in the college. She asked to join in, and later dedicated her poem 'The Rosary College of Surgeons' to him.

That day, the gunboat *Helga* sailed up the Liffey and the boom of shelling was heard all over the city when it fired at Liberty Hall, which, unknown to the British, was by then empty except for the caretaker. Later, the sound of shelling became more frequent when heavy artillery was used against the GPO. At night, the sky glowed red with incendiary shells. From their post, members of the Royal College of Surgeons' garrison could hear the spatter of rifle fire at Mount Street Bridge, where a British contingent, marching into the city from Kingstown, came under fire from three outposts manned by Volunteers from Bolands Mills. After a day and night of fierce fighting, thirty British soldiers lay dead, with a further 157 wounded. Six Volunteers died.

On Thursday morning, to the rebels' delight, sixty-four rifles were found in the college. Word of other skirmishes came through. In north County Dublin, Volunteers made successful attacks on four Royal Irish Constabulary police barracks. In Ashbourne, County Meath, a bloody battle lasted for five hours. At the Magazine Fort in the Phoenix Park, a group of Fianna boys, pretending to play football, almost succeeded in blowing up the explosives held in the fort. When they failed to find the key to the high-explosives room, the disappointed boys set fire to the building. One soldier and a civilian died, with at least one Fianna boy wounded. Against all the odds, the Easter edition of *Workers' Republic* was published that day with a rousing poem called 'Our Faith' by Constance replacing the regular Irish Citizen Army column.

There was heavy fighting at the South Dublin Union, which, from its position off James' Street, controlled Kingsbridge Station, the terminus for trains from the Curragh military camp. From the Union, the rebels hoped to block southside approaches to the Four Courts. Cumann na mBan's Margaretta Keogh was shot dead when she rushed to help a wounded Volunteer – the only female rebel to die during Easter week. At Marrowbone Lane and at the Mendicity Institute on the south quays both sides suffered casualties. British fire was concentrated on the GPO, and Sackville Street, from the Liffey bridge to the GPO, was reduced to smoking rubble. At the Four Courts, Seán Heuston, one of Constance's Fianna boys, held out from Monday to Wednesday, with much of the fighting taking place in the maze of streets surrounding the building. Little fighting occurred outside the capital. MacNeill's summons on the Sunday to call off the Rising had made it impossible. While Galway and Wexford saw some action, most Volunteers stayed at home.

Inside the Royal College of Surgeons, messengers came and went, bringing food and news. By holding the building, they had already done more than Wolfe Tone, Constance told the garrison members. A rumour began that they were to flee the college and head for the Dublin and Wicklow mountains where they would continue the fight using guerilla tactics; this is what Mallin had expected would happen.

By Thursday, the British had thrown a cordon around the city isolating the main positions held by the insurgents. The GPO was surrounded and Connolly badly wounded. His wife, Lillie, staying at Constance's cottage, could see the smoke and fire enveloping the city below. She had found one of the few newspapers printed that week and read in it that her husband was dead; Nora arrived at the cottage and reassured her that Connolly, though badly wounded, was still alive.

On Saturday, the Royal College of Surgeons' garrison prepared for a possible charge by the British by attempting to demolish the staircase. The rebels celebrated the arrival of food, including a side of bacon, unaware of the official surrender that had been negotiated between Pearse and Brigadier-General Lowe earlier that day. On Sunday 30 April, Elizabeth Farrell, a Cumann na mBan member who had carried details of the GPO garrison's surrender a day earlier, was driven to Grafton Street by a British army officer. From there, she walked to the College of Surgeons carrying a white flag and a surrender order. Pale-faced and nervous, she went to the side door of the college at York Street and asked for Commandant Mallin. When she was told that he was sleeping and that the next in command was Markievicz, she gave the surrender order to Constance, who was indignant. 'Surrender? We'll never surrender!' she said, before waking Mallin with the news. A call went out for all the rebels in the Green area to report to the college immediately. Initially, there was a mixture of anger and excitement at the news. Constance argued that it would be better for them all to be killed at their posts. An exhausted Elizabeth Farrell became increasingly excited as the discussions continued, saying that the soldiers outside would blow her head off if she did not come out soon.

Once the rebels were all assembled, Mallin read the surrender order and he, Constance and Partridge each spoke of a job well done. An ambulance came to collect Skinnider and bring her to hospital. Her last words with Constance concerned a will, which Constance had slipped into the lining of Skinnider's coat with instructions to see that it got to her family. Mallin and Constance then led the group through the side door of the college, where they surrendered to Captain de Courcy Wheeler of the Kings' Royal Rifle Corps. After smartly saluting the captain, to whom she was related by marriage, Constance kissed her revolver before giving it up. 'I am ready' she said. Her flamboyant gesture may have been designed to distract attention from Mallin, a family man with four children and another on the way, who was well aware of his responsibilities as a provider, and had never planned on dying for Ireland. Constance refused de Courcy Wheeler's offer of transport to Dublin Castle and marched with Mallin and her comrades down Grafton Street and left into Dame Street.

Crowds lined the streets and one woman who waved encouragingly at Constance was arrested and spent over a week in jail. Constance's breeches came in for much comment. Most of the crowd waved hats and Union Jacks at the Staffordshire Regiment escorting the prisoners and yelled 'shoot the traitors' and 'mad dogs' at the rebels. Particularly virulent were the 'separation women'; because the GPO was destroyed, they would not get their allowance that month.

After a brief stop in the yard of Dublin Castle, the company set off for Richmond Barracks in Inchicore, where they were given tea and biscuits. Nora O'Daly carried the Red Cross flag throughout the march but, at the entrance to the Barracks, a soldier snatched it from her hands. Constance and Madeleine ffrench-Mullen were separated from the rest of the women. Once inside, Constance saw a number of women from the GPO and the Four Courts, among them Julia Grennan, who had spent Saturday night in a small park near the Rotunda. She ran over to shake hands and ask for news of others, but was bustled away.

Later in the evening, the company marched to nearby Kilmainham Gaol, a grim prison that had housed a long list of Irish rebels, among them Charles Stewart Parnell. With Constance was the medical student Brigid Lyons, who had been part of the Four Courts garrison. It was dark when they arrived, the gloom relieved only by the flickering candles carried by soldiers. Nora O'Daly saw Constance once again. She was on an upper landing smoking a cigarette when the other women were brought up. 'Put out that fag,' a guard shouted at her. When she refused, he knocked it out of her hand. She ignored him and smiled encouragingly at the other women before being put in a separate cell. O'Daly wondered at her self-control.

The rebellion was over. On the British side, including the military, the Royal Irish Constabulary and the Dublin Metropolitan Police, 120 were killed and 392 were wounded or missing. Of the rebels, an estimated 64 were killed, including nine at the GPO, six at St Stephen's Green and five at City Hall. A further 116 civilians died. The high casualty rate among civilians was blamed on their foolhardy curiosity.

Vindictiveness caused other fatalities, with fifteen civilians shot or bayonetted in their homes, allegedly by the British, during military operations in the North King Street area; some were killed even after the surrender of the GPO. The most shocking deaths occurred on

Wednesday 26 April, when Francis Sheehy Skeffington and two loyalist journalists were shot on the orders of Captain Bowen-Colthurst. Sheehy Skeffington was picked up on Tuesday evening when walking home after attempting to stop the looting in the city centre, while the two journalists were arrested when Bowen-Colthurst raided what he thought was a republican pub. The trio witnessed a rampage of violent behaviour from Bowen-Colthurst, including the shooting dead of an unarmed seventeen-year-old boy called J.J. Coade who was returning from church on the Rathmines road. On Wednesday morning, the captain suddenly ordered his men to execute the three men, possibly because of what they had witnessed.

Bowen-Colthurst's actions caused outrage, although army headquarters at Parkgate initially defended his behaviour. Thanks only to the determined actions of Dublin-born Major Francis Fletcher Vane, along with lobbying by Eva and Josslyn Gore-Both, Bowen-Colthurst was found guilty but insane by a military court on 16 May. Sheehy Skeffington, a pacifist, became the first martyr of the 1916 Rising.

CHAPTER TWELVE

Condemned to Live

Initially, the citizens of Dublin, far from sharing in the dreams and ideals of the rebels, turned against them for ruining their city and disrupting their lives. The trams had stopped running and, with both Bolands and Jacob's bakeries seized, bread was scarce. Shops were emptied of food and, for two days, no newspapers were published, making rumour the sole source of information. More crucially, the Irish, by and large, supported Britain in the world war then raging, with at least 150,000 signing up for the British army, as well as many more from the Irish community in Britain. Despite that, as the week wore on, the courage of the rebels and the fair-minded manner in which they treated civilians won them sympathy.

With a bitter and bloody war raging on the Continent, Army top brass were determined that the Irish rebels would pay for their cheek. When the chief secretary, Augustine Birrell, resigned in the immediate wake of the Rising, General Sir John Maxwell was sent to Ireland. Using the excuse of a possible connection with 'German intrigue and propaganda', Maxwell declared the Rebellion 'treason in time of war', punishable by death. As a military man, fresh from the failed invasion of Gallipoli, the political implications of his decision did not enter his head.

On 3 May, Patrick Pearse, Tom Clarke and Thomas MacDonagh were marched into a small courtyard at Kilmainham Gaol and shot by a firing squad. A day later, it was the turn of Edward Daly, Joseph Mary Plunkett, Michael O'Hanrahan and William Pearse, whose only crime was that he was the brother of Patrick. Because the male prisoners were held in the floor above the women, they could hear the priest when he came to the cells for a final call.

Alone in her damp Kilmainham cell, Constance lay awake, waiting for the morning when the door would clang open and she would be marched out to face the firing squad like her comrades. When a prison chaplain, certain that she would be shot, suggested that she wear a dress instead of her military uniform, Constance answered: 'I fought in these clothes and I'll die in them.'

In London, her sister Eva thought she was already dead; newspapers reported that her body had been found in St Stephen's Green. Her brother Josslyn noted in his diary for Sunday 30 April that the rebels had surrendered; a day later, he writes tersely 'No news'. On Tuesday, he drove to Annaghmore and asked the local MP, Charles O'Hara, to write to the Lord Lieutenant Lord Wimbourne on his sister's behalf.

On the morning of 4 May, Constance was taken from her cell and brought to a preliminary hearing presided over by Sir Alfred Bucknill, the deputy judge advocate-general – a 'fuzzy little officer with his teeth hanging out to dry'. Walter McKay, the seventeen-year-old page boy working at the University Club on St Stephen's Green, said that he had seen Constance drive up to the Green in a motor car, blowing her whistle and leaning out to give orders to a 'Sinn Féiner' after he had shut the gate of the Green.

> She then drove towards the Shelbourne Hotel – I saw her again about 1.15pm. She was then behind one of the monuments in the Green, she had a pistol in her hand which she pointed towards the club and fired. I ran upstairs and saw where the bullet struck. After firing she walked up towards the Shelbourne Hotel dressed in knickers and puttees.

The only other witness was Captain Henry de Courcy Wheeler who had accepted the surrender of the rebels at the Royal College of Surgeons. He described 'the accused' as armed with a pistol and ammunition in a Sam Browne belt. Bucknill later wrote that Constance broke down and cried. 'We dreamed of an Irish Republic and thought we had a fighting chance,' she had said. Her tears, Bucknill wrote, were 'a natural reaction to stress and disappointment'. It may be this hearing that William Wylie, the prosecutor for the trial, remembered when he described Constance as a broken woman pleading for her life who disgusted him. His account is at odds with all the available evidence.

A formal court martial was held later the same day, with more witnesses called. Although, like the other rebels, Constance had no legal representation, she was allowed to question witnesses. She made short work of the page boy, demonstrating that he could not have seen what he claimed from the University Club. When Constance asked him where he had been to school, and he revealed that he had been in an industrial school, he burst into tears when she then asked him if he had been sent there for thieving or some other crime.

Dr Charles de Burgh Daly, the man aimed at by Constance when he stood by the window of the University Club, told his story. He described her as wearing 'a man's uniform, green with a brown belt, and feathers in her hat'. At about one o'clock, she 'leaned up against the Eglington monument and took a deliberate pot shot at me in one of the open windows of the University Club. I was ... in uniform and the distance was about 50-60 yards. She could not tell that I was a doctor but, I suspect, considered I was a combative officer as I had ribbons on'.

Daly added that he had no knowledge of her killing anyone and added that she mixed up 'kindness and killing in accordance with her convictions'. He hoped that one day she might use her talents for the real benefit 'of our country'. Constance herself was to say that she saw Daly 'retire in time' and that the bullet hit the top of the window. According to the official report of her court martial, released only in 2002, Constance later said: 'I went out to fight for Ireland's freedom and it doesn't matter what happens to me. I did what I thought was right and I stand by it.'

The next morning she waited in her cell, listening for a third time to the crack of British rifles in the yard below. It was the turn of Major John MacBride, the estranged husband of Maud Gonne, to face the firing squad, although Constance did not know this. That night, an English soldier, on guard outside her cell, waited until all was quiet and then unlocked the door and offered her a cigarette. He sat down to smoke with her and told her that Pearse, Clarke and MacDonagh had been shot the first day, Daly, Plunkett, O'Hanrahan and Willie Pearse on the second and MacBride that morning. She was sure she would be next. Marie Perolz had asked Constance after her trial whether she had heard any news. 'I have been sentenced to death,' she said, although as yet she had heard nothing official.

On 6 May, she was standing looking out of the small window of her cell when a young officer entered. Obviously uncomfortable, he read her the results of the court martial. Like most of the rebels, she had been found guilty of taking part in an armed rebellion and of waging war against His Majesty the King and attempting to cause disaffection among the civilian population. The sentence was: 'Guilty. Death by being shot. The Court recommend mercy for the prisoner solely and only on account of her sex.' The sentence would be commuted to penal servitude for life. It was signed by General J.G. Maxwell, convening officer, and C.J. Blackader, Brigadier-General, president of the court.

The young officer had mumbled his way through the sentence. Constance asked him to read it again more clearly. When he finished, her response was simple: 'I wish you had the decency to shoot me.' She had been condemned to live; spared to contemplate the implications of the failed Rebellion without her comrades-in-arms. Constance was probably unaware that her commandant during the Rising, Michael Mallin, had made an extraordinary statement at his court martial, claiming that Constance had ordered him to take command of the men at St Stephen's Green. Many did think – including her old friend Lady Fingall – that Constance was in charge and Mallin probably believed that the British would never execute a woman. The pair may have concocted the scheme together; when Mallin's fifth child was born, she was named Mary Constance.

A frequent visitor to Kilmainham was the Capuchin friar, Father Albert Bibby, who smuggled out lines of poetry and other writings scribbled by Constance on scraps of brown paper. These he transcribed into a notebook before sending the originals to Eva in London. In a letter to Gertrude Bannister, a cousin of Casement's, Constance described lying awake at daybreak clinging to a crucifix given to her by Father Albert while 'the English murdered our leaders'.

Constance probably owed her life to Edith Cavell. A year earlier, the Germans had executed the British nurse, provoking outrage, and the British did not want to make the same mistake. Eva, anxiously waiting for news in London, was convinced that the personal intervention of the prime minister, Harold Asquith, saved Constance's life. After she was sentenced, Constance was moved to Mountjoy and, from her cell as Prisoner Number B374, she could hear the newsboys calling on the street outside. On 8 May, Mallin, Ceannt, Colbert and Heuston were executed; Colbert and Heuston were among the original Fianna boys from the first *sluagh* at Camden Street. That same day, Laurence Ginnell was forcibly ejected from the House of Commons after accusing Asquith of murder. John Dillon of the Irish Parliamentary Party made a powerful speech, appealing to the prime minister to stop the executions: 'it is not murderers who are being executed; it is insurgents who have fought a clean fight however misguided'.

A day later, Thomas Kent was executed in Cork and then came the news Constance had most dreaded: on 12 May, James Connolly and Seán Mac Diarmada were shot. Connolly, probably dying from gangrene in the leg that had been shattered during the fighting, was propped up in a kitchen chair when he faced the firing squad. Constance wrote a poem in honour of her great friend and pledged on his 'murdered body' that she would dedicate the rest of her life to the causes they had espoused.

> You died for your country and left me here
> To weep – No! My eyes are dry
> For the woman you found so sweet and dear
> Has a sterner destiny –
> She will fight as she fought when you were here
> For freedom I'll live and die.

The three-verse poem was given by Constance to a wardress as a souvenir before she was moved to an English prison.

With the executions, General Maxwell had seriously miscalculated, as George Bernard Shaw pointed out in a letter to the *Daily News* published on 10 May. The Irish rebel leaders were prisoners of war, entitled to mercy. 'It is absolutely impossible to slaughter a man in this position without making him a martyr and a hero. The shot Irishmen will now take their places beside Emmet and the Manchester Martyrs in Ireland and nothing in heaven or earth can prevent it.'

While the Rebellion had initially failed to ignite the patriotism of the Irish, the drip-feed of information about the executions changed that. The heartlessness of the executioners, often taking two volleys, and the callous treatment of James Connolly inspired appalled revulsion, not only in Ireland but across the United Kingdom. On the night after Pearse's trial, General Blackader, one of the three military judges presiding over the courts martial, dined with the Countess of Fingall. In her memoirs she reports the General saying of Patrick Pearse: 'I have had to condemn to death one of the finest characters I have ever come across. There must be something very wrong in the state of things that makes a man like that a rebel. I don't wonder that his pupils adored him.'

In the shop windows of Dublin, postcards of the executed rebels were displayed prominently. With nationalist organisations forced underground, religion provided a focus for discontent. The first manifestation of the deep public feeling came at the month's mind for the dead leaders – a mass celebrated a month after a death. The first of these, in Rathfarnham, remembered Patrick and Willie Pearse. Others followed at Merchant's Quay, John's Lane and elsewhere, with those attending flaunting their rebel badges. All Souls' Day on 1 November provided another opportunity for public commemoration.

Ignoring the rising political temperature, the British military continued to make wholesale arrests. A further 137 were sentenced to penal servitude and twenty-three to prison with hard labour. By 1 July 1916, 3,149 men and seventy-seven women had passed through Richmond Barracks, with 1,862 detained without trial. Prison would become a university for spreading the doctrines of nationalism. As well as the ill-treatment of the prisoners and the incompetence of officers, the insolence of the military in the streets, looting by soldiers and foul language used to women was causing increased anger among the public. Pearse had achieved his objective: whatever about the Rising itself, the extreme response of the British gave Sinn Féin and the nationalist movement the boost it needed.

At Mountjoy, Constance was allowed visitors, and her sister Eva and Esther Roper travelled from London, sailing into Kingstown on 12 May. On a glorious spring morning, the two women got an inkling of what was to come when they witnessed hundreds of khaki-clad soldiers crowding around the gangplank of their ship. She and Esther took a taxi through shattered streets with a 'muddled, desperate look' and, after a brief visit to Eva's cousin, the writer Susan Mitchell, who had obtained permission for the visit, they travelled on to Mountjoy. Only then did

Eva notice the newspaper placards with the headline 'Execution of James Connolly' written on them in large letters.

Inside the jail, Constance, calm and smiling, appeared behind 'a sort of a cage' set into the wall of a bleak whitewashed room. 'Nobody who has not gone through the ordinary prison visit can realise how unsatisfactory it is, nor what a strain it is, to fling one's conversation across a passage with a wardress in it, to a head appearing at a window opposite,' wrote Eva later. Her only thought was whether Constance had heard that Connolly – and Seán Mac Diarmada – had been executed that very day. It proved an unnecessary anxiety: 'she knew everything'.

With little time available, Constance rapidly told her sister about the shock and grief of the surrender, as well as the details of her court martial. She was worried about Agnes Mallin, in hiding and penniless, and gave Eva directions so that she could find her. She expressed her bewilderment at the execution of Francis Sheehy Skeffington, who did not even believe in fighting. She had little to say about her own treatment. She was a 'convict' and a 'lifer' and that was that. It had been splendidly worthwhile – for one glorious week, Ireland had been free. After twenty minutes, the 'oddly becapped head disappeared from the window'. Eva would not see her sister for another four months.

At Kilmainham, when she was sure she would be executed, Constance asked Father Ryan to be with her at the end. After she was reprieved and transferred to Mountjoy, she registered as Catholic, though she was Church of Ireland by birth. On that final night in the college, Constance had knelt with the others in prayer. Suddenly she had 'a vision of the Unseen'. It brought her peace. In Mountjoy, Father McMahon, the Catholic chaplain, found her attitude to her new faith puzzling and he discussed it with Hanna Sheehy Skeffington:

> She wants to be received into the Church, but she won't attend to me when I try to explain transubstantiation and other doctrines. She just says, 'Please don't trouble to explain. I tell you I believe all the church teaches. Now, father, please tell me about the boys.'

Constance had shocked the good father by referring to Lucifer as 'a good rebel', but Sheehy Skeffington suspected that she was teasing; it was part 'of her habit of leg-pulling of authority'.

Sheehy Skeffington reflected that Constance belonged to the church of St Francis of Assisi rather than to that of St Paul. 'The ritual and the ceremonies, the music and the beauty of the Catholic Church, its art and cultural background attracted the mystic in her.' Over her bed was a picture of da Vinci's Christ.

Four days after her sister's visit, Constance wrote her first letter from prison. It was full of instructions. She missed her dog Poppet – who appeared to be with Lillie Connolly – and gave her sister explicit instructions for closing up Surrey House, mentioning mothballs and starch, a collection of wigs and how to get into a locked desk without a key. In there, Eva might find a bank book and papers for recovering income tax. She obviously hoped to use her things again: 'I don't want anything thrown away.' There were bills to be paid and St Mary's to be rented out. 'I think my name should be suppressed and it should be let in yours.' She had left a bag in Liberty Hall, where her bicycle was probably 'knocking round'.

She wanted her old housekeeper, Bessie Lynch, and servant, Bridie Goff, looked after and the rent paid on the 'little hall' in Camden Street. After Constance's sentence was commuted, her brother, Josslyn, was appointed administrator of her affairs, to her annoyance. Constance had wanted Eva to do the job, as was clear from this letter, and when Eva failed to tell Josslyn of their sister's instructions, relations became strained. Constance sent a rambling letter to her brother with wild suggestions about what he should do to raise money from her investments. She also wanted her false teeth returned.

In her letters to Eva, she was determined to keep cheerful. 'The life is colourless, beds are hard, food peculiar, but you might say that of many a free person's life ... So darling don't worry your sweet old head.' Mountjoy was heaven compared to her later experiences of prison life. She described it in a letter from England:

> There was so much life in Mountjoy. There were seagulls and pigeons – which I had quite tamed. There were 'Stop Press' cries, little boys splashing in the canal and singing Irish songs shrill and discordant, but with such vigour. There was a black spaniel too with long silky ears, and a most attractive convict baby with a squint – and soft Irish voices everywhere. There were the trains

'Broadstone and North Wall trams' and even an old melodion and a man trying to play an Irish tune on a bugle over the wall!

By the time Eva and her friends visited Surrey House, it had been thoroughly ransacked, first by the military authorities and then by looters in search of souvenirs. The furniture was smashed, and papers, ornaments, books and pictures were strewn about, many of them trampled and destroyed. A box of lantern slides had been overturned and every single slide had been crushed. A beautiful leather dressing case had been slashed by a bayonet. The garden had been dug up in search of arms. Among the items confiscated were the letters from Canon Hannay about the underwear Constance should wear in *Eleanor's Enterprise*. Margaret Skinnider claimed that the soldiers 'had the effrontery' to sell the books, fine furniture and paintings they had looted on the street nearby. Severals paintings, including Casimir's *Bread*, were left behind.

When Eva left the house, she was mistaken for Constance by bystanders, but although this made Dublin a dangerous place for her, she and Esther Roper trawled the shattered streets the next day in an attempt to find Agnes Mallin. In Inchicore they finally met Father Ryan, who knew the whereabouts of Mrs Mallin's family; they eventually found her and gave her some money.

Rumours had begun circulating that Constance had shot dead an unarmed policeman on the first day of the Rebellion. Neither Eva nor Josslyn knew whether this was true. Nor did they know what had happened at the court martial. Eva wrote to her brother: 'Can you find out exactly what happened at the court martial? I only heard half from Con and we ought to know this to contradict the vile stories some people are making.' Josslyn began an energetic campaign of writing letters, firstly to the British army in Ireland, then to the Chief Secretary and finally to the War Office. They replied telling him he could obtain a copy of the court martial if he made a formal application, providing Constance did not object.

There were two more letters to Eva from Mountjoy, one in tiny writing on toilet paper smuggled out by a sympathetic apprentice warder from Wexford. She told Eva that 'alas!' she was being exiled to Aylesbury. On 3 August, Roger Casement was hanged in Pentonville Prison, London, despite a vigorous campaign by supporters, among them Eva and Alice

Stopford Green, to have him released. Eva had attended his trial on at least one occasion and helped organise a petition for presentation to King George V at Buckingham Palace. It was to no avail.

Constance repeated that she did not mind being in jail and that her only desire was 'to be of some use to those outside in the long tedious struggle with England'. She explained that she was not going on hunger strike 'as I am advised by comrades not to do so'. She asked Eva to try and get news to Casimir, stating that 'It would have to be very diplomatically done to evade the censor.' The second letter was scribbled on the back of an envelope and mentions her daughter: 'I am glad that M was amused and not shocked!'

On 7 August, Constance arrived at Aylesbury, a forbidding Victorian prison in Buckinghamshire, first opened in 1847 as a county jail and converted to a women's prison in 1890. The entrance was through double doors; the first door was always banged shut and locked before the second was opened. Inside was a mixed bag of petty thieves, prostitutes, swindlers and murderers. Political prisoners were rare. She had enjoyed the ferry journey across the Irish Sea, with a 'sunny porthole and a fresh breeze', reporting that her escort had never been to sea before and suffered from seasickness. When they arrived, she saw a big airship like a Zeppelin: 'I long so to fly!'

Constance was put in solitary confinement and she quickly got used to the routine. The day began at 6.30am when prisoners washed and dressed and then ate a breakfast of six ounces of bread and one pint of tea, usually cold, in their cells. Work followed, hard or soft or none at all, depending on the sentence. In Constance's case, it was hard labour and she got two ounces of cheese and a small piece of bread at ten o'clock to keep her going. Lunch at noon consisted of two ounces of meat, two ounces of cabbage, one potato, thick flour gravy and six ounces of bread. On Thursday this was changed to suet pudding with black treacle. On Fridays there was fish instead of meat. Supper at 4.40pm was a pint of cocoa or tea and six ounces of bread. At 5.30pm, the prisoners were locked up for the night. During her sentence, Constance's weight dropped from a healthy eleven stone to a gaunt seven and a half stone.

Although her fellow prisoners were 'the gutter rats of England', Constance described 'a certain community of hatred that gave one mutual interests and the mutual sport of combining to pinch onions, dripping or rags!' The prisoners were perpetually hungry and always on the look-out for an extra turnip or onion. It kept them going, she said. She also commented: 'All prison does for people is to teach them to use bad language and to steal.'

Despite the cheerful tone she maintained in her letters to Eva, Constance hated being constantly observed though a painted 'eye' in the door of her cell and, in her first week at Aylesbury, she spent her nights awake and pacing. After some time, she was sent to the sewing room – the warmest room in the prison – where she made prisoners' nightgowns and articles of underwear from coarse unbleached calico. Because Constance had been entered in the record as Catholic, she was allowed to arrange the flowers for the chapel. The chaplain, Father Scott, won her affection for his goodness to even the most hopeless of prisoners. Prisoners were allowed one book a week and, after a few weeks, they were permitted to write one letter a month.

Staskou wrote to Josslyn in August. Like most of the family, he regarded the Easter Rising as a 'sad stupid business' and added that it was a blessing that his stepmother 'cannot get into more trouble'. Since the censors prevented Constance and Casimir from writing directly to each other, Casimir wrote to Josslyn in September from Kiev, treading very carefully around the subject of his wife and asking for news of the entire family. Constance was concerned about Casimir and Staskou, believing that very few of her letters to them ever got through and exasperated at having to deal with her husband's many creditors. She suggested to Josslyn that now he had found an address for Casimir, he should send all his bills on to him; Josslyn had been covering his brother-in-law's debts. In another letter, she asked Josslyn to send on a photograph of her daughter Maeve, whom she thought was too young to visit her mother in jail.

Constance started sewing, stealing a needle from the workshop and pulling coloured threads from rags for use as embroidery cotton. From these meagre offerings, she fashioned things of beauty, rising early to sew and then hiding away her precious pieces of cotton. Among the small items she made was a pincushion embroidered with the words 'Easter Week 1916' along with her initials worked with her own hair. It became the prized possession of a prison nurse originally from Galway. After an embroidered picture of the Madonna and child was found in her library book, her cell was searched and the needle and rags were confiscated.

Whatever about sewing for herself, sitting still for hours in the sewing room did not suit Constance's restless spirit and she asked to be moved. Her next job was cleaning the prison kitchen, where she became an expert at scrubbing floors – an art she would later demonstrate to Kathleen Clarke, though initially she proved so bad at this routine task that she was ordered to start again. This she did without grumbling; prisoners who complained risked being certified as insane and sent to Broadmoor Criminal Lunatic Asylum. She was determined to be a model prisoner and, apart from her undercover sewing, on only one other occasion did she rebel. When the Germans were making a successful push, the prisoners were ordered to go to the chapel and pray for the success of the British troops. Constance, along with a German spy and an Irish-born swindler called Mary Sharpe, refused to do so. Sharpe, originally from County Longford, and better known as the notorious 'Chicago May', would later write her memoirs. She remembered Constance as the 'grandest' woman she had ever met and admired her for her courage. 'No kind of hardship ever fazed her,' she said.

When the women refused to pray, they were punished, wrote Sharpe:

> For spite, they made the three of us women carry enough gruel around the prison to feed the entire 200 convicts. We had to carry immense, heavy cans up winding stairs. While we were doing this, the Countess recited long passages in Italian from Dante's *Inferno*. The place looked like Hell, all right, with the lights dimmed and musty-smelling bags tacked across the windows, as a precaution against bombing.

Constance was to criticise the prison service strenuously, arguing that it only bred criminals and should be abolished. She painted a graphic picture of the dirt and filth endured by all prisoners. Dinner was served in rusty old cans, with no facility for washing them. Along with another convict, she did her best by using a bowl on a kitchen table and towels. Often the water was cold and there was no washing powder or soda.

I could give you endless examples of English cleanliness. It may be summed up as follows: Brasses, floors, doorknobs, all that jumps to the eye immaculate, but dirt and carelessness behind the scenes. I have seen vermin found in the baths.

Because she was a 'Star Class' prisoner, she could associate only with others in this class. Of the twenty-six women in Aylesbury at the time, twelve were serving sentences for wilful murder, three for manslaughter and one for woundings. All worked in the kitchen. In an article about her time at Aylesbury, which was published later, Constance criticised the then governess – Dr S.F. Fox – as possessing neither heart nor imagination. She described the filth of the conditions, the constant fear of picking up 'loathsome diseases' and the disturbed mental state of many prisoners. One section of the prison contained 150 prisoners, and their food tins were often returned to the kitchen in a state too disgusting to describe. One of the 'girls' in the 'Borstal section' tried killing herself by cutting her throat while another set fire to her cell and nearly died of the burns. Several tried to hang themselves with the rope used for making mailbags; others swallowed buttons and huge needles. 'Poor girls! It seemed so wicked and futile to drive them to this.'

While Constance kept herself scrupulously clean, she was not particularly tidy. Because she had lost so much weight, her skirt had to be hitched up, with the two sides rarely even. Her blouse hung out and there were glimpses of a grey petticoat. Prison cells did not contain a mirror. Talk was forbidden and the lack of companionship proved the greatest of hardships for Constance. 'Even the miserable little grain of comfort you can get from a few minutes' talk with another prisoner can only be procured by endless trickery and deceit.'

The Irish male prisoners of the Rebellion had won the right to associate with other prisoners for an hour each day, but this privilege was not extended to Constance and the five other Irish women deported to England. Marie Perolz and Brigid Foley spent time in Aylesbury but had left before Nell Ryan, Winifred Carney and Helena Molony arrived. As internees, they were held in a different wing of the prison to Constance. Twice a day they would stand on a high step and wave across a wall as she passed on the way to the small wash-house. They also saw her in church on Sundays and occasionally smuggled her a note of greeting.

In August 1916, the committee and members of Cumann na mBan elected Constance president at their annual convention. This was more than a gesture; with so many men in jail, it was left to women to argue the case for Ireland and its prisoners internationally. A number of women travelled to the USA, among them Min Ryan, Nellie Gifford, Nora Connolly and Hanna Sheehy Skeffington, who brought with her a letter for President Woodrow Wilson. This was signed by, among others, Margaret Pearse, Jennie Wyse Power, Louise Gavan Duffy and Mary Colum, as well as Constance in her capacity as president of Cumann na mBan. It put forward Ireland's claim for self-determination and appealed to Wilson to include Ireland among the small nations for which the United States was fighting.

During the autumn of 1916, the other Irish women at Aylesbury asked for a move to the same wing as Constance. They were prepared to give up all their privileges, including visits, food and letters, to do so and undertook not to communicate further with the outside world. Their request was 'disallowed'.

Constance remained resilient; she was determined not to let prison break her and she kept her letters to Eva upbeat. Her first letter from Aylesbury, dated 8 August 1916, was closely written on two sheets of an official form. There were strict rules when it came to correspondence. Prisoners could write only to a 'respectable friend', watching their language and sticking to personal matters, with no mention of politics and no complaints allowed. The letters were censored.

She wrote that she had recently seen herself in a mirror – thin and sunburned with her teeth turned black. Compared to Mountjoy, Aylesbury was 'queer and lonely'. She found it difficult to understand what anyone said to her. She was impressed by the garden, with its hollyhocks and a 'great crop of carrots'. This she passed every day when they exercised going 'round and round in a ring – like so many old hunters in the summer'.

She had dreamt of her sister a few nights before and remarked that she dreamed a great deal in prison. She asked Eva when her next book was coming out, 'the one with some of my pictures'. She regretted that they 'were very bad' and that she could do much better now. 'I was just getting some feeling into my black and white when I left Ireland. I made quills out of rooks' tail feathers that I found in the garden, they are much nicer than most pens – you can get such a nice soft line.' She tells Eva not to worry about her. 'I am quite patient and believe that everything will happen for the best.' The letter was signed 'Yrs Con-(vict G12)'.

The book she referred to arrived a few weeks later. It was *The Death of Fionavar*, a verse play describing the 'world-old struggle in the human mind between the forces of dominance and pity, of peace and war'. Over the winter of 1915–16, Constance had decorated it with borders of primroses, birds, lilies, butterflies, cocoons and winged horses – a favourite symbol for both sisters. The book was dedicated 'To the Memory of the Dead. The Many who died for Freedom and the One who died for Peace'.

In Eva's poem in honour of the rebels, she writes:

> Poets, utopians, bravest of the brave,
> Pearse and MacDonagh, Plunkett, Connolly,
> Dreamers turned fighters but to find a grave,
> Glad for the dream's austerity to die.
>
> And my own sister, through wild hours of pain,
> Whilst murderous bombs were blotting out the stars,
> Little I thought to see you smile again
> As I did yesterday, through prison bars.

Shortly after, Eva received a few unauthorised letters, undated and unsigned, written on toilet paper. Constance had found 'a real friend' who was taking 'awful risks' for her, bringing titbits of news and 'tuck'. She asked Eva to meet her and to find someone with 'not too grand an address' who could act as an intermediary. She had learned the art of discretion. 'You had probably better not try and see her again, as most likely you are both under watchful and protective eyes.'

In a second illicit letter, Constance tells Eva that she had been moved back to the workroom and given sewing to do. She comments, 'Don't count on me getting out for ever so long. Unless a real fuss is made (home and America).' She thought that the trade unions should have an inspector or visitor in the jails. She loved the book with its dedication: 'I love being in poetry and feel so important!'

A third note was little more than a list of questions relating to conditions within the prison:

> These questions should be asked me and all political prisoners at a visit: What do you weigh? What was your normal weight? What do you get to eat? Can you eat it? How much exercise do you get per day? How often do you get clean under-clothes? Are you constipated? Can you get medicine? What temperature is the room you work in? What is your task, i.e. how much must you do in a week?

In September, Constance had her first visit from Eva and Esther Roper. 'You don't know what a picture the two of you made, all nice soft dreamy colours. (Moral! Always visit criminals in your best clothes.)' The prison matron, E.W. Sharp, sat in on this visit and, in her report, she relayed a story that Constance told Eva of throwing a glove with a message inside it to friends when she was taken away from Mountjoy by taxi cab. Constance asked Eva to give Marie Perolz a certain dress that she was to wear like 'Elijah's Mantle'; an elliptical way of telling Perolz that she was to carry on her work. She asked Eva to find nineteen-year-old Lily Kempson, who had fought with her during the Rising and delivered messages to and from the GPO, describing her as her 'right hand' and one of her 'chief messengers'. She begged her to see her daughter Maeve and also asked Eva to contact the veteran Clan na Gael man John Devoy in the USA if help was needed.

A police report commenting on the matron's report confirmed that Constance had thrown her glove to three women standing on the corner of Berkeley Road immediately after she left Mountjoy in a taxi cab, but they had felt the gesture was merely 'bravado'. Lily Kempson (or Lizzie Anne Kempston as she was called in the report) had sailed for New York from Liverpool on 1 July en route to San Francisco. She would marry there and, when she died in 1996 at the age of ninety-nine, was the last remaining survivor of 1916.

Since there was so little news to report in her letters, Constance remembered old friends and family, wrote down pieces of verse and told of her dreams and anything beautiful she had noticed. Very little outside news filtered through to the prisoners, restricted as they were to occasional 45-minute visits. However, news of Constance and the other prisoners was trickling out. They may have been behind bars but their influence was spreading and the British authorities were well aware of this. It was one of the reasons they were not kept in London prisons, where their supporters could have gathered.

Although Asquith had been replaced by David Lloyd George as head of a coalition government in December 1916, Sir Edward Carson remained in the cabinet as First Lord of the Admiralty and wielded considerable influence. In the House of Commons, John Dillon had brought up the question of the Irish prisoners several times and, by 21 December, Henry Duke, the chief secretary for Ireland, had decided it was time to free them. The following day, 600 untried prisoners were released from the Frongoch camp in Wales; among them was a young Michael Collins. More were released from Reading on 23 December and Winifred Carney and Helena Molony, the two untried women still in Aylesbury, were sent home on Christmas Eve. Despite efforts by the British authorities to keep the homecomings low key, the released prisoners returned home to bonfires and celebrations.

Constance was not released, despite a letter of entreaty to the Home Secretary written by Eva after her sister had served six months in prison: 'The fact of there being no legal limit to the terms of her imprisonment owing to the absence of any form of trial is a cause of great anxiety to her relatives and friends'. Captain Jack White wrote to Henry Duke on Constance's behalf: 'Constance Markievicz is one of my greatest friends and in many ways one of the finest women that ever breathed'. He argued that she should be removed to Lewes prison where she could associate with the other Irish prisoners: 'it's horrible to think of her in the surroundings she now is'.

In a letter she wrote at Christmas, Constance mentions her sorrow at the death of an old friend, Ernest Kavanagh, a caricaturist whose drawings had appeared regularly in the nationalist press. He had been killed by British fire while working in his office at the front of Liberty Hall on the Tuesday of Easter week. Constance had only just heard of his death.

She was thrilled with the forty-six Christmas cards she had received and, by way of a return Christmas greeting, she drew a picture of a woman behind bars, looking outwards. There were birds on the window ledge and in the air and a verse on either side of the picture.

On one side:

> The wandering winds at Xmas time
> The twinkling of the stars
> Are messengers of hope and love
> Defying prison bars.

On the other:

> The birds that fly about my cage
> Are vagrant thoughts that fly,
> To greet you all at Xmas time –
> They wing the wintry sky.

Her sister's card to her did not arrive until a week after Christmas, having caused some alarm at the Home Office. Eva had drawn a similar card, which Constance thought better than her own. She pictured a woman looking through a barred window at an angelic figure with a harp. Four children surrounded the singer, while on the border women sat, kneeled or stood.

The verse read:

> Do not be lonely, dear, nor grieve,
> This Christmas Eve
> Is it so vain a thing
> That your heart's harper, Dark Roseen,
> Crowned with all her sixteen stars,
> A wandering singer, yet a queen,
> Crowned with all her seventeen stars,
> Outside your prison bars
> Stands carolling?

The authorities thought the verse was code for a prison escape, although no such plan was ever concocted. Constance's letter of 29 December 1916 shows her extraordinary acceptance of her fate:

> All my life in a funny sort of way seems to have led up to the last year, and it's all been such a hurry-scurry of a life. The great wave has crashed up against the rock and now all the bubbles and ripples and little me slip back into a quiet pool of the seas.

Constance was always delighted to see her sister, who usually brought Esther Roper with her. Roper marvelled at Constance's courage. She had even won over some of the prison staff. 'No prisoner was allowed to talk in the passages, but the first sound we heard while we waited was always her gay ringing laugh as she came along the corridor from the cells, talking to the wardress in charge of her.'

After a few weeks, Constance had been given a large notebook of cheap lined paper for sketching and jotting down verses. Each page was numbered so none could be torn out, and it was regularly censored. After a time, she got a second notebook of better-quality paper, which was unlined. On the first page of the original book was a sketch of a bookplate for her sister. That was followed by sixty pages of verse and many drawings, mainly images of Irish heroes or horses; she was good at horses. The second notebook contained mostly finished examples of the drawings from the first and illustrated poetry – her own, and her sister's. Two pictures show Joan of Arc kneeling with a sword in her left hand, rosary beads in her right and angels hovering.

Like Josslyn, Constance was a keen gardener and, even on her busiest days in Dublin, she had usually found time to tend to her garden. An attempt to grow a rose in her prison cell failed and when she told her sister, Eva wrote a verse:

> There is nothing good, there is nothing fair
> Grows in the darkness thick and blind
> Pull down your high walls everywhere
> Let in the sun, let in the wind.

On one of the last pages of the second book was another poem by Eva called 'To C.A.', which refers to St Francis. This Constance had illustrated with a striking picture of St Francis surrounded by birds and animals.

In Ireland, the provincial press, indifferent to the Rising when it happened, was now supportive. The *Sligo Champion*, which had pointedly ignored Constance's activities since 1911, commented sympathetically on her plight, and Sligo was one of many towns appealing for rebel prisoners to be better treated. At the behest of her family, the barrister J.F. Cunningham wrote a number of letters to Henry Duke asking for her release on health grounds. Since all 'the nationalists' had been released, he was 'begging this concession' on behalf of a family of unionists. He argued that, by holding the Irish internees, the British government was giving the Kaiser 'a trump card'. England was being 'placarded before Europe as inflicting a miserable fate on the people of Ireland'. When a peace conference assembled, the case of Ireland – a country England 'had no real quarrel with' – was sure to come up. In a later letter dated 26 January, he said, 'The Gore-Booths are no more rebels than I am, or than you are, or than Mrs Pankhurst, or Annie Kearney'. Cunningham was prepared to offer all his wealth 'and his head to boot' to guarantee her future good behaviour. Constance would have been horrified at the tone of his letters.

In January, Ernley Blackwell, the Undersecretary of State at the Home Office, writing from the Home Office in Whitehall, argued that it was impossible to organise a 'woman's side' at Lewes prison, since she would be the sole woman so accommodated. 'She has all the other privileges of the male prisoners and the length of her visits has been extended to three quarters of an hour'. He denied that she was living in the 'atmosphere and conversation of a brothel', as Eva had argued.

On 26 January 1917, Constance was visited by Esther Roper and Lady Clare Annesley, a feminist and pacifist from Castlewellan in County Down. She was now allowed daily visits. According to the principal matron's report, she told them that she had been accused of being in command of the army that attacked Dublin Castle, which was totally untrue. An unexpected visitor was Sir John Leslie, an admirer from years earlier, who brought her drawing materials. Other visitors included Alfie Byrne, later the Lord Mayor of Dublin, who interrupted her while scrubbing in the kitchen, and the Dowager Duchess of St Albans, who worried that she was not saying her prayers.

Alfie Byrne and Captain White, along with Eva and Esther Roper, continued to hound the authorities with petitions and questions in parliament about her status. Constance, because she was jailed at Aylesbury, was the only political prisoner in a British jail not allowed the privilege of association with comrades. With her health suffering, Eva finally gained for her the concession of a glass of milk a day. She was always hungry.

On 17 February 1917, Louie Bennett, on behalf of the Irishwomen's International League, sent a petition to the Home Secretary asking him to grant Constance the ordinary privileges of a political prisoner. On 25 February 1917, C.P. Scott of the *Manchester Guardian* raised Constance's case with David Lloyd George. He was unimpressed: 'a little solitary confinement will do her no harm'.

In a by-election held in Ireland that month, Count Plunkett, father of executed rebel Joseph, who was strongly supported by Sinn Féin and the Irish Volunteers, was elected MP for Roscommon. It was a first defeat for the Irish Parliamentary Party in the area for forty years and a bitter blow for John Redmond. In March, Eva received a letter from Father Albert Bibby of the Capuchin order who, as chaplain to the IRB Supreme Council, had ministered to the 1916 leaders before their executions at Kilmainham. He told Eva of a meeting called by Dublin's lord mayor to discuss the release of 'all our dear friends'. In April, the direction of the world war changed when the USA came in. The British were well aware of the anti-English beliefs of some twenty million Irish-Americans, many of them families starved out of their country during the Famine. Rumours that Markievicz was being ill-treated in prison were spreading in Irish-American circles.

A few weeks after the Americans entered the war, Count Plunkett called a convention in Dublin to formulate a programme for Irish independence. Among those on the organising committee were Arthur Griffith and Helena Molony. Delegates from seventy groups agreed to form a National Council to put forward Ireland's position at the peace conference they hoped would take place soon.

Eva continued her campaign to have her sister's prison sentence reduced, enlisting the help of friends, organisations and the press in both Ireland and England. They sent letters to town councils begging for support and suggested forwarding resolutions to the Home Office.

Questions were asked in the House of Commons and, in May, Cumann na mBan sent a series of letters to countries drawing attention to the treatment of the 122 Irish prisoners of war still jailed in English convict prisons. Constance's friend Æ wrote a tribute to the rebels, which he circulated privately:

> You, brave on such a hope forlorn,
> Who smiled through crack of shot and shell,
> Though the world cry on you with scorn,
> Here's to you, Constance, in your cell.

On 9 May, the Irish Parliamentary Party suffered another blow when Joseph McGuinness, then a prisoner in Lewes, won the South Longford by-election, beating the IPP candidate by thirty-seven votes. A month later, on 10 June, a large protest meeting on behalf of Irish political prisoners was held at Beresford Place and was addressed by Count Plunkett and Cathal Brugha. Lloyd George, anxious to reassure his new American allies that the British were attempting to solve the 'Irish problem', called for a convention in July to discuss Home Rule. Although Sinn Féin, supported by labour organisations, decided to ignore the convention, it did have one positive side effect. In order to promote an atmosphere of conciliation, Andrew Bonar Law, the leader of the House of Commons, announced on 15 June that all rebels held since the 1916 Easter Rising would be released.

A day later, the men were freed. At the gate of Pentonville, Éamon de Valera was handed a telegram telling him that he would be the Sinn Féin candidate for the West Clare by-election caused by the death of John Redmond's brother, Willie, in the war.

Constance's last letter from Aylesbury was dated 6 June. She wrote about a book on St Francis sent to her by Father Albert, of the decoration for a poem by Eva, about horoscopes and about spiritual communication with her sister at a certain time each day. She remembered how she had conducted meetings with 'the fun of bursting thro' all the red tape' and confessed that she was beginning to believe in anarchy.

On Sunday 17 June, Eva got a message from the Home Office; she could go to Aylesbury the next day and collect her sister. In a drawing expressing her joy, Constance showed an open cage, with the bird ready to fly with wings outstretched. The next morning, Eva and Esther Roper went to the prison, 'armed with all the gay clothes we could beg or borrow'. Soon Constance had cast off her prison clothing and, resplendent in a blue dress, she left Aylesbury prison for ever.

By the time the little group reached Eva and Esther's flat at 33 Fitzroy Square, crowds of journalists and well-wishers were waiting. Among them were Marie Perolz, Kathleen Lynn and Helena Molony who had taken the ferry to England as soon as they heard of Constance's pending release. In London, Constance enjoyed tea and strawberries on the terrace of the House of Commons with Eva, Esther, Alfie Byrne and Captain Jack White 'resplendent in top-hat and spats'. She graciously acknowledged the bows of her political enemies.

After three days of celebration and catching up, Constance was seen off at Euston Station by exultant supporters singing 'The Soldiers' Song' while she stood to attention. When the call came for three cheers, Constance kissed the bunch of roses she held in her arms and flung it into the crowd. At Holyhead, flag-waving supporters sang and cheered as she boarded the *MV Leinster.*

With Eva by her side, she arrived at Carlisle Pier in Kingstown late on the afternoon of 21 June. So many supporters were waiting that she struggled to get on the Dublin train. All along the ten-mile route, supporters lined the railway track. At Westland Row train station, her followers jostled one another to get a better view of their heroine, who was dressed in an old cardigan suit, topped by a magnificent new hat. Small boys climbed lamp posts. A great cheer and a display of republican flags greeted her when she took her place with Eva in Kathleen Lynn's car, driven by a uniformed Volunteer. She passed through the crowds, standing in the car, holding a large bouquet of flowers. A pipe band headed the procession, followed by representatives of all the organisations to which she had contributed.

From the station, the cavalcade moved along Great Brunswick Street and Tara Street before crossing Butt Bridge to Liberty Hall. The cheers continued when she walked up the steps and into the building. When she appeared at one of the windows, she had but a few words to say. 'I thank you more than I can say for the welcome back to Dublin that you have given me – I find Ireland rebel at last. We shall go on working until Ireland is free once again. I am going home now to rest in order that I may start work at once.' On her way to Dr Lynn's house in Rathmines, the car passed the GPO, the Royal College of Surgeons and Jacob's, all bearing the scars of the 1916 Rising. Outside Dr Lynn's house she spoke briefly, with a police observer carefully noting every word. 'I will now only say goodnight to you but we will meet again tomorrow or the next day and every day and we will all go on working until we die and until Ireland is a republic.'

When released, Constance had no home and no money. Ensuring that she had enough to live on was the union that she had so staunchly supported; she also received a generous £500 from the Irish National Aid Association and Volunteer Dependants' Association as well as money from Josslyn. Her daughter Maeve, now aged sixteen, was refusing to hear anything of her notorious mother. When sent to a small private school in New Milton, Hampshire, she was teased about her background.

There was only one thing left for Constance to do. On 24 June, she was formally received into the Catholic Church at Clonliffe College, taking the baptismal name of Anastasia. Among those present was Agnes Mallin. Joining the Catholic Church was Constance's way of identifying completely with the cause of Ireland. Casement was a convert to Catholicism for much the same reasons, as was Maud Gonne MacBride. Others thought differently: Dr Kathleen Lynn remained staunchly Church of Ireland all her life, while Rosamund Jacob, a Quaker, believed that the Catholic Church was one of the greatest influences for evil in the world.

Constance soon resumed her work with the labour movement. She was on the Irish Citizen Army executive and she raised money for the James Connolly Labour College. In 1917, with Helena Molony, Kathleen Lynn, Louie Bennett and Helen Chevenix, she was working to promote the rights of Irish women workers and was elected president of the Irish Women's Workers Union. Two strikes were settled by the union, although Constance was not involved. The nationalist cause remained her top priority.

CHAPTER THIRTEEN

Sinn Féin – We Ourselves

In the months following the Easter Rising, Irish nationalists grieved for their lost leaders. Replacing them would not be easy.

Friction between the various political groups opposing British rule was never far below the surface, with Arthur Griffith and Count Plunkett holding very different views. In early June 1917, a meeting was called to draw up a new unified republican policy. As well as Sinn Féin and the Irish Republican Brotherhood, the Liberty Clubs, the Irish Nation League, Plunkett's Mansion House Committee and the Released Prisoners' Organisation were represented. A leader emerged in the form of the American-born Éamon de Valera, the only commandant from the Easter Rising to have avoided the firing squad.

De Valera, tall and austere, was implacably republican and socially conservative. Born in the United States and brought up by his grandparents in Bruree, County Limerick, he took the Sinn Féin view that an independent Ireland must be protected from the corrupting influences of the British system and global industrialisation. The Roman Catholic faith of the Irish, he believed, not only distanced them from Britain but – as its name implied – formed a link between Ireland and a wider European community. While he respected the role of women in the political sphere, he believed that their roles as wives and mothers were paramount. During the Rising, when he commanded the brigade at Bolands Mills, he resolutely refused to have any women under his command.

De Valera made a dramatic start to his by-election campaign in County Clare by quoting the Easter Week Proclamation. A vote for de Valera, his election posters proclaimed, was 'a vote for Ireland a nation, a vote against conscription, a vote against partition, a vote for Ireland's language, and for Ireland's ideals and civilisation'. Against him, the Redmondites opted for Patrick Lynch, who was a crown prosecutor.

Constance, a big draw since her release from prison, was in Ennis on 7 July to support de Valera and address several meetings. There was no further need to call for a rebellion, she proclaimed, because Sinn Féin's policy was focused on gaining and using political power, backed by a strong Volunteer force, whose immediate duty was to keep order. At one meeting, with a number of soldiers' relatives in the audience, her rousing republicanism so provoked them that the leaders of the Labour League of Ennis were forced to rescue her. Although her clothes were torn and her hat bent, her spirits remained high.

De Valera won the seat for Sinn Féin, receiving 5,010 votes, compared to the 2,035 won by Lynch. After his victory, de Valera appeared on the steps of the courthouse in Ennis wearing his Volunteer uniform. Beside him were Constance, Count Plunkett and Arthur Griffith.

In the month following Constance's release from prison, the city of Kilkenny and her native Sligo both made her an honorary citizen. She was one of the few women ever so honoured and the occasions were a convenient excuse for Sinn Féin rallies. For the ceremony in Kilkenny on 19 July, Constance travelled by train with de Valera, Laurence Ginnell and William T. Cosgrave, the Sinn Féin candidate for the forthcoming by-election in the city.

The following week, Constance returned home to Sligo. When she wrote to fix a date, she acknowledged that she was overwhelmed by the honour. 'I long to see Sligo again. I used to think and dream of our hills and rivers and of the sun setting out over the sea and of all the people at home. My thoughts were often with you all this weary year I spent in an English jail.' She signed her name, followed by ICA (Irish Citizen Army) and q12, her Aylesbury convict number.

On the evening of Saturday 21 July, foghorns and cheers greeted the arrival of her train. A brass band played nationalist tunes, including 'Easter Week' and 'A Soldier's Song', and a torchlight procession brought her to the Sinn Féin hall on Teeling Street for a speech of welcome from the Mayor Councillor Dudley M. Hanley. Not everyone was pleased to see her; Sligo had its share of British sympathisers and anti-nationalists. A 'separation woman' charged at the group that was carrying the large Sinn Féin banner at the front of the procession and was hustled away. At Old Market Street, a group of women waved Union Jacks and indulged in 'very objectionable expressions'. One woman got a punch in the face when she tried to snatch the Sinn Féin banner. During the speeches, these women remained on the fringes of the group, booing and singing. A group of young men squared up to them, while the speakers on the platform appealed for calm. Sinn Féiners, for their part, felt 'insulted' by the large Union Jack fluttering over the Constitutional Club, the meeting place of the local Orange Order. Members of the Gore-Booth family kept their distance and the church at Drumcliff was the closest she got to Lissadell that weekend; she stayed in a local hotel.

In her speech of thanks, Constance told the crowd that they should not vote to send any man to Westminster 'to help England govern Ireland'. 'I cannot say many more words, as you will notice I am hoarse. That is what happens when you are kept in jail for a year and when you are allowed to speak only in a whisper.' Darrell Figgis, who had escorted her to Sligo, ended his speech by appealing to the crowd to disperse quietly.

After mass on Sunday morning, Constance spent the day addressing meetings in Drumcliff, Maugherow and Grange. The group had split up in order to attend as many meetings as possible in north Sligo; they made it to fourteen of them. That evening, a concert was organised in her honour. As soon as Constance arrived, the packed hall rose to its feet, applauding her for over five minutes. After the musical interlude, Constance rose and gave a rendition of the piece she had recited to her regiment on Easter Sunday. When she finished 'it seemed as if the audience would never stop cheering'. She returned to recite a humorous piece called 'A Recruiting Ballad for the British Army'.

On Monday morning, Constance went on a cruise of Lough Gill and, in the afternoon, she met Éamon de Valera, Count Plunkett, Laurence Ginnell, Joe McGuinness and other visitors who had arrived in Sligo on the midday train. That night, she was conferred with the freedom of the borough at Sligo Town Hall, built on the site of a Cromwellian fortress well known to earlier generations of the Gore-Booth family. A group of fifty Sinn Féin men positioned themselves to ensure that there was no more disturbance and 'some parties who were making themselves objectionable were quietly removed.' When the Mayor spoke, he was rushed by a soldier, who was ejected by Volunteers. He recovered to introduce Constance as 'the mother of a new Ireland'.

In reading the address of freedom, the town clerk said they were honouring not just Constance, but also 'a family of which she was the most distinguished member'. Constance, in reply, acknowledged that she had moved far from her origins: 'I became a rebel because the older I grew and the more I thought and the more I used my eyes and the more I went amongst the people of Ireland, and particularly Dublin, the more I realised that nothing could do Ireland only to get rid of England bag and baggage.'

While the Irish Parliamentary Party had made great promises, young men and women were 'drifting away in a great stream out of the country – our fairest, our youngest and cleverest ... Our mills were empty and I saw nothing but cattle and sheep on lands where we should have human beings.'

She was proud to have called James Connolly 'a friend' and to have worked beside him during the 1913 lock-out. She urged her audience to work for Ireland and expressed the hope that Irish independence would be recognised at the peace conference, 'not only on grounds of sympathy but on logical grounds'. In his speech, Éamon de Valera said that the Countess's speech should convince everyone that they were 'neither wild dreamers or red revolutionaries'. Laurence Ginnell described Constance as 'the Joan of Arc of Ireland'.

While in Sligo, she got news that her Irish Citizen Army comrade William Partridge had died; his funeral would take place at Ballaghaderreen, which was within reach of Ballymote. On Tuesday, Constance attended the funeral, wearing her Easter Week tunic. She spoke in Ballymote and, after going to mass the next day, was taken to Keash, where there were sports, and lunch at the priest's house. She spoke to young women about her life and work and showed them the rosary beads given to her by William Partridge, which she wore around her wrist. Later she made a speech to 4,000 people.

Two weeks later, she was in Cork. News came through that William Cosgrave had won the Kilkenny by-election and, as the train travelled south, cheering crowds and bonfires on the hills celebrated another Sinn

Féin victory. Constance was photographed in Kilkenny with Cosgrave, Darrell Figgis, de Valera and Laurence Ginnell; she was dressed in a long, silky coat and was holding a bouquet.

Cork presented Constance with an 'Address from the Remnant of the Irish Republican Brotherhood of Rebel Cork of '65-67 to Countess Markievicz'. She prized this as much as her address from the ITGWU. She gave two speeches that weekend in Cork and another in Clonakilty, took part in several meetings organised by transport workers, Cumann na mBan and the Fianna, and demonstrated on behalf of prisoners arrested under the Defence of the Realm Act.

Her speeches followed a pattern – first she would exhort her audiences to work for any of the several republican societies connected with Sinn Féin. She would then compare the 1916 Rising to Bunker Hill, a lost battle that helped win a war. Victory for Sinn Féin was defined as recognition for Ireland at the peace conference. Any nation whose people rose up and held its capital city for a week was entitled to be represented at such a conference; or so Sinn Féin believed.

The by-election victories for Sinn Féin in North Roscommon, South Longford, East Clare and Kilkenny City were the first fruits of the Rising. A party with no funds, no central organisation and no staff had taken seats from an Irish Parliamentary Party that had powerful local organisations and financial support. For the British administration in Dublin Castle, the new Sinn Féin policy was an affront. It ignored the existence of the Castle administration and treated British law in Ireland as illegal. The administration began making arrests.

By September, fourteen men had been arrested for supporting Sinn Féin's new constitutional movement. They denounced the court, ignored the judges and demanded to be treated as prisoners of war. Among those arrested was Thomas Ashe, charged with sedition for a speech he made in Ballinalee, County Longford, where Michael Collins was also speaking. He was detained at the Curragh and then transferred to Mountjoy Gaol in Dublin to serve two years' hard labour. In Mountjoy, Austin Stack acted as the prisoners' commandant and, with Ashe and others, demanded prisoner of war status. On 18 September, when their demands were refused, they went on hunger strike. On 25 September, Ashe died at the Mater Hospital after being force-fed by prison authorities. Dr Kathleen Lynn, who saw him before he lost consciousness, was sure that food had found its way into his lungs. At the inquest into his death, the jury condemned the staff at the prison for the 'inhuman and dangerous operation performed on the prisoner, and other acts of unfeeling and barbaric conduct'.

Constance wrote to Eva about Ashe's 'heroic' death. She felt that the British were trying to goad republicans into another rising so that they could wipe them all out. On every street were machine guns and armoured cars, manned by 'masses of soldiers'. When she had given a talk in Cork, the British had mobilised a regiment with four machine guns in a neighbouring street.

Ashe's funeral on 30 September was an opportunity for nationalists to show their strength. An advance guard of armed Volunteers, followed by nearly 200 priests, led the procession of 30,000 mourners. Many were armed and wearing the forbidden uniforms of the Volunteers, Cumann na mBan, the Fianna and the Irish Citizen Army. The funeral oration was given by Michael Collins who, until then, was unknown to most. After the last post sounded, three volleys were fired and Collins spoke: 'The volley we have just heard is the only speech it is proper to make above the grave of a dead Fenian'. The British army looked on silently.

On Sunday 21 October, Constance received an overwhelming reception in the small Limerick village of Athea, the home town of Con Colbert, one of her Fianna boys, who had been executed for his part in the Rising. So packed were the streets that one spectator worried that the buildings themselves might collapse under the pressure. Following an open-air meeting in a field, Constance was the guest of honour for lunch in Colbert's home, Gale View.

Ordinary politics had resumed and, at Sinn Féin's tenth annual *ard fheis* on 25–6 October in Dublin's Mansion House, the various strands of the movement came together. Éamon de Valera emerged as the new leader of the revamped organisation when both Arthur Griffith and Count Plunkett graciously withdrew their names. Although the original Sinn Féin abhorred physical violence and had never sought a complete break with Britain, it was decided to hold on to the old name, by now associated with all Irish nationalists. A new constitution was accepted that declared Sinn Féin's intention to deny the right of the British parliament to legislate for Ireland was accepted.

An issue that threatened to split the convention was raised by Constance. Like many, she found Eoin MacNeill's efforts to stop the Easter Rising at the last minute hard to forgive. Pearse, in his final address to his soldiers during Easter week, had struck a conciliatory note. 'Of the fatal countermanding order which prevented those plans from being carried out, I shall not speak further. Both Eoin MacNeill and we have acted in the best interest of Ireland.' De Valera, in prison, had resolved not to let the matter split the Volunteers. When MacNeill arrived with a group of prisoners at Dartmoor, where de Valera was held at the time, he ordered his men to salute MacNeill. If Sinn Féin was to win an election, presenting a united front was vital.

Constance opposed the election of MacNeill to Sinn Féin's 24-member executive on the grounds that he had changed his mind many times. She was supported by Kathleen Clarke and a few others. Clarke, who had told Constance she would not support such a motion, changed her mind when she saw the hostility 'a woman who had come out and risked her life' faced at the meeting. De Valera spoke in MacNeill's defence, pointing out that he had never made any claims to be a revolutionary. MacNeill had retained the respect of the majority and was elected to the executive with 888 votes – more than the 617 received by Constance.

During the discussion on the constitution, the resolution 'that the equality of men and women in this organisation be emphasised in all speeches and leaflets' was introduced, with women determined not to be sidelined. Kathleen Lynn and Jenny Wyse Power stressed the need for talented women as well as men in the new Ireland. The pair were supported by Seán T. O'Kelly and the motion was passed. Kathleen Lynn, Kathleen Clarke and Josephine Countess Plunkett as well as Constance were elected to a new 24-member executive. Jenny Wyse Power was co-opted soon after, replacing Countess Plunkett. These politically active women still faced a wall of indifference if not downright hostility: at the convention, just seventeen of the thousand delegates who attended were women and only Waterford-based Rosamund Jacob came from outside Dublin.

At the Irish Volunteers convention in Croke Park a few weeks later, de Valera was elected president, making him the military as well as the civil leader of Irish republicanism. Cathal Brugha was chief of staff of the Volunteers and his great rival Michael Collins became director of organisation. Collins was an IRB member, as was the Fianna founding member Seán McGarry, who was the general secretary. De Valera had given up his brief IRB membership.

As well as her work with Sinn Féin, Cumann na mBan and the Fianna, Constance was on the committee of the Irish Republican Prisoners Dependants' Fund. She was re-elected president of Cumann na mBan at its 1917 autumn convention and remained chief scout of the Fianna, who made Éamon de Valera their president. With the Fianna, she believed that there was a continuing need for a link with the Volunteers, although – interestingly – she did not fully support the idea that all Irish of military age be trained in the use of arms, believing that this should be an individual decision. In early December she was in Belfast where, a few days after her visit, two Fianna were caught carrying a sackload of bombs that they had smuggled from Scotland.

At the first meeting of the Sinn Féin executive on 19 December 1917, Constance was appointed to head a Department of Labour along with Cathal O'Shannon, who represented the labour movement. No documents of the time explain this decision, although the account of a meeting on 4 March 1918 mentions vaguely that Constance had submitted 'a report' of some kind and that it was accepted.

Although loved by the public, especially in Dublin, Constance was not entirely accepted in nationalist circles. The Sinn Féin Club at Tulla, County Clare, threatened to burn a lookalike model of the 'dreaded' Countess and the superior of the Christian Brothers in Ireland was not amused when he discovered that the Countess was invited to visit CBS Tullamore and speak to the boys. In 1918, Griffith expressed his annoyance at her flamboyant rhetoric and 'idiotic revolutionary speeches'.

Her relationship with the labour movement was also changing. After the Rising, Thomas Johnson, a moderate Home Ruler, became leader of the Labour Party. Constance would never establish the same kind of warm personal relationship with him, or with the ITGWU's William O'Brien, as she had enjoyed with Connolly and Larkin. Party politics were played down in the labour movement after 1916; the ITGWU, whose membership had grown from 5,000 in April 1916 to 68,000 by 1918, concentrated on economic rather than political goals.

She found time, as always, for children, holding a Christmas party for nearly 700 youngsters at Liberty Hall in December 1917. In early 1918 she travelled to Manchester with Cathal O'Shannon to raise funds for the James Connolly Labour College and, in Cork, spoke on the place of international labour in an independent republic. In February, suffragists celebrated their first victory when the vote was given to all women over the age of thirty. In that spring of 1918, the Irish Women's Workers Union was registered as a trade union with Louie Bennett and Helen Chevenix as honorary secretaries; membership by then had risen to 5,000. At the time, women's wages were generally less than a third of a man's average.

In March 1918, John Redmond died from complications following an operation for gallstones. A few weeks later, with no Redmond to hold him back, the British prime minster, Lloyd George, extended the Military Services Bill to Ireland; in effect, he was introducing conscription. Lloyd George saw two good reasons for doing this – it would provide badly needed troops for the war effort and would reduce the numbers tempted to join the republican army. In an attempt to prevent a backlash in Ireland, he linked the move to a new Home Rule bill, so alienating both nationalists and unionists.

Every member of the Irish Parliamentary Party voted against the new bill and, when it was passed, they all walked out of the House of Commons in protest, returning to Ireland to link up with Sinn Féin in organising resistance. Never again would southern Irish MPs sit in the House of Commons. De Valera, after a stirring statement reminding the British of the unselfish heroism of Irishmen in Flanders, Suvla Bay, Gallipoli, Egypt, Arabia, Mesopotamia, Mons and Ypres, persuaded the Irish Catholic bishops, then meeting in Maynooth, to denounce the bill.

After a conference in Dublin's Mansion House on 18 April held by Lord Mayor Laurence O'Neill, an Irish Anti-Conscription Committee was convened, representing all shades of political opinion. An anti-conscription pledge was read out at masses all over the country on Sunday 21 April. In all, two million men and women signed a declaration to resist any effort to force Irish men into the British army. Constance joined other leaders in an anti-conscription campaign that brought the Irish Women's Franchise League, Cumann na mBan and other women's organisations together to express their opposition. De Valera came up with an anti-conscription pledge: 'Denying the right of the British Government to enforce compulsory service in this country, we pledge ourselves solemnly to one another to resist conscription by the most effective means at our disposal.'

On 23 April, nearly the whole of Ireland (Belfast excepted) took part in a one-day strike organised with the approval of the Irish Labour Congress. Esther Roper's brother, Reginald, came to Dublin as an observer and met Constance. Machine guns were placed on the Bank of Ireland building on Dublin's College Green in anticipation of another rising. The British, with its army desperate for men, were determined to enforce the bill. Field Marshal Lord French, the newly appointed viceroy, took a hard-line view: 'If they do not come, we will fetch them'. His sister, the militant feminist Charlotte Despard, was one of thousands to oppose him. After a mass meeting at the Mansion House, a national women's day was organised, while women all over the country pledged not to take over jobs left open by men if they were conscripted.

With fury mounting among all sections of Irish society, Edward Shortt, the newly appointed Chief Secretary for Ireland, came up with a plan to arrest all known activists and to put extra troops on standby. To provide a reason, Dublin Castle concocted with a risible tale of 'treasonable communication with the German enemy' after Joseph Dowling, a former member of Roger Casement's Irish brigade, was arrested when he came ashore from a U-boat off the Galway coast allegedly with a message for Sinn Féin from German leaders. On the night of 17/18 May, seventy-three prominent members of Sinn Féin were arrested and deported immediately.

Constance, whose many 'seditious' speeches had been noted by the authorities, was among them. She had left the Sinn Féin headquarters on Harcourt Street, walked to Maud Gonne MacBride's house on nearby St Stephen's Green and then set off for Rathmines where she was living at the time with the Ginnells. Near the entrance to Portobello Barracks, she was stopped by six soldiers and two detectives and told to get into an armoured car. Her brown cocker spaniel, Poppet, jumped in with her. She was taken first to Dublin Castle and then to Kingstown early the next morning, along with the others who had been arrested. Among them were Maud Gonne MacBride, Kathleen Clarke, Arthur Griffith, Count Plunkett, Éamon de Valera and William Cosgrave.

After they were loaded into the hold of a gunboat, they crossed the Irish Sea in the mid-afternoon, arriving in Holyhead at 10pm. The following day, the men were taken to Usk and Gloucester jails, while Constance was kept in the Holyhead police station and then brought to London by train. On her way, she was asked to pay six shillings for her dog's ticket.

At Euston, she found Eva waiting. While travelling, Constance had experienced a strong urge to see her sister, regretting that she had not had time to tell her of her arrest. In London, Esther Roper felt a pressing urge to go to Euston and meet the Irish mail train. With Eva in tow, she set off for the station and, when they arrived, they split up to search the platform. Soon after, Roper spied 'the strangest little procession' coming towards her. It was led by a brown cocker spaniel, followed by a couple of soldiers with rifles, then Eva and Constance and finally an officer with a drawn sword.

A detective opened the door of a taxi and Constance got in accompanied by an escort; Poppet jumped in too. Eva heard the detective tell the driver to go to Holloway Prison. A few hours later, Poppet was brought to Eva's flat; he was later sent back to Ireland where he stayed with the Bartons in Glendalough, County Wicklow, until Constance returned. Robert Barton, an officer with the Royal Dublin Fusiliers during the 1916 Rising, resigned his commission in disgust at the heavy-handed British treatment of the rebels and joined the republican cause, as did his cousin Erskine Childers. Barton became Sinn Féin member for West Wicklow in 1918. His sister Dulcibella was a good friend of Constance's.

Joining Constance in Holloway were Maud Gonne MacBride and Kathleen Clarke. The three women were given cells after the 'Hard Nails Wing' of the prison was emptied. Between their cells were three empty ones. In each cell was a camp bed with slats and a mattress that seemed to be made of hay according to Kathleen Clarke; the hills and hollows that developed, along with the board-hard pillows and coarse blankets and sheets made sleep difficult, although Constance made no complaint, cheerfully maintaining that she could sleep on stones. The three women were given just one hour a day for exercise. For the remaining twenty-three hours, they were locked up.

As internees, the women were allowed to have food, clothes, books and approved newspapers sent in. Early on, Kathleen Clarke remembered asking Constance whether she was paying to have her meals sent in; Constance confessed that she was doing so because she was recovering from a bout of measles. The arrests were good propaganda for Ireland. On 23 June, Arthur Griffith, then held in Reading jail, won a by-election in East Cavan, beating the Irish Parliamentary Party's candidate. Constance was elated. 'Such a victory, our arrests did it ... Putting us away cleared the issues for us so much better than our own speeches ever could.'

She was growing increasingly sceptical about the value of leaders, who could be 'such a curse' since power so often got 'into the hands of a clique'. She shared her distaste for parliamentary politics with many Irish activists, believing that the national revolution would be in vain if the existing structures were left intact. As a supporter of the co-operative movement, she believed that, with their leaders in prison, people would be forced to think for themselves.

The practical joker in Constance was never far from the surface. She had her fun with the censor who read her letters, writing that she was probably accused of taking part in the 'German Plot' because of the German measles she had contracted just before she was arrested. Her first few to Eva were signed *Auf Wiedersehn*.

As the most experienced of the three 'jailbirds', Constance worried about her companions. When Maud Gonne MacBride was arrested, her son Seán had despairingly run after the Black Maria that was taking her away. In Holloway, she was not allowed to sign a cheque to provide for him. Kathleen Clarke, after the horror of losing both husband and brother during the Rising, worried about her three children. She found the prison diet of cocoa, margarine and 'a thing they called skilly' repulsive. When she became alarmingly thin, the doctor put her – and MacBride – on a 'hospital' diet that included tea, rice pudding and milk. Constance persuaded the doctor to allow them two hours of exercise and fresh air every day; later, they were permitted as much time as they liked out of doors. Under this regime, Constance's health improved and she stopped having her meals sent in.

Kathleen Clarke continued to fight for a better diet and persuaded the doctor to give them an egg each a day. When she continued to lose weight, she refused a move to the hospital, as the doctor wished, unless places were also found for her friends, even though Constance's fussing exasperated her. 'I told her one day that if she wanted an occupation to look elsewhere, that I was in no humour to provide her with an occupation or thrills, but that did not choke her off', she wrote in her autobiography. In the end, the doctor found beds for all three in the hospital.

A consequence of moving to the hospital was that the women were allowed visitors. First to arrive on 27 August was Eva Gore-Booth. 'Madame came back from her sister's visit in a wild state of excitement, bringing a large basket of fruit and flowers', reported Clarke. After a warning not to speak of politics, their conversation was witnessed and noted by a prison observer. Constance elaborated on her arrest and trip to Holloway, claiming that Poppet, her dog, was taught to 'strafe' anything English on the journey. She asked where the dog was now, wondered whether Eva had received a cheque for £20 (she hadn't) and put in a request for sketching materials. She wondered why the male prisoners got larger sheets of writing paper than the women and why her post was held up.

Maud Gonne MacBride had a visit from her son Seán and daughter Iseult, while Kathleen Clarke's sisters were to travel from Limerick. A few weeks later, a report in the *Irish Independent* described the conditions enforced for the visits. These, Clarke felt, 'were designed to humiliate us and our visitors', and so she cancelled her request to see her sisters. Constance agreed with Mrs Clarke; MacBride did not.

The author Patricia Lynch was a frequent caller at Holloway, leaving food, flowers, books and other treats. Knowing that both Constance and MacBride were keen gardeners, friends sent them potted plants. When these wilted in the dank cells, the pair left them in the exercise yard on alternate nights to help them grow. To brighten up the grey ugliness of their 'cage', they decorated their cells with bunches of grapes, ribbons and coloured clothes.

In the early days, Clarke heard MacBride and Constance arguing about their respective social status. Constance claimed that she had belonged to the inner circle of the vice-regal set, while MacBride was 'only on the fringes of it'. The women would then complain about each other to Clarke. She found it quite a strain, although she came to like both her companions. Clarke felt that Constance patronised her, wondering why such 'an insignificant person as myself' was put in prison with her. Her attitude was that the British were a 'blundering lot of fools to arrest someone like me'.

Throughout 1918, the arrests and the restrictions did little to improve the state of chaotic anarchy in Ireland. All nationalist organisations were proscribed, including the GAA, since a crowd could assemble easily at a football or hurling match. In defiance of the ban, 1,500 hurling matches were held on 4 August while, on 15 August, nearly 2,000 Sinn Féin meetings were held in one hour. By August, Sinn Féin had 81,000 members in 1,025 clubs, each with a company of Volunteers. In that month, Hanna Sheehy Skeffington, arrested outside the offices of the Irish Women's Franchise League after her visit to the USA, spent one day in Holloway. Constance had not seen her since Easter week.

In October, to the great relief of Constance and Kathleen, Maud Gonne MacBride was sent to a nursing home in London. She had become morose and depressed while in jail. Clarke was told that she could be released on similar grounds if she appealed to the British government; she said she would never appeal to the British government for anything. The remaining pair were given a gas ring and Constance took to making stews; Kathleen became the practical joker, on one occasion giving Constance soap to flavour the stew. When she was offered whiskey as a stimulant, she passed it on to Constance, who, unlike her, was not a teetotaller.

On 9 November, May Power wrote to Constance to tell her that a boy had won first prize in an essay competition conducted by the *Catholic Bulletin* on the subject of 'My Favourite Heroine'. His essay was just one of many written about Constance.

The long and bloody world war ended on 11 November 1918. From 21 November, when the Parliament (Qualification of Women) Act 1918 came into force, women over thirty were not only allowed to vote but could stand for election to parliament for the first time. This had the effect of tripling the British electorate from 7.7 million in 1912 to 21.4 million by the end of 1918. Women now accounted for about 43 per cent of the electorate and, had those over twenty-one been enfranchised, women would have outnumbered men. When an election was called for 14 December, Sinn Féin asked Constance to stand. It would be the first general election in the United Kingdom since December 1910. She agreed, for 'sport'.

The opening meeting of the Sinn Féin campaign was held on 11 November with jubilant Armistice Day celebrations as a backdrop.

Sinn Féin would put up candidates in all the existing constituencies. Of the seventy-three Sinn Féin candidates, forty-even were in jail – better propaganda than any number of speeches, as Constance noted: 'Sending you to jail is like pulling out all the loud stops on all the speeches you ever made or words you ever wrote!'

Constance was standing in Dublin's St Patrick's Division, one of the four Dublin constituencies at that time. It consisted of the Merchant's Quay, Usher's Quay and Wood Quay inner-city wards. The Irish Women's Franchise League and Cumann na mBan did most of the hard work on the ground, although Sinn Féin did hold a rally on her behalf. She managed to send out an election address, dated 11 November:

> It is with great pleasure that I have been accepted as SF candidate for St Patrick's constituency. As I will not procure my freedom by giving any pledge or undertaking to the enemy, you will probably have to fight without me. I have many friends in the constituency who will work all the harder for me. They know that I stand for the Irish Republic, to establish which our heroes died, and that my colleagues are firm in the belief that the freeing of Ireland is in the hands of the Irish people today ... There are many roads to freedom. Today we may hope that our road to freedom will be a peaceful and bloodless one; I need hardly assure you that it will be an honourable one. I would never take an oath of allegiance to the power that I meant to overthrow ... The one thing to bear in mind is that this election must voice the people of Ireland's demand to be heard at the peace conference ... We are quite cheerful and ready for anything that comes.

She sent a note from Holloway urging co-operation between Sinn Féin and the Irish trade union movement. Since the first principle of Sinn Féin was to end the connection with England, 'Sinn Féiners affiliated or amalgamated with English trade unions should be recommended when possible to sever the English connections'. She also believed that they should make it their business to secure a living wage for workers.

Constance also wrote to the Irish Women's Franchise League: 'One reason I'd like to win is that we could make St Patrick's a rallying ground for women and a splendid centre for constructive work by women. I am full of schemes and ideas.' In the election address sent to the Sinn Féin director of elections in Dublin, she wrote that she stood for a republic such as Connolly 'wrote about, worked for and died for'.

> Real democratic control with economic and industrial as well as political freedom. To organise our new nation on just and equitable lines, avoiding the mistakes other Nations have made in allowing the powers of Government, law, force, education, foreign policy, etc, to be the birthright of the moneyed classes to be used by them for the further accumulation of wealth and the building up of a class tyranny daily more subtle and more difficult to seize and overthrow.

Women, she argued, must 'trust women to speak for them, to work for them and fight for them and to look after their interests in the Irish Republic'.

Because the winter was bitterly cold, Kathleen Clarke spent much of the day in bed and, to keep herself busy, requested material for knitting, crochet, lace-making and embroidery. Inspired by her friend, Constance acquired materials for sketching and painting and many of the watercolours she painted in Holloway have survived. She painted remembered scenes of Ireland and heroic figures from the past. She tried her hand at an illumination on the topic of Connolly's 'The Cause of Labour is the Cause of Ireland'. Among the pictures was a caricature of Kathleen trying to thread a needle with her face all puckered up. Clarke liked it: 'It really was very funny, and very clever.'

Constance had a habit of smoking when she came into Kathleen's room, which had a gate to it rather than a door. She would drop cigarette ash and flick the paint and water off her brush. Because Kathleen liked order and Constance's untidiness 'distracted' her, she told her to leave the room. Constance sat in the corridor, heaving deep sighs. Next morning she asked very meekly if she could come in. 'No', said Kathleen, 'I have had enough of you'. Constance tried again, promising to bring a plate for her cigarette ash and a jar for her paint brush. Still Kathleen would not relent. 'But Kathleen, I'm lonely,' said Constance. Kathleen gave in.

The pair tried to make their humdrum life as pleasant as possible and such quarrels were rare. Constance stole the wardress's report book in which was noted every move either of them made and they had much fun reading it. Reading helped pass the time, with Constance favouring poetry, especially Robert Browning. She also ordered books on economics, labour, socialism and history from the library and flicked her way through them. 'She would skim through a book, trying in her quick way to get the sense of it,' said Clarke.

On 14 December, Irish women marched to the polling booths for the first time, led by ninety-year-old Anna Haslam, who, with her late husband, Thomas, had founded the Dublin Suffrage Society in 1874. The issue was clear: a vote for Sinn Féin was a vote for a free and independent Irish republic. By a majority of 70 per cent, the Irish people voted for Sinn Féin. The Irish Parliamentary Party dropped from eighty seats at the beginning of the year to a paltry seven. Their fight for Home Rule was over.

One Sunday morning in December, Constance had a visit from the governor and the matron, bringing the news that she had been elected a Member of Parliament – the only one of the seventeen women candidates to make it. Among others who stood were Winifred Carney in Belfast and Charlotte Despard in London. 'Madame got so excited she went yelling and dancing all over the place,' said Clarke. In the St Patrick's Division, Constance polled 7,835 votes; William Field of the Irish Parliamentary Party, who had held the seat for twenty-six years, got 3,741 and Alderman J.J. Kelly won 312 votes.

Outside the Sinn Féin headquarters on Dublin's Harcourt Street, an excited crowd had watched as the figures from the counting centres were displayed on a giant noticeboard in a second-floor window. That Sinn Féin could win by such a huge margin was the stuff of dreams. 'The humbug was now over,' as Joseph Cleary said when speaking on behalf of a triumphant Markievicz. Not everyone was pleased with her election. A leader in the *Irish Independent* questioned her 'mental balance'; this 'mean and unjustified attack' provoked angry letters to the paper from Maud Gonne MacBride and Jenny Wyse Power.

On Christmas Day, after Constance decorated the small passage outside the Holloway cells with flowers, she and Kathleen had a 'grand dinner' with food sent by Clarke's sisters in Limerick, and a bottle of champagne from Eva. Soon after, Kathleen became ill with heart trouble, possibly connected to the flu epidemic then raging. Not wanting another

Irish martyr, on 19 February the authorities decided to release her and she stayed with Eva until she was fit enough to return home. Constance remained in Holloway for a further three weeks: 'Of course, I miss K very much, though for the first time in my life, I was thankful to see the back of a dear friend.' In an affectionate letter, she sent Kathleen 'heaps of love' and wondered 'whose head you are snapping off now'.

She was hungry for news of Ireland and worried about her husband who 'hated wars, revolutions and politics' and of whom she had heard nothing since 1916. She knew indirectly that her stepson, attached to the Russian Volunteer Fleet at Archangel as an interpreter, was still alive. 'Poor Staskou, I'd hate him to be killed or wounded; he did love life so.'

From Holloway, she wrote a letter to the young playwright Frank J. Hugh O'Donnell, about his play *The Dawn Mist*. Praising his ability to write about 'the idealism and spirit of self-sacrifice that is the keynote of the true Irish character', she takes a cut at depictions of stage Irishry 'merely picturesque results of our history' and signs off in Irish – *Mise ar gCúis na hÉireann* (Yours in the cause of Ireland). The letter was used as a foreword to the printed edition of the play.

No one watching the elections could doubt that the Irish wanted to rule themselves. On 7 January 1919, twenty-six of the elected Sinn Féin members met at Dublin's Mansion House to make plans for convening an Irish parliament three weeks later.

CHAPTER FOURTEEN

Nineteen Hundred and Nineteen

On Tuesday, 21 January 1919, the first Dáil Éireann met in the Round Room of Dublin's Mansion House, watched closely by the press and many international visitors; long queues had formed on the street outside. Dublin Castle had decided to ignore the Dáil; the viceroy, Lord French, thought the occasion so ludicrous that he had withdrawn the need for a police permit.

Presiding was Cathal Brugha, since both the president (de Valera) and vice-president (Arthur Griffith) were in jail. Members were called *Teachta Dáil* – the Irish for deputies of parliament; the word *Dáil* meant 'assembly'. By an extraordinary coincidence, as the new members of parliament walked into the Mansion House at around 3.30pm, members of the Royal Fusiliers were departing after a celebration lunch.

A prayer from the 'Rebel Priest', Father Michael O'Flanagan, opened the ceremony, which was conducted mainly in Irish, to the bemusement of the visiting press but also to many locals, few of them fluent Irish speakers. Only twenty-four members were present with a further thirty-five described as *Fe ghlas ag Gallaibh* or 'In a foreign prison'. All were Sinn Féin members and most were young, urban, middle-class men, with Constance, a 51-year-old woman, the notable exception. Unionists had declined the invitation to join the new assembly.

Among the documents hastily prepared for the occasion was a 'Democratic Programme' based on the 1916 Proclamation, with the labour leader Tom Johnson its main architect. Its radical programme might have been a ploy to influence the International

Socialist Conference taking place in Bern, Switzerland; the 'Second International', formed in 1889 and dissolved in 1916, had supported the demands of Irish republicans, as had Russia. An Irish Declaration of Independence was read, firstly in French and then in English, followed by a 'Message to the Free Nations of the World' in French and English aimed squarely at the Versailles Peace Conference then meeting in France. Under a provisional constitution, the Dáil gave itself full powers of legislation and absolute control over finance. With the business of the day complete by 5.20pm, a celebratory dinner followed.

In the wider world, the Red Army had occupied Sebastopol in the Crimea as the Bolshevik effort to drive the Allies out of Russia continued. There were fears that Bolshevism could sweep through the continent of Europe. Farther afield, Britain faced revolts in Egypt, Afghanistan and India.

In the early months of 1919, the Catholic Church had warned of links between Bolshevism and Sinn Féin, and Bishop Kelly of Rosse criticised the leaders of the Dáil, especially Constance, for their extremist tendencies. Constance declared to a Sinn Féin meeting that if President Wilson failed to support Ireland, they should turn to the Bolsheviks, who had consistently supported the Irish cause. Republicans at the time were friendly towards the Bolsheviks and news of Bolshevik atrocities and barbarity was received with suspicion. With Woodrow Wilson, in Constance's view, 'a dark horse' likely to lose sight of Ireland's cause, she suspected that the League of Nations might not favour small nations after all, leaving them open to other alliances.

Through Nora Connolly, Constance had 'first-hand news' of the industrial advances in Russia but she heard also of terrible ruthlessness towards perceived enemies of the Republic, including 'cruel and drastic' executions.

She disliked autocracy of any kind but was optimistic:

> ... surely if they have the sense to organise education, they can abolish class. While they are menaced by the moneyed classes of the whole world, their only hope lies in the success of a strong central government: a tyranny in fact, but once the pressure is relieved, Lenin survives, and he has not lost his original ideals. We may hope. Of course, they may go mad with the idea of Empire,

and go out with their armies to force the world to come under their ideas and do awful things in the name of freedom, small nationalities, etc, but even so they have done something.

She believed that the Bolshevik revolution was the natural successor to the French revolution. Both had overthrown undemocratic autocracies and attempted to build new societies based on equality for all. To see violence as justified and necessary in order to discard a discredited regime was part of the prevailing tradition of romantic nationalism. Later, Constance would admit that she knew little of the Bolsheviks but, at the time, she argued that they were akin to the ancient Irish in their commitment to 'decentralisation' through 'soviets' or local councils.

The first task of the new assembly was to press the case for Irish independence at the Versailles Peace Conference that had started on 18 January and would continue for a year. As far as republicans were concerned, they had fulfilled the conditions for nationhood set down by President Wilson in his 4 July 1918 speech: 'What we seek is a reign of law based on the consent of the governed and sustained by the organised opinion of mankind.' Éamon de Valera, Arthur Griffith and Count Plunkett were nominated as delegates by the new Dáil and Seán T. O'Kelly set off for Paris to secure their admission to the conference. In March, he was joined by George Gavan Duffy. In the USA, friends of the Irish cause persuaded Congress to pass a resolution asking that Ireland be admitted to the peace conference.

In the early months of the year, appeals and protests about the continued imprisonment of Constance and the other Irish internees went unheeded. Invitations from the prime minister, Lloyd George, in 10 Downing Street, hoping that 'it might be convenient for the newly elected MPs to attend the opening of the new parliament on 11 February', were forwarded to the Irish MPs in their jails in England. Constance received hers a week after parliament opened and she enjoyed composing a suitably acerbic reply, though she suspected it never went further than the prison censor. She was continuing her studies of political systems, going through the works of H.N. Brailsford, a man who fought against secret 'diplomacy', and the hard-line Bolshevik Maxim Litvinov who, like Connolly, argued that power must lie in the hands of the working class.

England was in the grip of the worst flu epidemic in its history and one of its victims was Pierce McCann, an Irish internee held in Gloucester jail. Aware that they might be creating a new set of Irish martyrs, the British decided to release the remaining Irish internees. Constance left Holloway on 10 March and spent a few days with Eva and Esther in London before returning to Ireland. Eva had organised meetings with British trade union leaders and socialist activists for her sister. Constance could not resist a visit to Westminster, where she dropped into the members' vestibule and was amused to see that the place reserved for her coat and hat in the cloakroom was next to that of Sir Edward Carson. Many thought her refusal to take her seat a missed opportunity for women. It would be another few months before Lady Astor, elected the Conservative MP for Plymouth after her husband was elevated to the Lords, would become the first woman MP to sit in the venerable chamber of the House of Commons.

When Constance returned to Dublin, arriving by the 6pm mail boat at Kingstown on Saturday 15 March, she received an even more jubilant reception than twenty-one months earlier following her release from Aylesbury.

> Madame O'Rahilly and Mrs Humphries met me at Holyhead, and they had secured sunny seats on the boat. The sun on the rippling sea was divine, and the seagulls gave the finishing touch to the reality of freedom. I was met by deputations of everybody! We motored in to Dublin to Liberty Hall. Last time was nothing to it. The crowd had no beginning or end. I made a speech, and then we formed up in a torchlight procession and went to St Patrick's. Every window had a flag or candles or both. You never saw such excitement.

Police were under orders from the Under-Secretary not to interfere. As an elected member of parliament, this was Constance's first opportunity to address her constituents and she had a right to do so. Furthermore, the reception of released prisoners so far had 'fallen very flat', said the chief secretary Edward Shortt, mainly because of the Castle's policy of ignoring them.

One of her first visits was to Kathleen Clarke, who had spent seven weeks in a Dublin nursing home after her return from London and had then gone to stay with her sisters in Limerick. Four rooms at the Clarke household on Richmond Avenue were filled with Markievicz's furniture. At the time of her arrest, Constance was living with the Ginnells, and had brought her furniture and valuable paintings with her. When the Ginnells were forced to move, Kathleen Clarke offered Constance the use of her house while she recuperated from her illness. After Clarke returned from Limerick, Constance asked to stay on and Clarke agreed: 'Though we quarelled occasionally, I was fond of her; she had some very fine qualities.'

Éamon de Valera had not waited to be released. In February, with the help of Michael Collins, Harry Boland and the wax impression of a key, he had escaped from Lincoln Prison along with two other prisoners. He remained in hiding until the release of all the Irish prisoners was announced. Plans were made for him to return to Dublin on 26 March, where he would be greeted by the Lord Mayor of Dublin in a manner befitting the official head of state. Dublin Castle had no intention of either endorsing the new republic or acknowledging de Valera's status, and the streets of Dublin rumbled to the sound of tanks and armoured cars. The first aeroplanes flew over the city. Fearing bloodshed, de Valera cancelled his reception.

When the Dáil met for its second session on 1 April 1919, fifty-two members were present, including Constance. De Valera was elected president and formed a cabinet. Constance was appointed Secretary for Labour, making her the first official female cabinet minister in western Europe (Alexandra Kollontai had been appointed People's Commissar for Social Welfare in Soviet Russia). Her brief included social welfare. She told Kathleen Clarke that she had threatened to quit Sinn Féin and join the Labour Party if they did not give her the job. Since she had headed the Sinn Féin labour committee in 1917, she felt that she had earned the right to be minister.

Others appointed as ministers were Arthur Griffith (home affairs), Cathal Brugha (defence), Count Plunkett (foreign affairs), Eoin MacNeill (industries), Michael Collins (finance) and William Cosgrave (local government). The Dáil continued to meet, though sporadically, holding six meetings in 1919 and three each in 1920 and 1921. To raise the money it needed to finance its activities, a National Loan was launched at home and in the USA by Michael Collins as Minister for Finance. Although conducting ordinary parliamentary business was difficult, the Dáil was successful in taking control of local government and the court system.

Constance was delighted with her new position and wrote to her sister on notepaper headed 'Dáil Éireann, Department of Labour, Mansion House'. 'It is so funny, suddenly, to be a Government and supposed to be respectable!' Her first job as Minister concerned the plight of two child prisoners-of-war. On 21 January, while the first Dáil was meeting in Dublin, Dan Breen, Séumas Robinson, Seán Hogan, Seán Treacy and at least five others had provided a stark reminder that the gunmen were very much prepared to fight on. In an ambush on South Tipperary County Council, employees carrying explosives to Solobeaghead quarry and their armed Royal Irish Constabulary (RIC) escort, Constables Patrick McDonnell and James O'Connell, were killed, provoking widespread criticism, even within Sinn Féin. During its investigation, the RIC seized an eight-year-old boy, John Connor, and questioned him for over four hours. Along with his fifteen-year-old brother Matthew and eleven-year-old-friend Timothy Connors, he was held for ten weeks.

When questioned in the House of Commons, the Attorney General for Ireland, A.W. Samuels, replied that the children were not arrested, but rather 'removed from the neighbourhood' to ensure their 'personal safety'. Constance's committee reported the safe release of the boys, as well as of other republican prisoners.

In August 1919, the Dáil founded a National Conciliation Board for the settlement of trade disputes that came under Constance and the Department of Labour. In one of the first industrial disputes involving her ministry, the Irish Transport and General Workers' Union was negotiating with a Dublin manufacturer of beads who was underpaying his employees. The meeting at the Sinn Féin offices in Harcourt Street was dragging on, with no apparent hope of settlement. Constance thought up a ruse to hurry matters along. She rushed into the meeting room with the urgent news that the military were on their way in fifteen minutes. Still neither side would give an inch. Five minutes later, she told them that they had only ten minutes left. Neither side listened. Only when she warned the meeting that the military would arrive in just five minutes did the employer sign an agreement.

Seán O'Faoláin maintained that Constance was received with scant courtesy by her fellow Dáil members between August 1921 and June

1922. Her memoranda were shuffled from one meeting to another and often ignored. Collins, who funded the various departments, had described the Department of Labour as 'a bloody joke' with little to do. Labour got the smallest allocation of funds of any ministry and Constance did not demand more. In 1920, it was allocated £450; later Constance got a further £500 for the Labour Arbitration Tribunal. By comparison, the Irish language department got £5,000 and propaganda received £900. Yet Constance, although she was on the run, worked hard, setting up conciliation boards and arbitrating disputes, while her department issued guidelines on wages and food prices. The problem was a general lack of interest in labour matters.

Following her second spell in prison, Constance embarked on a whirlwind programme of Dáil meetings, committee meetings and meetings with workers and employers all over the country and occasionally abroad. Much of her work was conducted in secret; there were no limousines, plush offices or lengthy lunches for the new cabinet ministers, although they were paid an annual salary. Constance insisted that deputies' expenses be monitored closely, that public funds should cover only a third-class rail ticket and that the per diem maintenance allowance be no more than fifteen shillings.

At the end of April, Constance was in Glasgow, addressing a huge meeting; on 11 May, she presided at the Fianna *Aeridheacht*, an open-air gathering. The following weekend, she was in Cork attending meetings. She had been invited to attend a *Feis Mór* in Newmarket by the local branch of the Gaelic League and, after arriving late on Saturday evening, she gave a brief speech. 'Boycott English manufacturers and burn everything English except their coal,' she said, quoting Jonathan Swift. After the meeting, her short journey to the Railway Hotel was observed closely by the local police. When they saw a woman who looked like Constance leaving the hotel, they followed her to the local train station where they saw her take a train out of town. What they did not realise was that the woman they had seen off was Madge McCarthy, who acted as a decoy while Constance slipped away from the hotel, spending the night at the Corney Lenihan home in Drom an Airgil. On Sunday morning, Constance sat on the platform for the *Feis Mór*, with only a few policemen in evidence.

The following week, Constance revisited Glasgow before returning to Dublin to meet the three members of the American Commission on

Irish Independence. Edward F. Dunne, a former governor of Illinois, Frank P. Walsh from New York and Michael J. Ryan of Philadelphia had come to Ireland from Paris at the invitation of de Valera and with the approval of the British. They spent a month touring the country and their report, issued in June 1919, was sent to British government officials, to newspapers and to American delegates attending the Versailles peace talks. It formed part of the official USA government publication on the treaty talks.

At Holyhead, the Americans were shocked by the number of armed British soldiers waiting for the ferry to Kingstown. At the time, Ireland was occupied by over 100,000 men, equipped with lorries, armoured cars, tanks, machine guns, artillery and bomber planes. In addition, 15,000 RIC policemen – whom the Americans described as belonging to a branch of the military – lived in barracks and were armed with rifles as well as side arms.

Despite initial opposition from the governor, the American trio visited Mountjoy Gaol, where they discovered that only twelve of the prisoners were non-political. They experienced first-hand the restrictions on movement around the country and witnessed numerous assaults on republican men and women on public streets. On 9 May, the Americans attended a special session of Dáil Éireann. Afterwards, on their way to a Mansion House reception, they were stopped by the military, and de Valera was not allowed to pass. Later, the Americans witnessed soldiers brutally assaulting Eoin MacNeill.

The influence of Constance was apparent in the Americans' descriptions of attacks on women and children taken in for interrogation by the police. She had supplied information on education, infant mortality rates, the organisation of labour and the appalling destitution and hunger suffered by many. The Americans had met labour leaders and were impressed:

> Ireland has the best organised and most coherent labour movement in the world. It is being thwarted and suppressed by the army and constabulary. Wages of unskilled workers are below a line which means to them hunger, cold and privation. The wage of skilled labour is far below the minimum for decent existence.

They noted that many Irish labour leaders believed that, unless they were freed from foreign control and exploitation, they would follow the example of the Russians, setting up 'soviets' or workers' governments and refusing to produce wealth for their oppressors.

The Americans' report, signed on 3 June 1919, recommended that the peace conference appoint an impartial committee to investigate the Irish situation: 'today – the darkest of the dark spots on the map'. President Wilson, wary of alienating his British ally, was not prepared to accept their recommendations. If anything, the work of the committee hardened his heart against the Irish cause and parts of the report were used as an excuse to deny safe conduct to Paris for the three Irish delegates. President Wilson's priority at the Versailles conference was setting up a League of Nations, which, he argued, would help smaller nations like Ireland in the future. For this he needed British support and, in June, he announced that the United States, Britain, France and Germany would have a veto on who was admitted to the conference. Sinn Féin had badly misunderstood the purpose of such conferences, which was to decide the fate of the defeated nations and the countries they had annexed. Had the Germans invaded Ireland, then the Irish would have been welcomed unreservedly. Privately, Constance described the League of Nations as 'pompous rubbish (for the benefit of democracy I suppose) about the reduction of armaments when all they wanted was information on their neighbours so they could get one up on them'.

In mid-May, while the Americans were in Ireland, the British suffragist and socialist Sylvia Pankhurst had visited Dublin, speaking at the Trades Hall in Capel Street on 'Russia Today', with Constance chairing the meeting. She had never met Pankhurst before and was impressed. A week later, a messenger from Michael Collins arrived at the Clarke household on Richmond Avenue in Fairview with a warning for Constance to clear out; a raid was expected. She got dressed and hurried to Margaret Skinnider's house on nearby Waverly Avenue, forgetting her glasses; she was forced to call out Margaret's name several times before she found the correct house. She stayed at Waverly Avenue for some months, disguising herself when she went out, most often as an old lady.

On 5 June, the Socialist Party of Ireland planned a Connolly Birthday Concert at the Mansion House. Shortly before it was due to begin, the police drew a cordon across Dawson Street to stop people attending. Near St Stephen's Green, four police and two civilians were injured after an exchange of gunfire. Fearing that this might happen, the Trades Hall in Capel Street had been booked as an alternative venue and here Constance presided over an evening of speeches, music and appeals for funds.

Ten days later, on 15 June, Constance was arrested for the speech she had made in Newmarket four weeks earlier. She was taken to Mallow by special train, accompanied by thirty soldiers and an equal number of police 'armed to the teeth'; it was a 'Gilbertian' comic-opera journey according to a letter she wrote to Hanna Sheehy Skeffington. The American delegates accused the British of arresting her because of the help she had given them. The British denied this, claiming that, in her speech, she had urged people to regard the children of the police as spies, to ostracise them, treat them as lepers, and refuse to sit near them in church or school.

During her trial, she refused to recognise the court and called no witness in her defence. She wished only to deny the charges. Firstly, she would never have advocated the persecution of policemen's children, and, secondly, she had not urged shops to boycott the police because it would be impossible to do so and would achieve nothing.

When she was sentenced to four months in jail, she stood up. 'Three cheers for the Irish Republic,' she cried. The crowd continued to cheer while she was escorted from the building. The authorities had planned to have her moved to Mountjoy Gaol in Dublin, but the governor feared she would escape and so requested a 'strong guard' outside the female prison 'day and night'. The RIC pointed out that employing four shifts of twenty policemen for this purpose would be 'to the very serious detriment' of the city. The proper place to guard prisoners was inside the prison walls.

A suggestion that Constance be moved out of the country was dismissed on the grounds that she had been tried in Ireland. By 10 July, the move to Mountjoy was still under discussion and two large motor lorries, one small lorry and a supplementary escort of twenty military were held in readiness. It was then decided to defer the move until after the peace celebrations, since it was 'not improbable' that Sinn Féin would try to seize her. By 28 July, given her good conduct, it was decided to leave her in Cork.

She 'seemed in good health and contented' when visited by a medical officer of the General Prison Board. Her cell was bright and airy and the exercise ground 'spacious, neat and orderly'. She was well aware of the propaganda value of her detention: 'As long as the jails are full, that keeps the heart in the people – Ireland always hatches a plentiful supply of Phoenix eggs – and of dragon's teeth not a few!'

Her stretch in Cork was not too onerous. She was allowed visitors; friends sent in food and she had all the reading and writing material she wanted. She made a rock garden for the governor and studied history and economics – most notably John Mitchel's *Jail Journal*, which argued that Young Ireland had failed because it could not frame a coherent policy. There was no evidence that her letters were censored. 'This is the most comfortable jail I have been in yet. There's a nice garden, full of pinks, and you can hear the birds sing', she wrote to Eva. Nora Connolly visited a few times and noted the number of young soldiers employed to guard one woman. She observed that, with no-one to talk to, a sociable woman like Constance must be lonely.

In September, Constance was delighted to get word through Eva of Staskou. She had heard no news of him since he had left Dublin in June 1915 to visit his father. Nor had she heard anything of her husband. He had been in Kiev, which was 'rather a bad place just now' and, with his love of 'fine ideas', he might 'just as easily be a Bolshevik as anything else'. She remembered that, in Dublin, Casimir could lunch with the enemy and sup with the enemy and 'between the two make a wild rebel speech'. She had not written to either her stepson or husband, afraid they might be put on a 'black list' by corresponding with 'a rebel like me'.

That September, while Constance was still in jail, the Dáil and Sinn Féin were both declared illegal, along with the Irish Volunteers, Gaelic League and Cumann na mBan, as well as their journals and newspapers. From then on, the Dáil would hold only a few secret sessions, while the cabinet met 'on the run'. Constance was released on Saturday, 18 October and attended a reception and concert organised by the Irish Women's Franchise League in Dublin to celebrate her release. She was delighted to be back among her friends, returning to live with Kathleen Clarke.

At midnight that day, Constable Michael Downing of the Dublin Metropolitan Police (DMP) was shot dead in High Street, Dublin, after he approached three suspects while on patrol. For some time, 'The Squad', a group of trained assassins recruited by Michael Collins, had targeted members of the DMP's G Division, but Downing was not a member of that division. Tensions in the city rose and Cumann na mBan's annual conference, scheduled for the Mansion House on 20 October, was banned, with twenty DMP constables along with a superintendent, an inspector and two sergeants assigned to patrol Dawson Street. Most republicans stayed away, although Maud Gonne MacBride appeared, as did Countess Plunkett on a tricycle. According to the police reports, Constance stepped off a tram at about 2pm, accompanied by a 'low sized dark sallow-complexioned lady wearing glasses'. She walked up to the Mansion House and, when stopped by a policeman, asked to see the Lord Mayor stating that she was the 'Minister for Labour' under the 'Irish Government' elected by the Irish people.

When asked whether she was connected with the banned meeting, she retorted:

> What meeting? What an impertinent question. Do you represent the hirelings of the British government? What Irishmen! I got four months in Cork for telling people about you and I'm glad I did so! You won't let me in then; very well. I have been here to test it and I hope you won't be too badly punished.

She then walked away towards the Green. The police authorities were not prepared to dismiss Constance's words as the bravado of a woman only just released from prison, describing her as a 'pestilential harridan' from the 'most extreme section' of the republican movement. They believed that her release from Cork jail had been celebrated by the murder of Constable Downing and that she posed a grave danger to public order: 'While she and those associated with her move freely about, assassinations will continue.'

The Dáil met once more on 27 October, with its departments doing their best to continue functioning, despite being banned and under constant surveillance. Constance's Department of Labour was located in North Frederick Street and masqueraded as a letting agency for apartments. It also contained pianos on one floor so women on the staff could pretend to be music teachers if raided. Because of Constance's scrupulous attention to detail, her Ministry was the only Dáil department to escape a raid.

She maintained her connection with the Irish Citizen Army, doing what she could to improve the education of the workers. During that year, she stayed for a time in the house of Thomas Johnson, the first leader of the Labour Party in Dáil Éireann. Some labour activists believed that communism, as preached by Karl Marx, would see a return to a more communal way of life. Among them was Constance, although she had little time for labels. 'We're fighting for the working class,' she would say, 'call us what you like.' Like many traditional Sinn Féiners, she wanted to see a co-operative economy based on agriculture that would reduce the need for imports and see off the 'gombeen' middlemen.

In November 1919, Dublin Castle made an unsuccessful attempt to deport Constance as an alien, seeing her as a continuing danger to the public peace. The Home Secretary had pointed out that it was contrary to established practise to deport a British-born woman. Even worse, it 'might give the lady and her sympathisers a most undesirable advertisement' and it presented considerable practical difficulties. The whereabouts of her husband was unknown; he was either Polish or Russian, but no one knew which and then there was the problem of which country would be willing to take her; France and Holland were among the countries mentioned. Far better to keep control of her under Article 11 of the Aliens Restriction (Amendment) Act 1919, he suggested.

A crackdown in December saw a raid on the house where Constance was living. Dáil Éireann headquarters was raided and the Mansion House, official residence of the lord mayor, was occupied by troops. A total of 187 raids resulted in thirty-two arrests on political charges and nine deportations, although no charges were brought. The annual *Aonach* Christmas Fair was cancelled. No one knew when they would be arrested or for what reason. Constance was away when they came to arrest her. She asked Eva to try and find out what they wanted to charge her with this time – their English cousin, the Communist MP

Cecil L'Estrange Malone might know. She believed that the British were trying to provoke another rebellion so that they could eliminate the problem of Irish nationalism once and for all.

She continued to give the military the slip: 'It's awfully funny being on the run. I don't know whether I am most like the timid hare, the wily fox or a fierce wild animal of the jungle.' She moved from house to house with little difficulty. 'I fly around the town on my bike for exercise and it's too funny seeing the expression on the policemen's faces when they see me whizz by.'

At the end of 1919 came an appeal by Irish women activists to their 'sisters in other countries' for Irish internees to be recognised internationally as political prisoners. The document was signed by Constance for Cumann na mBan, Hanna Sheehy Skeffington for the Irish Women's Franchise League, Helena Molony for the Irish Women Workers' Union, Louie Bennett of the Irishwomen's International League, Maud Gonne MacBride for Inghinidhe na hÉireann, and Kathleen Lynn for the League of Women Delegates. An American Committee for the Relief of Ireland was established and shiploads of food and clothing were sent across the Atlantic, while fundraising continued. By the end of 1922, over £1.5m had been collected. Tensions remained high and, on 19 December, Lord French, the viceroy, was ambushed by Volunteers at Ashtown, just outside the Phoenix Park. One of the Volunteers, Martin Savage, aged twenty-one, was shot dead.

Dáil Éireann continued its effort to run the country while Ireland descended into a state of anarchy. Democratically elected members of the new parliament, most of them civilians, moved from house to house attempting to evade arrest and raids. On the streets, British soldiers, many of them shell-shocked or, at the very least, traumatised after long years in the trenches of Europe, behaved with savage brutality.

Yeats, in his poem 'Nineteen Hundred and Nineteen', put it graphically:

... a drunken soldiery
Can leave the mother, murdered at her door,
To crawl in her own blood, and go scot-free...

CHAPTER FIFTEEN

The Shadow of a Gunman

L ate in 1919, Sinn Féin had begun planning for the municipal elections scheduled for 15 January 1920. For the first time in Ireland, proportional representation would be used in an attempt by the authorities to undercut the republicans. Sinn Féin had no fear of the new system – at the Sinn Féin *ard fheis* held in April, Arthur Griffith, Eoin MacNeill, de Valera and Constance had all spoken in favour of it.

Although Constance attempted to get women to stand, she found them reluctant, many fearing for their own safety and with good reason. Whenever Constance spoke, the army or the police appeared soon after, although she usually managed to evade them. A directive of 14 January 1920 from W. E. Johnstone, Dublin Metropolitan Police Chief Commissioner, reported that Countess Markievicz had made appearances at two unannounced meetings in Dublin over the previous few days. He impressed 'on all who superintend' the grave importance of securing her arrest over the next day or two. 'To this end, enough force must be kept in reserve at Divisional Headquarters and a message sent to G Division the moment an unannounced meeting is discovered'. A motor van would also be kept available. Advice was also given that 'The police on the spot must act firmly and promptly, as the Countess never remains at a meeting for more than a few minutes and may possibly be heavily veiled and, therefore, difficult to recognise. Superintendents are advised to have at least three cyclists trawling the city on the look-out for impromptu meetings.'

In January 1920, under the initials C.M., Constance wrote an article for the *Irish Citizen*, pointing out the right of every family to have a good home, and urging women to vote in the municipal elections. She wanted new houses for workers built at once and her concern mirrored that of Labour and Sinn Féin. Constance advised women to demand a home with a good living room, two or three bedrooms, a boiler, gas cooker and coal cellar. This must have seemed quite luxurious to the working-class women of the time. She believed that living outside the city centre was better for children: 'crime and cruelty is found far less in these beautiful suburbs, where every housewife wears a dignified air of being mistress to a really good home with a lovely garden, where she can grow fruit, vegetables and flowers'. Like fellow nationalists, she saw the future Ireland as a bucolic idyll: 'We do not want a black country with all its slums, misery and crime to be built among the fair hills of Ireland.' Hostility to city life was not unique to Ireland; English and German intellectuals held similar views.

Women, as household managers, should ensure that the house was kept clean and tidy 'no matter however simple and poor it might be'. Constance argued that the state was but a larger version of the home, and advised women of every class to 'arouse themselves and take the keenest interest to abolish all slums and to see in Dublin a city built worthy of the lovely mountains and the surrounding country and sea'.

In another article, Constance appealed to women to start campaigning against assaults on children. Judging such cases, especially when they concerned girls, was proving problematic because most of the officers of the law, although they meant well, were men, as Constance had seen for herself when attending court cases. Women magistrates and solicitors were needed to counteract this bias. She liked to give women jobs and felt her time in jail had helped bring women into the open: 'The shyest are ready to do my work when I'm not there.'

A child, representing the future, was the responsibility not just of the parents but also of the community. She pointed out that it was mostly working women who were driven to desperate acts when their children were cold and hungry and who then ended up in jail, as she had witnessed at Aylesbury. Education was the key: 'only when all children of a nation have the same education will they have the same chances in life and learn to look after the people as a whole'. Working-class mothers were in a desperate situation, especially when their men were on the run. She commented that 'the whole economic position of

Ireland has reduced our workers to such a terrible state of poverty and uncertainty that one bows in admiration to the splendid mothers of the lovely children that they have given to Ireland with such unthinkable suffering and self-denial'.

Although she helped out at St Ultan's, the children's hospital Kathleen Lynn had founded at Charlemont Street in 1919, Constance had little to say about maternity and birth control clinics, possibly reflecting the predominantly Catholic ethos of the Dáil and the puritanism of the time. Nor did Constance demand state welfare, although she had supported the abolition of Poor Law doles and the provision of a widow's pension in her election campaign.

A total of forty-three women were elected to local councils and boroughs. Of the thirty-three county councils, twenty-nine had Sinn Féin majorities, along with 172 rural district councils, all of them pledging allegiance to Dáil Éireann. Republican justices or 'Brehons' were often women, among them Hanna Sheehy Skeffington, president of the Court of Conscience at Dublin Corporation. Anne Ceannt and Áine Heron served in Rathmines Pembroke before it was amalgamated with Dublin Corporation, and Kathleen Clarke was elected alderman for both the Wood Quay and Mountjoy wards. Yet there was a feeling that women's involvement in public affairs was merely a product of the extraordinary times. The important administrative, political and military decisions were still taken by men.

Overall, eleven of the twelve Irish cities voted republican in the election; Belfast was the only exception. The British continued to ignore the clear wishes of the people, as they had done after the general election. Every day came new tales of raids and reprisals. The military and the police continued to harass republicans, roaming the street with what Constance called 'covered wagons', rounding up and searching suspected republicans and, with bayonets fixed, charging at curious civilians who may have gathered, knocking women and children to the ground and causing untold injuries.

With the *Irish Bulletin*, the Dáil's official gazette, publicising details of British acts of aggression, international concern was increasing. Several fact-finding missions came to Ireland, registering a damning catalogue of brutality, destruction and murder in an atmosphere of sheer terror. After its visit in November 1920, the British Labour Party called for the withdrawal of British troops and the setting up of an Irish Constituent Assembly. Its appeal was ignored.

Constance was now fifty-two years of age and occasionally her cheerful mask slipped:

> It is rather wearying when the English Man Pack are in full cry after you, though I get a lot of fun out of it ... I have had some very narrow shaves. The other night, I knocked around with a raiding party and watched them insult the crowd. I was among the people and I went right up to Store Street Police Barracks where the military and the police lined up before going home. Night after night they wake people up and carry off someone, they don't seem to mind who. Some of the people they took lately did not belong to our crowd at all.

She became adept at disguise – a favourite was a particular Victorian bonnet that transformed her into a fragile old woman. She was recognised but never betrayed even when, on one memorable occasion, she raced for a tram, lifting up her long skirt. Nora Connolly remembered a trip with 'granny' into Dublin's city centre. Constance, with a gleam of mischief in her eye, hopped nervously on and off the footpath until an unwary policeman escorted her across Sackville Street.

There was a much-told tale of her hiding incriminating documents in plain view. Hearing a raid was imminent, Constance stuffed her papers into a trunk, hailed a taxi and, after some thought, brought it to a friend who owned a pawn shop. There the trunk was placed in the front window with an elevated price tag so that no one would be tempted to buy it.

In March 1920, Constance went to stay with the O'Carroll family. 'Auntie' remained for eight months and was remembered by the family for her enthusiastic gardening and her attempts to learn the Irish language. She soon threw off her little old lady disguise and returned to the work of her department, Mrs O'Carroll reported.

On 1 March, in a letter asking for support for the Republican Loan, she described the difficulties Ireland's representatives were having, with collectors in constant danger of imprisonment: 'On mutual trust and mutual help our Republic is being built up – a trust founded on our mutual love of Ireland and sanctified by our mutual participation in the Great Awakening when the Republic was proclaimed from the GPO in Easter Week 1916.'

Despite the best efforts of the British, Sinn Féin was quietly establishing itself as the government of the country. The Republican courts, functioning all over the country, had earned a reputation for fairness and became widely popular; cases appearing before the Assizes shrivelled. Running the courts was not easy since, wherever they were held, raids by the British military could be expected. The Republican Loan was heavily subscribed, despite its underground nature. Although they subpoenaed nearly every bank manager in Dublin, the British could not discover where the fund was kept and, when they brought in a detective, Alan Bell, to investigate, he was shot dead within a month by one of Collins's men.

Lessons had been learned from 1916 and the war against the British occupier was led not by armies but by 'Flying Columns' – small groups of guerrilla fighters who could move quickly, attack and then disappear. For a young man with an adventurous streak, membership of a 'Flying Column' was exhilarating; they lived as outlaws, sleeping in barns and fields and cadging food from sympathisers. Overseeing the new militancy was Michael Collins, who had stepped into the leadership vacuum when de Valera left for the USA in June 1919. In Dublin, Collins continued to operate his own 'executions squad'; his men posed as builders' labourers, wearing guns under aprons. Like Constance, Collins was miraculously invisible. He had spies everywhere.

As usual in war, it was the civilians who suffered: 'Shot in the back to save the British Empire, an' shot in the breast to save the soul of Ireland,' the character Seumas Shields says in Seán O'Casey's play, *The Shadow of a Gunman*. Shields expressed the views of many neutrals: 'I'm a Nationalist meself right enough ... but I draw the line when I hear the gunmen blowin' about dyin' for the people, when it's the people that are dyin' for the gunmen!' Many rebels and their families took to sleeping in the fields by night. Women were dragged into a conflict over which they had no control. All they could do was wait for news of their husbands, fathers, sons and brothers; it left many feeling helpless and bitter.

By February 1920, there had been 5,000 raids, over 500 arrests and ninety-eight towns sacked and burned. A total of 203 were killed by the British forces and 48,474 families had their homes raided. Of the seventy-two Sinn Féin members of parliament, sixty-four had been arrested and a further two deported. The six remaining, including de Valera, were abroad. A curfew from midnight to 5am was extended to 8pm to 5am. In April 1920, prisoners in Mountjoy went on hunger strike and, after eleven days, they were released, helped by a general strike in Dublin. The British were starting to show some respect for Sinn Féin.

During the last days of March 1920, the English cabinet had adopted a more aggressively military policy in Ireland, with Sir Nevil Macready appointed as Commander-in-Chief of the English Army of Occupation in Ireland. Because they were opposed to this policy, three Royal Irish Constabulary (RIC) officials were asked to retire. In the five months following, 133 Irish towns and villages were sacked, shot up or partially burned. Policing became a problem because of the dwindling number of local people signing up for the RIC, with barracks in many rural areas closing. To boost their number, the British had opened the ranks to the thousands of ex-soldiers who had failed to find work after the war, often with good reason. Because the dark green uniform of the RIC was in short supply, these new recruits were given Army khaki with an RIC cap and belt. They became known as the 'Black and Tans'. RIC officers had little notion of how to deal with the unruly ex-soldiers, many of them working-class Londoners, who had no experience of community policing, let alone rural life.

The Black and Tans were followed by an even more fearsome force: the Auxiliaries. These former army officers, wearing blue uniforms and glengarry caps, were paid £1 a day, compared to the ten shillings given to the Black and Tans. While the Republicans hated the Black and Tans, they both loathed and feared the Auxiliaries who were often drunk and, on the flimsiest of excuses, repeatedly assaulted men and women alike in a vicious manner. Although the Lord Lieutenant estimated that there were at least 100,000 Sinn Féin members, only 15,000 of these – at most – were in 'active service'. They would have to employ all their ingenuity to deal with a well-organised British army of 20,000, and a further force of 20,000 policemen.

One effective method of hampering British army movements was employed by Transport Union staff who, in the six months from May 1920, refused to work on trains carrying the British army or to handle military equipment or stores at the docks. Sinn Féin also benefited from a superb intelligence system, including spies in Dublin Castle, organised by Michael Collins.

In May 1920, Dublin Corporation, dominated by Republicans, acknowledged the authority of the Dáil as the duly elected government of Ireland. That month, Constance received a death threat 'from the Black Hand gang in the police'. It was printed on paper 'they had taken the precaution of stealing from us'. She wrote to a friend that the police were clearly plotting to murder her and others, and were manufacturing evidence 'to prove that we assassinated each other'. In the same letter, she reports that, at the annual Fianna *Aeraiocht*: 'The boys made Aunt Sallies in the form of hideous caricatures of police and soldiers painted on boards – these were a great attraction'. On 14 May, she defied the authorities when she made a dramatic appearance at an open-air meeting in Croke Park held to commemorate the dead leaders of 1916. In June, she attended the annual Wolfe Tone commemoration at Bodenstown.

On 29 June 1920, the Dáil met for the first time since October; it was maintaining its efforts to function as the respectable face of nationalism, with TDs wearing suits and carrying briefcases. With de Valera still in the USA, Arthur Griffith presided. He highlighted the success of the National Land Bank, which had helped settle a land crisis in the west of Ireland, as well as of the Land Arbitration Courts and the Industrial Commission. As Minister for Finance, Michael Collins had managed the greatest feat of all – the Republican Loan was over-subscribed by £40,000.

Earlier that month, on 19 June, Colonel Gerald Smyth, recently appointed divisional commissioner of police for Munster, had made an explosive speech at the RIC barracks in Listowel – the only police barracks in Munster that had refused to co-operate with the military. Forgetting that he was addressing policemen, not soldiers, he advised officers to do their best to wipe out Sinn Féin. If a police barracks was burned down, then the RIC was to take over the biggest house in the locality and throw the occupants in the gutter. If civilians on the roads did not respond to a 'Hands Up' order, they were to be shot: 'innocent persons may be shot, but that cannot be helped ... The more you shoot the better I will like you.' His listeners were aghast and when Constable Jeremiah Mee was asked whether he was prepared to co-operate, he removed his cap, belt and bayonet and called Smyth a murderer. Smyth ordered his arrest, but backed off when Mee's comrades swore the room would run with blood if the order was carried out. Mee and thirteen others immediately resigned. Other Munster barracks stood by their Listowel comrades.

Not until 10 July was Smyth's speech printed in the *Freeman's Journal*, with explosive effect. A day later, Mee and some of his colleagues went to Dublin to meet Dáil members, among them Michael Collins and Constance, in the offices of the Irish Labour Party. In Westminster, Lloyd George, after promising a full investigation into the incident, called Colonel Smyth back to London. Two days after his visit, Colonel Smyth was shot dead by the Irish Republican Army (IRA) at Cork County Club. His funeral in Banbridge, County Down on 20 July was followed by a three-day pogrom against local Catholic homes and businesses, with one Protestant man shot dead and three Irish nationalists convicted of firearms offences.

Patience was running short on all sides. The daily newspapers of 24 July announced that, in future, hunger strikers would not be released until they had served their full term of imprisonment and that the holding of inquests on Sinn Féin victims would be made illegal. Colonel Smyth may have been dead but the policy he had outlined in Listowel was very much alive.

Between July and September 1920, the Labour ministry sorted out 129 strikes. Constance came to believe that workers all too often opted to go on strike without any coherent policy, distracting attention from the fight for Irish independence, which she still saw as fundamental. She supported strikes that could weaken British control, such as the munitions transport strike. Workers' living conditions needed attention and the ministry decided to investigate the wages and hours of employees in agriculture, industry and commerce. Unemployment was a critical problem, with another recession biting and 100,000 jobless. Among them were hundreds of ex-RIC men; about 1,590 RIC men resigned in 1920 alone.

Unrest in the countryside remained a concern and she proposed investigating farm profits, establishing co-ops and taking over the Irish Packing Company; all practical ideas. The cabinet listened and did nothing. Constance ran into trouble with a fishing co-op in Kerry, where money went astray. Even with co-ops, difficulties could arise: 'The old problem always remains: how to prevent all the money and power, etc. getting into the hands of a few, and they establishing themselves as a ruling tyrant class.'

During the land agitation of 1920, Constance helped to settle a number of land disputes. She seconded a proposal to distribute vacant land and farms to the unemployed and landless. This was not supported, largely because Sinn Féin had its heartland in rural areas, where the 'big farmers' created most of the country's wealth. In the Dáil sessions of 6 August and 17 September, ministers heard of more arrests and reprisals, and also of attacks on creameries, mills and bacon factories as part of British strategy to slow the economy.

Lissadell had experienced its own labour problems, with Alderman John Jinks of Sligo recruiting farm workers for the Irish Transport and General Workers' Union and calling for a strike after a dispute about conditions. Constance wrote to Josslyn, reminding him that he came from a family of 'tyrants and usurpers'. Josslyn was far more concerned about the plight of his dairy cows, which had to be milked twice a day. When the workmen came back to work, they milked the cows on to the ground. There were also IRA raids; in one, which took place while the family was at church, the raiders failed to find the guns they were looking for, but took Josslyn's favourite gun case, which he later found hidden in a gorse bush.

Over the summer, Constance broke the curfew to visit Alfie Byrne, who spent much of his time travelling between Ireland and England attempting to help political prisoners. After tapping on his window, she handed him a roll of music that contained a warning for nine of 'our boys' in London who were going to be arrested. Byrne immediately set out for London and reached the men before the police.

Early in August, Constance summonsed Jeremiah Mee to her office at 14 North Frederick Street, receiving him with Michael Collins 'in the most friendly manner'. She wanted him to take charge of a bureau she was setting up to find jobs for ex-RIC members. Mee was given his own room and Constance delighted in introducing him as 'an RIC man from Kerry' to the prominent IRA men who came to meet her. Although initially Collins was not ready to trust Mee, after a month, he admitted that his first impressions were wrong.

Mee found Constance 'a grand person to work with' and one of the few to understand that 'the question of the RIC was an economic rather than a political one'. With Mee's help, she composed a letter to likely employers seeking work for ex-RIC men 'as clerks, agricultural workers, stewards, watchmen, agents, motor drivers, caretakers, etc'. She placed advertisements in the daily papers, with the authorities interpreting this as 'spreading disaffection among His Majesty's Forces', an offence punishable under the Defence of the Realm Act. To boost morale within the police force, the British authorities, led by Chief Secretary Hamar Goodwood, started a paper called Sir Hamar Greenwood's *Weekly Summary*, in which both Constance and Mee figured prominently.

On 26 September 1920, Constance went on a brief trip to Wicklow with Seán MacBride, who was bringing a French writer, Maurice Bourgeois, to see his mother Maud Gonne. When she heard of the trip, Constance insisted on joining them. MacBride was driving a borrowed car that kept breaking down and on their return to Dublin, the car was stopped in Rathmines by police because of a faulty tail lamp. When MacBride admitted he did not have a permit to drive the car, the police lit a match and, peering into the car, realised that one of the passengers was the notorious Madame Markievicz. Also in the car, along with Bourgeois, was a stranger who had missed the last tram and was walking home when offered a lift. 'All the King's horses and all the King's men with great pomp and many large guns' then arrived and a weary night in prison followed for all four. Bourgeois was in Ireland to collect material for the French War Museum and to write articles on Ireland. When he arrived, he had been hostile to Sinn Féin, but after spending two days in a filthy cell, despite showing his diplomatic passport, he became one of the organisation's stoutest champions.

Constance found herself back in Mountjoy Gaol, where she was to spend ten trying weeks with no access to painting materials and limited visitors. Her first thoughts were of her sister, then in Italy, and she wrote to Jennie Wyse Power asking her to send Eva a postcard assuring her that she was well. She added that she was attempting to learn Irish but found it difficult. Her Department of Labour continued its work firstly with Joe McGrath and, after he in turn was arrested, with Joe McDonagh.

While she was in jail, the focus of the world again turned on Ireland with the death on 25 October of Terence MacSwiney, the Lord Mayor of Cork, on the seventy-fourth day of a marathon hunger strike. MacSwiney had been arrested, along with ten others, on 12 August at a meeting in Cork and he had been charged with possessing documents that might 'cause disaffection to His Majesty'. With the others, he went on hunger strike in protest at the continuing arrest of public representatives. On the third day, MacSwiney was taken to Brixton Jail. On 17 October, Michael Fitzgerald, one of the hunger strikers, died. MacSwiney lived for eight more days; within a few hours, Michael Murphy, aged only twenty-two, also died.

Thousands turned out when MacSwiney's tricolour-draped coffin was paraded through the streets of London accompanied by an honour guard of Irish Volunteers. On 31 October, he was buried in Cork. Constance wrote to Joseph McGarrity, a leading member of the Clan na Gael organisation in the United States, about MacSwiney's death: '[t]here is exaltation and joy in the fighter's death, with the passion and glory of the battlefield, but to lie in a prison cell ... requires a courage and strength that is God-like'.

The day after, on 1 November, Kevin Barry, an eighteen-year-old medical student, was hanged in Mountjoy Gaol; he was the first republican to be convicted under the new Restoration of Order to Ireland Act, by which republicans would be tried by military court martial. Barry had been part of a group that had ambushed a party of armed British soldiers during which one of the soldiers had been shot dead. Although there was evidence that Barry's gun had jammed and that he could not have been the killer, he was tortured before his execution by a hangman brought over from England. No local would touch Barry. In a poem she wrote at the time, Constance describes Barry as 'simple and pure and brave'.

Three weeks later, in the early hours of Sunday, 21 November, fourteen British MI5 officers, linked to the Cairo Gang of undercover agents, were shot dead on Collins's orders at various locations in Dublin, many of them in their beds. A further six were injured. Retaliation was swift. Croke Park was the location that afternoon of a big football match and the stands were full. With the match already underway, the

Black and Tans appeared and began shooting into the crowd. Hundreds were injured in the panic and, when the firing stopped, twelve lay dead, with another sixty wounded. It was a miracle that more had not died. From her prison cell in Mountjoy, Constance could hear the sound of the machine guns, reminding her of Easter Week. That night, three IRA men were shot 'while trying to escape' from the guard room at Dublin Castle. At the inquest it was clear that they had been beaten to death. An editorial in the *New Statesman* of 30 November wholeheartedly condemned the murder, theft and arson committed by the Black and Tans and the 'state of government terrorism' prevailing in Ireland.

In the autumn of 1920, the Manchester branch of the Women's International League had organised a fact-finding mission to Ireland. Following the publication of its report, a series of public meetings were held in England with 'magic lantern' slides of ruined homes and burned out-shops and buildings illustrating the shocking conditions. Resolutions were sent to the government demanding the liberation of prisoners and a truce.

On 2 December, Constance's courtmartial in front of eight judges began at the Royal Barracks. Based on Fianna literature found in a raid the previous September at 26 Nassau Street, where Eamon Martin was living, she was charged with organising the Fianna ten years earlier. In the courtroom were Maud Gonne MacBride, Hanna Sheehy Skeffington, Kathleen Lynn and the war correspondent Henry Nevinson. Photographers who took pictures were asked to surrender the plates.

On the second day in court, Constance cross-examined witnesses. She asked for proof that any Fianna boy had ever attacked the British armed forces. She denied the allegation that she was responsible for the shooting of a policeman who had arrested her. Since Easter week, she said, terrible things had been put into her mouth that she had never had a chance to disprove: 'I am willing to sacrifice everything to Ireland except my good name.'

She was sentenced to two years' hard labour on Christmas Eve and wrote to Eva telling her not to bother about her:

> As you know, the English ideal of modern civilisation always galled me. Endless relays of exquisite food and the eternal changing of costume bored me always to tears and I prefer my own to so many

people's company ... I have my health and I can always find a way to give my dreams a living form. So I sit and dream and build up a world of birds and butterflies and flowers from a sheen in a dew drop or the flash of a seagull's wing.

During the previous year, ninety-eight civilians had been killed by unprovoked fire, thirty-six assassinated while in prison and sixty-nine shot in their beds or on the street. The British public was beginning to express its revulsion. Still the violence continued. In December 1920, martial law was proclaimed in Cork, Kerry, Tipperary and Limerick and later extended to all the Munster counties as well as to Kilkenny and Wexford. Soldiers arrested and destroyed almost at random; anyone caught with guns or ammunition was liable to be executed. On the night of 11 December, Auxiliaries set fire to Cork city centre, and the city hall and downtown shopping area were destroyed. In the censored press, the fire was attributed to natural causes. Explosions, gunfire and violence had become a way of life in Ireland.

On 23 December 1920, the Government of Ireland Act became law. It allowed for two parliaments: one in Dublin, one in Belfast. During the year, British politicians had considered a bill that would provide for two parliaments linked by a joint council, with some powers reserved for the British parliament. That month, de Valera finally returned to Ireland after eighteen months in the USA. During his absence, the political landscape in Ireland had altered. Hardline republicans, including Constance, opposed the Government of Ireland Act. She pointed out that the ultimate powers under the bill were 'vested in a viceroy and a Privy council who are merely servants of the British Cabinet'. Ireland would have no control of its finances or of its industries. A total of £18m in Irish taxes would go to London 'for England's debts'. The British army of occupation would 'continue to terrorise, murder, insult and rob our people'. In summary, the proposed Irish parliament would be little more than a talking shop.

After she had been in jail for two months, Constance was joined by Eithne Coyle, a Gaelic League organiser originally from Donegal, but working in Longford and later in Roscommon. Coyle was arrested on New Year's Eve 1920 and, on 29 February 1921, was sentenced to three years' penal servitude for aiding IRA members. Coyle remembered

Constance's love of gardening and how she had asked for dung. Several sacks of manure were delivered, helping her to grow both sweet peas and eating peas, despite the starlings and pigeons 'making war on everything'. She was continuing her study of the Irish language and was on the fifth book of 'O'Growney' when Coyle arrived. Already in Mountjoy was Eileen McGrane, a lecturer at University College Dublin, who had also been arrested on New Year's Eve, along with Máire Rigney and Lily Dunne. Later, the Sharkey sisters and Peg McGuinness arrived from Athlone Barracks, followed by Linda Kearns from prison in England, along with Frances Brady and Molly Hyland.

The horrors continued. On 14 March, six men were executed in Mountjoy after an attack on an RIC patrol in Drumcondra, Dublin. In April, Father Sweetman visited Constance in Mountjoy, bringing a gift from Eva of a green and silver rosary blessed by Pope Benedict XV in Rome. Because of Eva's deteriorating health, she and Esther Roper had spent much of the previous year in Italy and, while in Rome, they had stayed with the Irish Papal Envoy, George Gavan Duffy, and his wife, Margaret.

On 24 May 1921, elections under the Government of Ireland Act were held. Sinn Féin took part in the elections but refused to recognise the two parliaments. Instead the party treated the elections in both parts of Ireland as elections to the Second Dáil, which would govern one united country. Since none of the 128 candidates put forward in the south were opposed, no polling took place. The 124 Sinn Féin candidates and the four from Trinity College would make up the Second Dáil; Constance was joined by five other women – Mary MacSwiney, Ada English, Kathleen Clarke, Kate O'Callaghan and Margaret Pearse.

Constance watched and listened from her prison cell. She never gave up hope:

> Italy certainly fills one with hope, Greece too and Poland. We are the only ones left in chains ... it all makes one feel that we must win; the spiritual must prevail over the material in the end; we suffer, and suffering unites us and teaches us to stand by each other. It also makes us friends everywhere, while the policies of our enemies is leaving them friendless.

On 15 May 1921, Lord French was replaced as viceroy by Lord FitzAlan, the first Catholic to hold the position. In June 1921, the Government of Northern Ireland was formally established and, on 24 June, Prime Minister Lloyd George wrote to Éamon de Valera proposing peace discussions. A truce came into force on 11 July. Three days later, de Valera met Lloyd George in London. Constance knew little of what was happening and, in one of her final prison letters, she wrote of her plans for her rock garden.

On Sunday, 24 July, with the Truce now in operation, Constance was told by the Mountjoy prison governor that she was free to go. Eithne Coyle had become so devoted to her that she cried for a week after she left and was comforted with drinks of hot milk by a friendly wardress. Constance was now homeless. St Mary's had been rented out for many years, but Josslyn had been forced to sell the house to help pay for his rebel sister's expenses. She had nothing left of material value.

CHAPTER SIXTEEN

'I have seen the stars'

Constance revelled in her freedom: 'It is almost worthwhile being locked up, for the great joy release brings.'

With the British army back in their barracks and freedom fighters no longer on the run, she returned to work at the Department of Labour. From February 1921, the Department had organised an economic boycott of Belfast after thousands of Catholics working in the Belfast shipyards were forced from their jobs. Tensions had been high since July 1920 when, after the killing of a northern police officer in Cork, loyalists (many of them unemployed ex-servicemen) marched on the city's shipyards to force up to 7,000 Catholic workers and their 'rotten Prod' sympathisers from their jobs. From mid-1920 to the autumn of 1922, 465 people died and over a thousand were wounded in sectarian outrages and riots.

Constance opposed the boycott; she believed that splitting Ireland into two trading centres would play into British hands, giving them a good excuse for partition. Nor would it help trade union attempts to unite workers from all religious backgrounds against their common enemy. Despite warnings, not just from Constance but from Ernest Blythe and Arthur Griffith, a groundswell of local support ensured that boycotts began in various locations around the country. In March 1921, there were 184 boycott committees; by May that number had climbed to 360.

When it came to labour relations, the Department of Labour continued to work closely with the unions in attempting to resolve disputes through a series of conciliation boards. Among the arbitrators were Darrell Figgis, Tom Kelly, Ernest Blythe and Seán Moylan. Disputes ranged from the agricultural – the harvest bonus for farm workers – to disagreements in factories, offices and shops. Constance was deeply troubled by instances of religious bigotry, as in one case when the Catholic owner of a quarry in the north ordered his manager to dismiss a Protestant worker. She threatened to put such matters in the hands of the police if they were not resolved.

Despite the prevailing air of optimism, neither side was convinced that the truce would hold. Many republicans were still in jail and, of the 3,200 who were interned, including forty women, fewer than half had been tried. Among the women, mostly imprisoned for possessing Cumann na mBan literature, were two sisters called Cotter and their cousin, who were weeding turnips in a field when a Black and Tan lorry was blown up nearby. Elderly sisters, one aged seventy and the other eighty, from Ballinalee were briefly held for harbouring Seán McKeon after an ambush. Mary Bowles, aged fourteen, from County Cork, got five years for 'endeavouring to save a machine gun from capture'.

The Bolshevik revolution in Russia was attracting wide coverage at the time and affecting political thought. Britain, enjoying a post-war boom, and with its political system relatively unscathed, despite the war, was hit by a series of strikes that were giving hope to socialist revolutionaries such as Sylvia Pankhurst, whose *Dreadnought* magazine Constance read while in prison. In October 1921, Constance sent a memorandum to the cabinet warning of the imminence of social revolution. She feared a sequence of events, starting with 'small outbreaks growing more and more frequent and violent, the immediate result of which will tend to disrupt the Republican cause'. All that was needed was a 'violent popular leader'. She had been reading Lenin, who believed that a revolution could only be achieved by the strong leadership of one person, or of a very select few, over the masses.

Her busy life of speeches and meetings meant that the only time she had to read and ponder was when she was in prison. She reflected that Ireland had 'never produced a tyrant'. There was, in the Irish nature, a feeling for 'decentralisation' that she equated with modern 'soviets' or worker-led social groupings. That streak had also prevented the Irish from ever getting together 'under one head'.

After de Valera's negotiations with Ulster and London, interned members of the Dáil were released on 6 August so they could meet and discuss the terms of Lloyd George's proposals for the truce. Constance, influenced by meeting the mother of a boy killed in the fighting, did not condemn the proposals outright.

Although she had retained her seat in the elections, Constance lost her cabinet position when de Valera, appointed as president, reduced the cabinet to seven – Michael Collins, Arthur Griffith, Austin Stack, Cathal Brugha, William Cosgrave and Robert Barton. A further nine ministers were appointed, with Constance remaining Secretary for Labour. When de Valera proposed a constitutional amendment to ratify the cabinet changes, Kate O'Callaghan vigorously opposed the demotion of the only female member of the cabinet. She was supported by Mary MacSwiney, who warned that it would set a dangerous precedent. She was right – not until 1979 would another Irish woman, Máire Geoghegan-Quinn, be given full ministerial office.

The October 1921 convention of Cumann na mBan – the first since 1917 that was not suppressed – was its largest ever. With memories of the War of Independence still raw, the convention took place in an atmosphere of battle-weary determination. Constance, presiding for the first time in four years, argued that it was time for action not speeches; women must be ready to fight. She believed that the struggle was far from over and women were instructed to

> go out and work as if war was going to break out next week ... go and prepare yourselves to do good work for Ireland in the way you have done it in the past. Put yourselves in touch with your local Volunteers, avoid quarrelling, look over deficiencies, and try and work everywhere together wherever you can.

Cumann na mBan had evolved. Women, active participants in the war, felt that they had earned the right to be consulted about the peace. Members were more politically aware and capable of holding their own in debates, while restructuring meant that each Irish Republican Army company had a Cumann na mBan branch attached to it. Some tensions remained. Women were not screened as thoroughly as men and had a separate oath: 'I pledge myself to support and defend to the best of my ability the Irish Republic and to uphold the aims and objects of Cumann na mBan and the IRA'. Yet, since members tended to come from staunchly republican families well known in their localities, problems with informers did not arise. Few women had the freedom to uproot themselves and start afresh elsewhere, as men did.

On Hallowe'en 1921, Eithne Coyle, along with Linda Kearns, Eileen Keogh and May Burke, slung a rope ladder over the Mountjoy Gaol wall and escaped, with other women playing a football match to distract the warders. Waiting were the cars of St John Gogarty and Dr Pat McLaverty. One of the helpers was a petty criminal called Seamus Burke, whom Michael Collins rightly suspected of being a British spy. After lying low in the McLaverty house for a week, Coyle and Keogh arrived at the home of Maud Gonne MacBride in St Stephen's Green. One of their first visitors was Constance, who gave Eithne £5 to tide her over, telling her she need not pay it back. Coyle repaid her at the first opportunity. Next stop was a convent in Kilcullen, County Kildare, but when Burke's double dealings were discovered, the escapees were quickly moved to an IRA camp in Carlow. While there, the pair received a letter from Constance, representing the Cumann na mBan executive. After a complaint from Eileen McGrane, they were to be court-martialled for escaping without informing the other women prisoners, a charge that Coyle strenuously denied. The charge was later dropped.

To her great joy, Constance had, at last, received a letter from her husband, now settled in Warsaw and working as legal advisor and commercial counsellor to the American Consulate General, as well as writing and producing plays. The family home at Zywotowka had been burnt down by the Bolsheviks and the family had scattered. After five years' service with the Imperial Marine Guards, her stepson Staskou had married a Russian woman, Alexandra Ivanova Zimina, in the Orthodox church, but because the Bolsheviks did not recognise the union, Alexandra could not get Polish identity papers. The couple lost a newborn baby to typhus in the hard winter of 1920. In January 1921, Staskou was arrested by the Bolsheviks and held prisoner for twenty-five months. His wife left him to his fate.

Always conscious of the police censor, Constance replied in neutral tones to her husband's letter, giving the Mansion House, Dawson Street, as an address. She made inquiries about Casimir's family, reported on their furniture and hoped that, if the truce held, he might come and visit. In reply to his question about her plans, she wrote that she had none because it was impossible to make any 'at a time like this'. She had come into contact with 'many of the old acting crowd' in recent times and everyone was asking for him. 'I'm so sorry to hear about Stas. I wonder why anybody considers it wrong to marry the girl you love. Surely it was not political, he hated politics so.' She ended by asking him to write again soon, before signing off 'Yours ever'.

Constance had stayed with friends in Percy Place for a few months after the Truce. Early in the winter, she moved in with the Coghlans at Frankfort House in Rathgar – close to where she had lived with Casimir when they had come to Dublin some twenty years earlier. The Coghlan children were told that a Mrs Murray was coming to stay and, for ever after, she was Auntie Murray. In October, she was re-elected president of Cumann na mBan.

Negotiations for the terms of a treaty agreeable to both the British and the Irish were continuing. After a protracted exchange of letters, a conference was arranged. Trade, defence and Ireland's association with the British Commonwealth were key points to be discussed.

On 7 October 1921, the five Irish delegates to the conference were given their credentials. They were Arthur Griffith, Michael Collins, Robert Barton, Edmund Duggan and George Gavan Duffy; Duggan and Duffy were the legal advisors. Appointed as secretaries were Erskine Childers, Finian Lynch, Diarmuid O'Hegarty and John Chartres. Making up the British delegation were Lloyd George, Lord Birkenhead, Sir Laming Worthington-Evans, Austen Chamberlain, Winston Churchill and Sir Hamar Greenwood. De Valera's refusal to join the delegation has been debated ever since. After his talks with Lloyd George, he knew that there was no chance of the British approving an Irish republic. There was a good chance of the talks collapsing; if that happened, he believed that it would force further negotiations and, at that point, he might become involved and introduce his plan to leave Ireland outside the inner circle of the Commonwealth while maintaining contact with it. He believed this 'external association' solution would be an acceptable compromise for both the British negotiators and the republican 'die-hards'.

The Irish delegates were given instructions to 'negotiate and conclude on behalf of Ireland a treaty or treaties of settlement, association and accommodation between Ireland and the British Commonwealth'. While they had full power to negotiate, the draft treaty would be sent to Dublin for review before it was signed.

From 11 October until 6 December – eight weeks in all – the marathon negotiations continued in London. It was to prove an exhausting process with long days of meetings punctuated by frequent trips across the Irish Sea by the delegates; this would not have been necessary had de Valera agreed to travel. Telephone calls were not considered an option because of the risk of tapping. Undertaking most of the hard negotiating were Griffith and Collins. By the end of November, a rough draft of a treaty was hammered out. The new Irish Free State would have far greater powers than before but would give up its aspiration to a 32-county Ireland.

Under the eighteen articles of agreement, the Irish Free State would have its own parliament and executive. It would enjoy the same constitutional status as Canada, Australia, New Zealand and South Africa, with its representatives taking an oath of allegiance to the Crown. The country would have religious and educational freedom. Ireland would have its own army, although strategically important harbours, among them Queenstown (now Cobh), would remain in British hands. Britain would also have access to Irish airports and airspace.

The critical article concerned the status of 'Northern Ireland', which would have the right to decide whether it would remain separate from the Irish Free State. Should the North reject incorporation into the new state, a boundary commission would establish a border. When the Dáil met to discuss the document on 3 December, hard-line republicans refused to acknowledge the many concessions gained by the negotiators, as well as the potential for more in the future. They preferred to dwell on the negatives. They argued that Ireland would not have full fiscal independence, it would have no independent foreign policy and that its defence would lie largely in British hands.

The majority were prepared to live with the proposed terms, which went far further than any Home Rule bill. More difficult to resolve were the questions of an oath of allegiance to the king and the issue of splitting the country in two. De Valera argued that, with this treaty, Griffith had achieved neither full independence nor the national unity for which Republicans had fought so hard. He was less concerned about the oath, which he believed was meaningless. Collins agreed; he described the oath as the sugar coating on the pill. Others, most notably Cathal Brugha, emphatically did not agree. An appeal to de Valera to return with the delegates to London was rejected.

So it was that the weary delegates took the mailboat and train back to London, with no solid idea of the cabinet's position on key issues. After a heated debate on the issue of Ireland remaining in the Empire, which provoked a walk-out by the British negotiators, the Irish argued again for an oath to the Irish Free State rather than to the Crown – a formula suggested by de Valera. Finally, at 2.30am on 6 December, under threat of 'immediate and terrible war' from the Ulster Unionists, the exhausted Irish delegates climbed down and signed the treaty, without referring to the Dáil. Lloyd George, theatrically waving two letters and asking which one he would send to William Craig in the morning, had lived up to his reputation as 'the Welsh wizard'. He had outmanoeuvred the Irish.

Griffith and Collins were realists; they believed that the deal was the best they could negotiate under the circumstances and were aware that a fledging Irish Republic could be crushed in days if the British decided to renew hostilities, although this was unlikely since the British public had no appetite for further conflict, nor could the country afford the expense. The British had played a strategic game; in a volatile and changing world, the Treaty was a warning to other annexed states like India and Egypt that complete independence was not an option. Yet had the negotiators held out against the lurid and unlikely threat of a unionist invasion, some of the finer detail in the Treaty, such as the contentious issue of the Boundary Commission, might have been worked out in a more satisfactory manner.

In Dublin, de Valera was angry that the cabinet had not been consulted one final time. He failed to appreciate that negotiations, especially those held over a long period away from home, take on a life of their own. Both Griffith and Collins were heavy drinkers and all the plenipotentiaries were exhausted after months of shuttling back and forth across the Irish Sea. They wanted an end to it.

Hard-line republicans, including Constance, Cathal Brugha and Austin Stack, felt the Treaty was a betrayal of the Republic that they asserted had been in place since Easter 1916. With the cabinet split, de Valera issued a public letter on 9 December stating that he could not recommend acceptance of the Treaty. The following day, the influential 1st Southern Division of the IRA in Cork, although answerable to the Dáil, made it clear that it would not support the Treaty. Although most Irish people – businessmen, the bigger farmers, the press, the labour movement, army leaders and the Catholic Church – responded favourably to the Treaty, de Valera and the hard-liners continued to argue that it went against the majority opinion as expressed in the recent election.

After the delegates returned to Dublin, ten long and often acrimonious sessions of the Dáil took place in the Council Chamber of University College Dublin at Earlsfort Terrace. Private meetings on 17 and 20 December were followed by the first public sessions running from 19 to 22 December. From the start, a deep chasm appeared between the views of the pragmatists who supported the treaty and the idealists who still clung to the notion of a mythical Irish Republic. As the sessions wore on, speeches became fractious and personal.

Constance and Liam Mellows were the only two to speak on behalf of the beleaguered working class, pointing out that the Dáil had pledged itself to a workers' republic and not to the replacement of the British administration by a similarly privileged Irish ruling class. Those in favour of the Treaty argued that, in the Irish Free State, new industries would provide desperately needed employment.

Arthur Griffith pointed out that the job of the plenipotentiaries had been to negotiate the best possible deal, knowing that full independence was not an option, while Michael Collins argued that it was a stepping stone to future independence. George Russell was just one of Constance's old friends who supported the Treaty. When he told Constance, her response was succinct: 'George, you are an idiot.'

The question of the oath produced much arcane argument. Was it a question of the slave bending the knee to its masters, or an agreement between equals? The debates divided those who trusted the British prime minister and those who did not. Constance may have unwittingly weakened anti-Treaty support when, despite de Valera's opposition, she seconded a motion to adjourn the debate until after Christmas. Some believed that had the Treaty been put to a vote on 22 December, it may have been rejected. However, with fifty deputies still waiting to speak, an adjournment was inevitable.

The main avenue of publicity open to anti-Treaty Republicans was a weekly journal called *Phoblacht na hÉireann*, published in Scotland to by-pass Free State censorship. Constance, who was on the editorial committee, wrote a front page article for the 3 January 1922 issue. Under the headline 'Peace with Honour', she stated her belief that peace in Ireland was possible: 'Let the Irish people send an offer of peace to the English people, a peace that will bring confidence to Ireland, security to England, in which there will be no attempt to impose anything on the people of Ireland.'

On 3 January, when the debate resumed, Constance, in her Cumann na mBan uniform, was in more militant form. 'I rise today to oppose with all the force of my will, with all the force of my entire existence, this so-called Treaty.' She saw the oath as the biggest obstacle to accepting the Treaty – an oath to an English king when they had fought for an Irish republic would be dishonest. She would rather die than pledge an oath to King George, she said. In an emotional appeal, she also condemned what she saw as English ideals: 'love of luxury, love of wealth, love of competition, trample on your neighbours to get to the top, immorality and divorce laws'. Mere independence was not enough – she aspired to a co-operative commonwealth where workers would be equal.

She objected to southern Irish unionists sitting in a second chamber. These 'anti-Irish Irishmen' stood for 'that class of capitalists who have been more crushing, cruel and grinding on the people of the nation than any class of capitalists of whom I ever read in any other country', she declared. They had 'used the English soldiers, the English police and every institution in the country to ruin the farmer, and more especially the small farmer, and to send the people of Ireland to drift in the emigrant ships and to die of horrible disease or to sink to the bottom of the Atlantic.'

Because of her own background, she could speak out in this manner:

> Now you all know me, you know that my people came over here in Henry VIII's time, and by that bad black drop of English blood in me I know the English – that's the truth. I say it is because of that black drop in me that I know the English personally better perhaps than the people who went over on the delegation.

At this point, a pro-Treaty deputy interjected: 'Why didn't you go over?' 'Why didn't you send me?' was her riposte:

I have seen the stars, and I am not going to follow a flickering will-o'-the-wisp, and I am not going to follow any person juggling with constitutions and introducing petty, tricky ways into this Republican movement which we built up – you and not I, because I have been in jail. It has been built up and are we now going back to this tricky Parliamentarianism, because I tell you this document is nothing else.

While Ireland is not free, I remain rebel, unconverted and unconvertible ... I am pledged to the one thing – a free and independent Ireland ... a state run by the Irish people for the people. That means a government that looks after the rights of the people before the rights of property ... My idea is the Workers' Republic for which Connolly died.

Constance, who had seen too much bloodshed, claimed to have 'quite a pacific mind' and, although she was prepared to die for the cause of Ireland, she did not like to kill. Other Irish women TDs – and male deputies such as Erskine Childers – were less 'pacific'. Because all of them had either been involved in 1916, or had menfolk who had died for the cause, the 'women and Childers party', as they were dubbed, were dismissed as bitter fanatics. As the arguments became heated, many of the speakers were close to hysteria. The normally unflappable Arthur Griffith referred to Childers as 'that damned Englishman' while Constance hit Collins with a barb about his fondness for power and suggested he might like to marry an English princess.

On Saturday, 7 January 1922, a vote was taken: sixty-four for the Treaty, fifty-seven against. Arthur Griffith pointed out that the Dáil could not simply turn itself into the government of Southern Ireland and promised to keep the Republic alive until a general election. Two days later, de Valera, taking that as a vote of no confidence and a form of legal trickery, resigned his office. His re-election was immediately proposed by Kathleen Clarke and Liam Mellows, but narrowly defeated fifty-eight to sixty. De Valera did not vote; nor did Liam de Róiste, one of the few to foresee the impending disaster: 'I refuse to plunge my country into fratricide.'

Ever the realist, Michael Collins made an appeal for co-operation between the two sides, pointing out that 'when countries change from peace to war or war to peace, there are always elements that make for disorder and that make for chaos'. As he spoke, he held out his hand to de Valera. Mary MacSwiney intervened, spitting out her belief that there could be no union between the Irish Republic and the 'so-called Free State'. The moment passed and civil war became almost inevitable.

On 10 January, during a debate on Michael Collins's motion that Arthur Griffith be appointed president of the provisional government, de Valera and his followers walked out, refusing to vote. A tirade of insults followed, Collins calling them deserters and Constance responding by calling those who remained 'Lloyd Georgists', oath-breakers and cowards. The Republic she had fought for was no more. Though disappointed by the result of the vote, Constance was concerned that the walk-out would cause a split. In December 1921, she had expressed her understanding and sympathy for the delegates although she did not agree with them; she hoped they could all work together for the good of Ireland. After the Treaty was accepted, she stressed that order and peace were needed; disruption and disagreement would have serious consequences. These conciliatory words of hers are often unacknowledged.

When all had calmed down, the sixty-one deputies remaining voted unanimously for Griffith as their new president. He then proposed six cabinet ministers: Collins, finance; Gavan Duffy, foreign affairs; Duggan, home affairs; Cosgrave, local government, and Richard Mulcahy, who took over from Cathal Brugha in defence. Joseph McGrath succeeded Constance as Minster for Labour. Mulcahy, an IRA general, assured the assembly that the IRA, which two years earlier had placed itself voluntarily under the control of the Dáil, would remain the army of the Irish Republic. As it turned out, the army was soon split into pro-Treaty and anti-Treaty factions, with most of the headquarters staff in favour of the Treaty and many influential commandants on the anti-Treaty side. On 14 January, the parliament of Southern Ireland was convened by Arthur Griffith. Anti-Treaty deputies ignored the occasion. A provisional government was elected and, on 16 January, Michael Collins, as chairman, formally took over the administration of the country from the British in a ceremony at Dublin Castle.

Winston Churchill, in the colonial office, became chairman of the Cabinet Committee on Irish Affairs and the evacuation of the hated Auxiliaries and Black and Tans, along with regular British army personnel, began at once. The Royal Irish Constabulary was disbanded.

Hundreds of untried prisoners were released from detention camps and nearly 400 prisoners in British jails were given an amnesty.

On 21 January, members of the now disastrously divided Dáil met at an Irish Race Congress in Paris, planned for over a year with the aim of supporting Ireland's struggle for independence and promoting Irish trade. Representatives of seventeen countries were attending. Relations between the Republicans and the Free Staters were so poor that they travelled separately. In Paris, an exhibition of Irish art, as well as a series of concerts and lectures, began. Among the speakers were Jack B. Yeats on painting, W.B. Yeats on lyrics and plays, Douglas Hyde on the Gaelic League and Eoin MacNeill on history. Constance, Mary MacSwiney and Éamon de Valera were the Republican delegates to the congress and 'Hymn on the Battlefield', written by Constance, proved a favourite at one of the concerts. Attempts by Robert Brennan, who had organised the exhibition, to persuade the two factions to put on a united face proved fruitless. The grand ideals of the Easter Rising and equal rights for all seemed far away.

At the Sinn Féin *ard fheis* in the Mansion House on 2 February, presided over by de Valera, it was agreed to hold off elections for three months to allow a constitution, then being drafted, to be presented to the membership. Cumann na mBan had held a demonstration outside the Mansion House when the first meeting of the provisional government took place; it had become the first national body to reject the Treaty, voting twenty-four to two on a motion put forward by Constance. Members began snatching the tricolour away when it appeared on pro-Treaty platforms. A special convention was convened for 5 February to allow the overall membership to have its say; 419 voted to reject the Treaty; sixty-three were for it. Constance was re-elected president and the six women members of the Dáil all spoke strongly against the Treaty. Some prominent members supported the Treaty, among them Jenny Wyse Power, Louise Gavan Duffy, Min Ryan and Phyllis Ryan. These women, along with Alice Stopford Green, Alice Spring Rice and Griffith's wife Maud, left Cumann na mBan and founded Cumann na Saoirse.

The anti-Treaty women turned out in force for an enomous Republican demonstration in Sackville Street with speakers spread over three platforms. De Valera spoke on all three; Constance also spoke. Meetings, demonstrations and speeches followed all over the country as the hardline Republicans explained their opposition to the Treaty.

Around this time, Constance spent several weeks in London staying with Eva and Esther. She addressed meetings in London and in the Midlands, arguing the Republican case.

In Munster, the first skirmishes in what would become a bitterly fought civil war took place. Constance's native Sligo was not immune and, in February 1922, Josslyn was kidnapped from his office at Lissadell. Elsewhere, eight IRA men, who claimed that they had been on their way to a football match, were to be hanged in Derry for the deaths of two Belfast prison warders. In retaliation, the IRA rounded up a number of prominent Protestants as hostages, among them Josslyn, whose photograph was published in the *Daily Sketch* with a caption describing him as 'the brother of Countess Markievic [*sic*]'. Josslyn was taken by gunmen in uniform to a cottage on a side road near Grange where, with a Major Eccles, he spent the day. In the evening, the pair were released after word came through that the prisoners had been reprieved following an appeal to Sir James Craig, who had succeeded Edward Carson as leader of the Ulster Unionist Party in February 1921. Around this period, letters to Lissadell were often opened before delivery and marked 'Censored by the IRA'.

The provisional government met on 28 February and again on 1 and 2 March for three sessions. In his opening statement, Arthur Griffith said that the Belfast boycott had been discontinued and pointed out that every minister was working to see that the provisional government worked in harmony with Dáil Éireann, which would not meet until 8 June. Many activists were members of both bodies in a particularly confusing period of Irish history. Kate O'Callaghan brought up the question of giving votes to women between the ages of twenty-one and thirty so that they might vote in the June election. Her motion was seconded by Joseph MacDonagh. Updating the register would also give the vote to young men who had turned twenty-one since the previous register, many of them IRA members and anti-Treaty supporters.

On 2 March, Constance spoke, remembering her early days with the Sligo Women's Suffrage Society:

> That was my first bite you might say at the apple of freedom and soon I got on to the other freedoms, freedom to be a nation, freedom to the workers ... I have worked in Ireland, I have even

worked in England, to help the women to obtain their freedom ...
It is one of the crying wrongs of the world that women, because of
their sex, should be disbarred from any position or any right that
their brains entitle them to hold.

She had never been happy about women's passive attitudes to public
life:

There has been less physical restraint on the actions on women
in Ireland than in any other country, but mentally the restrictions
seem to me to be very oppressive. It is hard to understand why
they took so little interest in politics as a sex, when you consider
that both Catholics and Dissenters (men) laboured under all their
disabilities and yet remained politicians.

As a member of the privileged class, however reluctant, she did not
always grasp the problems facing ordinary women in a changing society.

Griffith saw the motion as a trick to prevent the proposed election
and, while he agreed that the register of voters was hopelessly out of date,
he argued that any revision must wait until after the election. He pointed
to his own unwavering support for women's franchise. Constance was
not placated. She accused Griffith of acting like the English parties who
supported women's suffrage when it suited them. For her part, she was
speaking on behalf of young women whom she counted in every way
as her superiors. They had high ideals, and the education that had been
denied her. They had proved their valour during the years of terror,
which had dragged them out of their shells more effectively than years
of work in franchise societies. She appealed to the men of the IRA to
see that justice was done to 'these young women and young girls who
took a man's part in the Terror'. If women were good enough to fight,
they were good enough to vote. Even de Valera supported the motion
saying, 'I, for one, would like to see this Dáil fulfil the pledges that were
given to the women of Ireland by the men of Easter Week.' Despite his
words, the motion was defeated forty-seven to thirty-eight.

Constance, in a letter to Eva, expressed her disillusionment, pointing
out that women wanted to vote so they could have their say on the
Treaty and that they now found their position 'humiliating'. The register

was 'a farce' and Griffith clearly feared that if the register was revised, the Treaty would be beaten. She added: 'Things are awful here. There are more people being killed weekly than before the truce.' It was around this time that P.S. O'Hegarty launched his vicious attack on 'The Furies', the title he used for the women then active in politics who had lost loved ones during 1916 and its aftermath. He argued that with women in power there would be no peace.

On 26 March, a convention of the IRA took place and, although it was banned by the provisional government, anti-Treaty members attended, with Liam O'Leary named chief of staff of the IRA's military council. Although they were firmly anti-Treaty and some 4,000 boys had moved up from the Fianna to the army in the previous two years, the Fianna decided to go its own way. In January 1921, a composite council consisting of three Irish Volunteers and three Fianna had been established. Membership was variously estimated between 17,000 and 26,000, most aged between fourteen and sixteen. After the truce in the autumn of 1921, a training camp was established at Loughlinstown on the road between Dublin and Bray. At an Easter Sunday *ard fheis*, Constance was unanimously re-elected Fianna chief in her absence.

That spring, Constance was chosen by de Valera for a tour of the USA; a Free State delegation had already travelled across the Atlantic and their views needed a counterbalance. On 1 April 1922, she sailed from Southampton on the *Aquitania* with Kathleen Barry, sister of Kevin. When they arrived at the quarantine station in American waters, Constance became the centre of attention when fifty journalists boarded the *Aquitania*. Writing to Eva, she said she found ships rather like jail: 'small stuffy cabin and crowds of people around you that you don't want'. She thought it awful not to be at home in Ireland, where the difficulties ahead were 'colossal'. 'I sometimes wonder if the rank and file will ever trust a leader again. I wouldn't be a bit surprised if the army, or some of it, started out doing things on its own.' She found comfort in de Valera 'the one, strong, personal influence in the country', who, she believed, had always used that influence for unity, toleration and sanity. He could turn people's minds from vengeance to higher matters. She thought him too noble to understand crooks.

When they arrived at the Cunard Pier in New York on 7 April, they were greeted by Father O'Flanagan, Austin Stack and J.J. 'Sceilg' O'Kelly, editor of the *Catholic Bulletin* and president of the Gaelic League, as well as a crowd of sympathisers. Her mission, she told the waiting press, was 'to put the truth before the friends of Ireland in the United States'.

Constance was to discover that opinion on the Treaty was as divided in the USA as it was in Ireland. While she received an enthusiastic reception in some places, in others she was excoriated as a communist. *Gaelic American* criticised de Valera's speeches and wrote nothing of Constance's tour. During her five days in New York, she attended meetings, held interviews and met supporters, firstly in Lexington, then Newark and finally Jersey City, as well as holding a secret meeting with Clan na Gael. She took a day off to visit Jim Larkin in Sing Sing Prison in upstate New York, where the warden gave her a tour of the penitentiary. She was impressed, finding it much superior to any British or Irish jail she had known. She loved American food and coffee but was not so impressed by central heating. She developed an addiction to chewing gum, considered very unladylike at the time.

Next stop was Philadelphia, where the delegation arrived to an enthusiastic reception at Broad Street station on Good Friday afternoon. The following day, Constance was shown the historic buildings of the city, including Valley Forge, where she achieved her ambition 'to walk in the hallowed footsteps of Washington'. She was thrilled to meet up with 'Chicago May' Sharpe, her old comrade from Aylesbury jail.

On Easter Sunday, she and Barry were escorted to mass by Irish-American Volunteers in uniform and a brass band. After a long lunch, they went to the Irish American Club. She made a speech assuring her audience that the anti-Treaty Republican movement did not consist merely of fanatical followers of de Valera, but existed out of a profound conviction that Ireland 'must and will be a Republic'. It would need moral and financial support, she added. Later in the day, they were accompanied by a bodyguard of 200 Volunteers to a meeting at the Academy of Music, where Austin Stack and J.J. O'Kelly shared the platform and Joe McGarrity chaired. While the audience cheered every mention of de Valera and booed references to Lloyd George, it showed a charitable attitude to Griffith and Collins; relations between the Free Staters and the Republicans were still cordial.

They travelled on to Detroit, followed by a quick trip across the border to Windsor in Canada. In Akron, Ohio, they received a cooler reception;

a local newspaper had published a leader praising the Free Staters who had visited a few days earlier. Cleveland, St Paul-Minneapolis and Butte, Montana, followed – all of them Irish-American strongholds. Although their arrival in Anaconda was delayed by a snowstorm, Constance was greeted by a standing ovation. In Butte, they were met by the Pearse and Connolly fife and drum band at the head of a large delegation of sympathisers. 'Butte was one of the places that stand out for its reception for they met us with a band and an army. All Sligo seemed to be there!'

She was shocked to see how the town's copper miners lived and she insisted on seeing how the men worked. 'I saw a man drilling the copper ore without the water appliance to keep the dust down and breathing in copper dust eight mortal hours every day. They told us few men live to be old in Butte, Montana.' On Sunday, 30 April, there was a meeting in Butte High School.

Next Constance travelled across the Rockies and the wastelands of Montana to the Pacific seaboard cities of Seattle and Portland. In Seattle, she was met by her friend and comrade Lily Kempson, a veteran of the Easter Rising, who had settled in the United States. The small party travelled to Portland and then on to San Francisco arriving on 6 May to be greeted by a deputation dressed in ancient Gaelic dress. While in San Francisco, the delegation received news of the forthcoming 'pact' election. After visiting Los Angeles, where Tom Clarke's son Daly was waiting, it was time to head back to the east coast with a spectacular five-day railway journey weaving around mountains and crossing ravines. By 14 May, Constance was back in the town of Springfield, Massachusetts.

Almost everywhere she went, Constance addressed enthusiastic crowds and met old friends. She repeated her antagonistic view of the Irish Free State – it was not Irish, not free and not a state, she said. After her meeting in Springfield, she spent a day with J.J. Hearn in nearby Westfield, Massachusetts, sitting under an apple tree in blossom, revelling in the lilac and discovering a bird's nest. On a child's blackboard, she saw a slogan written in Irish: 'Colmcille's prophecy full of hope for Ireland' signed by Liam Mellows. She liked what she saw of American towns and houses – they were well kept, with good gardens, no walls to separate them and the wonder of built-in wardrobes. In

Cincinnati, she found another beautiful garden, full of flowering shrubs and roses, at the home of A.J. Castellini, whom she had met at the 1922 Irish Race Congress in Paris.

A visit to Chicago followed and, after that, a farewell week in Boston, beginning with an address to members of Cumann na mBan and followed by meetings in New Bedford, Lynn, Norwood, Lawrence, Full River, Worcester and in the Maple Street playgrounds, Holyoke. Constance's journey brought home to her the immensity of the USA with its diverse landscapes and climatic conditions. She had started out in the east in early spring, shivered in Montana's winter snowstorms and enjoyed summery conditions in San Francisco. In Los Angeles, she marvelled at the palm trees and orange groves and, in Arizona, she was awestruck by the barren desert.

On 22 May, Constance was cheered for six minutes by a crowd of five thousand at a meeting in New York's Madison Square Garden. She made a powerful speech denouncing the Treaty as 'nothing but a surrender'. Her companion, Kathleen Barry, recalled her twin personality: the private Constance who was 'thoughtful, interesting and interested in the young' and the public Constance who was confident, extrovert and charismatic. The crowds loved her and she was careful – as always – to tailor her speeches to her audience. On 30 May, she and Kathleen Barry set sail for home on the Cunard Line's *Berengaria*.

While in St Paul, Constance had begun a long letter to Staskou. She explained that she had not written before because she was afraid of compromising him. She had sent him many messages through Eva, who in turn, had passed his messages on to her. 'You know I've had a pretty stiff time of it, about three years and a half, and some of it was awful.'

She referred to the time he was held captive. 'I did what I could to help you and I think that some of the people whom I got to intercede for you may have been a little help.'

She longed to see him again and worried about Casimir:

You were always as dear to me as if you had been my own son. Also dear Casi, I hate to think of him having to work on a job. Of course, we are all frightfully poor now, for money won't buy anything. I wonder if he got the money I sent him from Ireland. He never wrote, at least I never got the letter.

She revealed her growing weariness with politics: 'what I begin to believe is that all governments are the same, and that men in power use that power for themselves and are absolutely unscrupulous in their dealings with those who disagree with them'. She ended the letter 'Now goodbye darling boy and much love from your loving Mother.'

During this trip, Constance spoke to Kathleen Barry about her daughter Maeve, whom she had not seen since before her imprisonment in Cork. Despite having little money, she bought many presents for her, including Hudson Bay furs in Seattle. When the two women finally reached London, Constance spent her first day with Eva, returning to her hotel at about ten o'clock. Kathleen went to bed but was interrupted by a housemaid who told her that a woman wanted to see Constance, but that there was no answer from her room. Behind the chambermaid was a tall young woman who said she must see Constance. It was Maeve, who had heard through Eva that her mother was in London. When Barry suggested that she look downstairs, Maeve confessed that she was not sure that she would recognise her mother. Armed with a description from Barry, she went downstairs but was soon back unsure about whether the woman she had seen having coffee with two friends was indeed her mother. It was.

In Ireland, having two rival armies in one country was promising nothing but trouble; de Valera and Collins urged moderation and did their best to recreate the unity the rebels had known when opposing the British during the Anglo-Irish War. Unfortunately, fighting men thrown up in a crisis rarely have the patience and the negotiating skills necessary for a peaceful life. Most ominously, Ireland had no tradition of peaceful opposition to fall back on; disagreements were traditionally resolved by violence and the hard men admired. With the election dividing the nation, pistols were cleaned and rifles retrieved from lofts and attics. The country would again fall under the shadow of the gunmen.

CHAPTER SEVENTEEN

Anarchy is Loosed

On 14 April, the anti-Treaty Republicans occupied the Four Courts building on Dublin's quays in defiance of the provisional government. Smaller groups moved into other buildings, including the Rotunda Hospital, and Fowler Hall on Rutland (now Parnell) Square, which was then an Orange lodge. The aim was to force a new confrontation with the British that might reunite the two Sinn Féin factions.

Although Griffith wanted to quell this rebel act immediately, Collins stood back, wary of plunging the country into civil war. A week later, at midnight on 20 April, anti-Treaty fighters attacked pro-Treaty troops stationed at the provisional government headquarters in Merrion Square. They also attacked the Bank of Ireland on College Green, the telephone exchange in Temple Bar, and City Hall. Three people were wounded.

In early May, the anti-Treaty Republicans took over the centre of Kilkenny, with provisional government troops sent from Dublin to dislodge them. While the country slid towards civil war, an uneasy truce between the two sides was announced in the Dáil. Towards the end of the month, de Valera and Collins presented a plan for a national coalition panel that would skirt around the tricky issue of the Treaty and form a government after the forthcoming election. The panel would represent pro- and anti-Treaty groupings, with numbers depending on the relative strengths of the groups.

Constance attended her last Dáil meeting on 8 June. A photograph of the time shows her pushing her bicycle on a visit to her constituency; she is surrounded by children and looks thin and haggard. On the eve of the election on 16 June, she spoke at a rally on York Street, declaring that Sinn Féin wanted law and order in Ireland, as well as food for the starving and work for the unemployed. For the house of 128 members, ninety-four Sinn Féin candidates were returned. Of these, fifty-eight were pro-Treaty and thirty-six anti-Treaty. The Labour Party, one of the parties urging unity, returned seventeen members, the Farmers' Party seven, Unionists (Trinity College) four, and Independents six. The four South Dublin City deputies consisted of two pro-Treaty members from the agreed panel, as well as one Labour and one Independent deputy. Pro-treaty Sinn Féin won 239,193 votes, compared to 133,864 for anti-Treaty Sinn Féin, with a further 247,226 voting for other parties. Constance lost her seat, as did Margaret Pearse, Ada English and Kathleen Clarke. Kate O'Callaghan in Limerick and Mary MacSwiney in Cork were both elected in strong anti-Treaty areas. As far as the British were concerned, the election results endorsed the Treaty and it was absolutely clear that the people wanted peace. However, the anti-Treaty Republicans were not prepared to listen.

On 22 June, Field Marshal Sir Henry Wilson was shot dead on his doorstep in London by two members of the IRA's London battalion. Wilson, an Irishman born in Longford, had been military adviser to the six-county government and was blamed by nationalists – and Michael Collins – for the reign of terror against Catholics in the North. His murder provoked a wave of anti-Irish fury, and Winston Churchill made it clear that if the situation worsened, Britain would take whatever steps necessary to safeguard its interests in Ireland.

On 26 June, a motor car agency in Dublin's Baggot Street had sixteen of its cars 'requisitioned' by anti-Treaty Republican troops as part of the 'Belfast Boycott'. The officer in charge, Leo Henderson, was arrested by pro-Treaty troops and, in reprisal, pro-Treaty deputy chief of staff J.J. 'Ginger' O'Connell was kidnapped and held by the anti-Treaty troops in the Four Courts. This was the final blow for Churchill, who warned Michael Collins that if he did not act against the anti-Treaty Republicans, Britain would be forced to. Collins reluctantly ordered an attack on the Four Courts after an ultimatum to surrender was ignored.

On 28 June, after a day of rumour, the citizens of Dublin awoke to the boom of heavy guns; the Civil War had begun. Constance, some three miles away in Rathgar, recognised it for what it was – an attack on the Four Courts. The bombardment of the beautiful Gandon building continued, first using two and then four eighteen-pounder field guns. Spectators lined both sides of the Liffey to watch 'the show'. On the second day of the battle, Free State troops stormed the east wing of the building, taking over thirty prisoners. Three were killed and fourteen wounded. After two days of constant pummelling, fires were raging and the west wing of the building was shaken by a powerful explosion when the fires spread to the munitions stored in the Public Records Office. Priceless records dating back to the Middle Ages went up in smoke. In the mid-afternoon of 30 June, men in the garrison surrendered after throwing their weapons into the fire.

Fighting continued on Sackville Street, where members of the anti-Treaty Dublin Brigade, led by Oscar Traynor, had occupied a number of buildings on the east side of the street. Cathal Brugha, Éamon de Valera, Austin Stack and Robert Barton were among those reporting for duty, while Constance was one of several Cumann na mBan members mobilised. She would spend time at Barry's Hotel on Great Denmark Street with John Hanratty and at the Hammam Hotel in Sackville Street. From Whelan's Hotel on Eccles Street, she organised a group of Red Cross nurses to go to the west, among them the novelist Annie M.P. Smithson. The plan was to hold out for as long as possible and give the Irish Republican Army in the provinces time to mobilise. Since Easter Week, the Republicans had learned much about street fighting and they could not be cornered easily.

Some seventy men and thirty women were mobilised in the block from the Hammam Hotel to the Gresham Hotel on Sackville Street. Across the road, on Henry Street, was a sniping post on the rooftops, manned by two or three riflemen. One of those riflemen described his experiences in a 1960 newspaper article:

It made my position in the shelter of the cornice as dangerous a one as you could find. I was due for relief and I wasn't sorry for that. But when my relief came, who was it but Madame. Played out as I was after two or three hours up there under continuous fire, I didn't like the idea of a woman taking over that position. But Madame just waved me to one side with that imperious air she could put on when she wanted to have her own way. She slipped into what little shelter there was, carrying with her an automatic Parabellum pistol – the kind we used to call a Peter the Painter. I couldn't rightly say how long she was up there, for I was so tired that I drowsed off to sleep. But when I woke up, the first thing I noticed was something different in the sound of the firing. The steady, continuous rattle of fire that I had learned to pick out from the sound of rifle and machine gun fire up and down the street had ceased; the sniper's post in Henry Street was silent.

On 5 July, a group of twenty, including three women nurses, were ushered out of the burning Hammam Hotel by Cathal Brugha. Among the last to go were Constance and some of the other women who walked out the back door of the hotel. Brugha went out the front with a gun blazing from each hand. He was mown down and died two days later from blood loss after a fatal shot to the thigh. It was the end of eight days of fighting in Dublin's city centre with over sixty killed, about 300 wounded and a large part of the city in ruins.

Two days later, on 7 July, Churchill sent Collins a message of congratulations. The fighting was not over and, within months, some of the bravest and the best were dead: Collins, Mellows, Childers, Griffith. On 30 July, Harry Boland was mortally wounded in Skerries by Free State troops who had come to arrest him. He died on 2 August. Boland had been one of Collins's closest allies but, when he changed sides, was shot on the orders of his friend, according to a statement by Constance in the semi-underground *Fenian* bulletin that was published from July to October of that year. Cumann na mBan provided the guard of honour at his funeral.

On 12 August, Arthur Griffith, aged fifty, died in a Dublin hospital of a cerebral haemorrhage, paying the ultimate price for the strain of the previous decade. Ten days later, on 22 August 1922, Michael Collins was ambushed and shot dead at Béal na Bláth in County Cork by anti-Treaty fighters. Denis 'Sonny' O'Brien, a former Royal Irish Constabulary man, was believed to have fired the fatal shot. Collins was regarded by many as the only politician capable of restraining a government that would rely increasingly on a regime of legalised terror.

The newly elected third Dáil and provisional government finally met in Leinster House on 9 September at the main lecture theatre attached to

Leinster House, then owned by the Royal Dublin Society; the building was bought outright from the Royal Dublin Society in 1924. Whether the new Dáil was a republican parliament or a crown assembly was not at all clear. Republicans elected in June did not attend, with the exception of Laurence Ginnell. When he stepped forward to sign the roll, he queried under whose authority they were meeting. After several unsuccessful attempts to get his question answered, he was forcibly ejected from the meeting. William Cosgrave was elected president in succession to Griffith. The constitution was debated and enacted.

With anti-Treaty Republicans under constant threat of arrest, Constance was on the run, staying with a succession of friends. She wrote articles for pro-Republican publications in the USA and helped Maud Gonne MacBride with the Women's Prisoners' Defence League. She was in Carrick-on-Suir in March and April where workers' co-operatives had taken over creameries and factories. Later that summer, she visited Clonmel, delivering an address from the steps of the town hall. Carrick-on-Suir was taken over by the Free State Army on 2 August and Clonmel on 8/9 August.

In the late summer and early autumn of 1922, Constance produced an anti-Treaty paper, writing most of the copy, drawing the political cartoons and printing it off on a Roneo duplicator until the machine was seized in a raid. In September, following the ambush on Collins, carrying a weapon had become an offence punishable by death under the Public Safety Act. Martial law and military courts became a reality on 15 October 1922. 'If murderous attacks take place, those who persist in those murderous attacks must learn that they have got to pay the penalty for them,' William Cosgrave told the Dáil, adding that, although he had always objected to the death penalty, this was a last resort in an effort to restore order to the country. General Mulcahy argued that the act would help regulate the anarchy and unlawful executions taking place on both sides of the divide. The Labour Party's Thomas Johnson opposed the Bill, likening it to a military dictatorship.

A total of eighty-one men would be executed by the Irish Free State, with Erskine Childers on 24 November the most notorious case. His crime was to possess a small pistol given to him by Michael Collins. He was followed four weeks later by the four men who had surrendered the Four Courts and had been held since then without trial in Mountjoy:

Liam Mellows and Rory O'Connor, both former Fianna boys, along with Joseph McKelvey and Richard Barrett. Since their crimes had been committed before the October proclamation, the executions were thought to be a response to the murder of Seán Hales and the serious injury to Pádraic Ó Máille, both of them Dáil deputies, on 7 December. Maud Gonne MacBride and the Women's Prisoners' Defence League organised a protest against the executions outside the house of the Minister for Defence, Richard Mulcahy. The Catholic hierarchy decided to excommunicate all Republicans who 'in the absence of any legitimate authority to justify it [were carrying out] a system of murder'.

Saorstát na hÉireann, the Irish Free State, was proclaimed on 6 December 1922, the first anniversary of the Treaty signing in London. William T. Cosgrave was elected president and the veteran Irish nationalist Tim Healy was named Ireland's first Governor General. When Cosgrave issued his list of thirty senators, it included W.B. Yeats, Sir Horace Plunkett, Oliver St John Gogarty and Jenny Wyse Power. Among the thirty elected senators were Alice Stopford Green and Colonel Maurice Moore. On 7 December, the Northern Ireland parliament voted to remain part of the United Kingdom.

On 27 December, Æ's open letter to Irish republicans was published in the *Irish Times*. While admitting his fondness for the 'underman' in a conflict, he appealed to the republicans to change their thinking.

> No ideal, however noble in itself, can remain for long lovable or desirable in the minds of men while it is associated with deeds such as have been done in recent years in Ireland ... I do not like to think of you that the only service you can render Ireland is to shed blood on its behalf.

His words were ignored. The homes of senators became targets, with the houses of Sir Horace Plunkett in Foxrock and St John Gogarty in Connemara among the thirty-seven burned to the ground. In the Curragh, seven 'Irregulars' were executed in one day and, in February 1923, the father of Kevin O'Higgins, the hard-line Minister for Justice, was shot dead in his home in Stradbally, County Laois, by anti-Treaty republicans. Constance made no mention of this brutality in a letter to Staskou, writing only of her efforts to send him money and to find a job.

In January 1923, Constance, accompanied by May Coghlan, took a ten-week break from the unrelenting horror of the Civil War with a trip to Scotland, followed by a visit to Eva in London. 'The Red Countess' was fully occupied addressing meetings, visiting Sinn Féin clubs and attending receptions and fêtes. She averaged two meetings every Sunday and two or three during the week, outlining the appalling treachery and tragedy of the Treaty and its aftermath. The British Special Branch followed her movements closely but did not attempt an arrest, possibly because the meetings did not attract big numbers. The month she spent with Eva in London from mid-March was the first extended stretch of time the sisters had spent together in years. She enjoyed walking streets that were full of memories for her, passing the homes of old friends, the church where she had been married and other familiar haunts, including the House of Commons.

Phobhlacht na hÉireann, promoting the anti-Treaty argument, had ceased publication in January 1923 and was immediately succeeded by *Eire, the Irish Nation*, published in Glasgow until April and after that in Manchester. Constance was always ready to contribute and wrote several articles under the general heading of 'My Experiences of Easter Week', referring mainly to the bravery of others. In April, on the anniversary of Easter 1916, she was in Dumbarton, Scotland, where she moved her audience to tears with her description of the sufferings inflicted on republican prisoners by Free State jailers. She seemed relieved to be away from Ireland and the threat of ending up in prison again. However, she had told de Valera that she was willing to do 'anything' he ordered her to do either there or in Ireland.

Constance argued that the conflict in Ireland pitted the ideals of an ancient Gaelic civilisation against the 'modern, moral anarchy of industrialism'.

> The Gaelic civilisation was founded on ideas of co-operation and de-centralisation, and the ambitions and talents of the people were directed towards learning art, beauty and holiness which alone can bring happiness and a lasting greatness to a people, and away from the terrible competition for luxury which had led to all the miseries and vices of an industrial nation.

For Constance, the new senate was an excuse to entrench the old Anglo-Irish landlord class in the new administration, while many Castle officials were finding jobs in a free state, which, in its structure and administration, mirrored what had gone before. While this was disappointing for a champion of the working class like herself, Constance would prove a pragmatist, unlike the dwindling rump of hard-liners.

During this time, the implacably republican Mary MacSwiney, along with Kate O'Callaghan, Dorothy Macardle, Máire Comerford and Sighle Humphreys, niece of The O'Rahilly, were on hunger strike in Kilmainham Gaol, demanding better conditions. On the nineteenth day of MacSwiney and O'Callaghan's hunger strike, the governor decided to move eighty-one prisoners to the North Dublin Union in Grangegorman, close to the Broadstone railway station. It took five hours to remove them forcibly. The next day, MacSwiney was released, with her aim of becoming a martyr like her brother thwarted.

By April, Constance was back in Dublin and she travelled to Clonmel where, on 10 April, she and de Valera narrowly escaped when a meeting of Republicans to discuss ending hostilities was ambushed by the Free State Army. Liam Lynch, the anti-Treaty army leader, was shot and captured. While the IRA could muster about 8,000 fighting men, the Irish Free State could call on an army of 38,000 and, after meeting army executives, de Valera for the Republican government and Frank Aiken (who would later become a key Fianna Fáil minister) for the Free State Army agreed to a ceasefire that would begin on 30 April 1923.

Less than a month later, on 24 May 1923, the Civil War ended with weapons and arms dumped. Hundreds of lives had been lost and the cost had spiralled to about £17m. In a message to his followers, de Valera admitted that further loss of life would achieve nothing: 'seven years of intense effort have exhausted our people ... A little time and you will see them recover and rally again to the standard.' An estimated 11,316, including 250 women, were held in prison – most without trial. To keep them there, the government rushed through the Public Safety Act in June. A confident government then called an election for 27 August, expecting to get unambiguous support for the Treaty.

In 1923, mainstream politicians were paying scant attention to the curse of unemployment – they believed it was a problem to be solved by public works and support for home industries. With her eye always on the poor and downtrodden, Constance sought to combine the policies of Sinn Féin and Labour, believing it important that labour and republicans fought the same battles. Yet, in the run-up to the election of August 1923, Sinn Féin did not present any economic or social programme. In contrast, Labour came up with a moderate reformist programme, their goal a republic run on the lines of a co-operative commonwealth. While the aims of Labour mirrored those of Constance, there was one essential difference: Labour was pro-Treaty and, some even argued, pro-British.

For the election, a reorganised Sinn Féin put forward eighty-seven candidates, although most were still on the run. De Valera, in a note to Constance, had said that he had decided to take the risk of speaking on 15 August in Ennis. He was arrested and remained in solitary confinement without trial for almost a year. Of the 153 seats in the Free State parliament, the government party won sixty-three, five more than in 1922, while the Republicans won forty-four, eight more than in 1922. The Farmers' Party, representing larger landowners, took fifteen seats, one more than the Labour Party. It was the first time that women aged between twenty-one and thirty had voted. Constance regained her seat in South Dublin City, but she and other Republican representatives refused to take their seats in the new government because of the contentious oath to the king of England.

These were bleak days for radicals and idealists, with the government continuing to make arrests. The Free Staters, now called Cumann na nGael, were governing in the interests of the business community, farmers and professionals. Constance had long repudiated the wealth, status and privilege that they found important. Economic policy was conservative, aiming at fiscal rectitude and deflation, with salaries and pensions cut back and no possibility of growth. Ireland remained the poorest region in the islands of Britain and Ireland. Many were forced to emigrate, not only because there were few jobs on offer, but because employees of the new state were obliged to swear an oath of allegiance before they could take up jobs as teachers, gardaí or civil servants. Those in power blamed unemployment on indolence or the restrictive practices of trade unions; the poor were largely believed to have brought their misfortunes on themselves. Cosgrave relegated the Department of Labour, once so proudly run by Constance, to a section of the Department of Industry and Finance. Women workers were ignored and sidelined.

The new government's administrative machinery was far from Connolly and Constance's ideal of a workers' republic run on co-operative lines. The new state supported Gaelic culture and the Irish language, but socially it was extremely conservative and the influence of the Catholic Church was considerable. Women returned to the kitchen, divorce was made impossible and films and books were censored.

In September, a series of three articles written by Constance for the British Labour *Forward* publication were reprinted in pamphlet form as 'What Irish Republicans Stand For'. She dedicated the leaflet to the memory of Wolfe Tone, John Mitchel, James Fintan Lalor and James Connolly and favoured facts over polemic, outlining the achievements of the Dáil during the Black and Tan days and comparing it to the current parliament. She repeated her lifelong belief in the co-operative movement. The Free State she described as: 'devised by the British cabinet of imperialists and capitalists and accepted by their would-be counterparts in Ireland, whom they supply with money, arms, and men for the purpose of breaking up the growing movement of the Co-Operative Commonwealth of Ireland'.

She attempted to clarify what had been achieved before the Treaty:

> As, step by step, the Republican Government became the *de facto* Government of Ireland, it began slowly to reorganise the national services on more democratic and Gaelic lines. Of course, we had to go very slowly and carefully, for not only were we faced with the difficulties which invariably face the development of any country on any lines, but we faced also the fact that an enemy army was in occupation of our country and that the whole nation was individually 'on the run'.

She outlined the achievements of the Home Office under Austin Stack, in particular the justice system and the work she had promoted in the Department of Labour.

'The only sane course for Ireland is co-operation,' she wrote, pointing out how the British had attacked co-operative creameries and other enterprises as part of their policy to break the republican movement. She gave many examples of the non-co-operative nature of the new Irish government. 'We Republicans ask: why encourage the "peaceful penetration" of Ireland by English capitalists, instead of trying to develop trade and industries ourselves on co-operative lines?' She would continue to work for 'a commonwealth based on Gaelic ideals'.

Ultimately, the interned republican prisoners got maximum publicity for their cause when they resorted to the most extreme measures: the hunger strike. On 13 October, 424 republican prisoners refused food in Mountjoy Gaol. The hunger strike spread to other prisons and camps and, within two weeks, nearly 9,000 were refusing food. Many of the women prisoners were interned at the North Dublin Union. Accommodation in the building, formerly a poor house and then a Black and Tan barracks, consisted of large drafty dormitories. Bathroom facilities were primitive and the building was haunted by 'ghosts of broken-hearted paupers'. The women passed their time drilling, sewing, knitting and reading.

Constance busied herself campaigning on their behalf. Her Sligo friend, Baby Bohan, from Ballymote was one of the women interned and her worried family had sent her sister Doty to Dublin to get news. One day, Doty came across a crowd gathered around a dray. It was Constance, 'our own Sligo heroine', appealing to the crowd to go to City Hall and sign a petition for the release of the prisoners. There seemed no possible justification for detaining either the women or other republican prisoners. At the Sinn Féin *ard fheis*, the virtues of passive non-military resistance were emphasised. The policy of armed resistance was abandoned.

On 20 November, Constance was arrested while on a day's canvassing with Hanna Sheehy Skeffington and two other younger women, mostly in Constance's inner city constituency. Late in the afternoon, three detectives stepped in front of their lorry at Kevin Street and Constance was arrested and taken by car to the Bridewell, where she was held without charge. When her captors offered her tea, she refused, saying that she would join the other prisoners on hunger strike; the day of her arrest, Dennis Barry, who had gone thirty-four days without food, died in Newbridge jail. In the evening, Sheehy Skeffington and Maud Gonne MacBride visited her with offers of food and clothing, which she refused. Next stop was the North Dublin Union, where Constance heard that Baby Bohan was so ill that she had been given the last rites. Constance's hunger strike lasted for only three days and she reported that the anticipation of suffering had been the worst part. She slept most of the time and had lovely dreams. She stated, 'I was perfectly happy and had no regrets.' She painted a good deal, making dozens of watercolours.

On 23 November, after forty-one days, the hunger strike in all the prisons was called off, though not before two men had died. Constance startled her jailers by insisting on scrubbing floors, with her skirt tucked into her bloomers. She busied herself getting Baby Bohan back to full strength, cooking for her and spending hours sitting on her bed, supporting her with her own body to ease her backache. She gave her mittens to protect her shrivelled hands from the cold. After Baby was released and went back to her family in Sligo, she sent Constance a pair of black cashmere mittens.

Five weeks after her arrest, on Christmas Eve, Constance was released. She was thin and pale, but found that her rheumatism had gone, as had her stomach trouble. On one of her first public appearances after her release, she delivered the oration at the grave of the ex-Fianna chief scout Liam Mellows on the first anniversary of his death.

To judge by a letter to Eva that December, she was increasingly sceptical when it came to both religion and politics: 'For every church and every sect is but an organisation of thoughtless and well-meaning people trained in thought and controlled by juntas of priests and clergy who are doing all the things that Christ would have most disliked.' The same she believed was true of 'all public bodies and governments'. What was needed was 'some scheme by which power can be evenly distributed ... and by which the foolish and uneducated can no longer be grouped in unthinking battalions dependent on the few pushers, self-seekers and crooks, and made slaves of and exploited.' She sounded deflated: 'Everything here is very dull. The main thing is the appalling poverty that meets one everywhere ...'

During the month, 3,481 prisoners were released, including all the women. It was a false dawn. In January 1924, the Irish government issued another Public Safety Act allowing for detention without trial. Once again, republican prisoners began filling the jails.

CHAPTER EIGHTEEN

No Enemy but Time

In 1924, Irish Republicans were rebuilding their shattered organisation, with the dream of establishing an independent republic undimmed. 'We were flattened. We felt the Irish public had forgotten us. The tinted trappings of our fight were hanging like rags around us' was how Sighle Humphreys described it.

At a general meeting of Cumann na mBan in April, Constance presented a plan to continue military training while, at the same time, adapting to changing conditions. There would be lectures on historical, social and economic subjects and first aid classes, as well as monthly military and physical drilling. Irish games and the Irish language were promoted, while the co-operative movement was highlighted as a solution to the plague of unemployment. Recent events were alluded to by Constance in her presidential address. 'No-one knows when we may be attacked again or when we may see our chance to strike again. Peace is beautiful and we want peace, but we cannot shirk the fight if it is the only way to win.' She still possessed an ability to strike the right note and, as she had done at the 1921 congress, she gave the women hope. Yet Cumann na mBan was losing members; many long-time members were tired and demoralised, while others felt the call of family life or needed to earn a living.

Constance worked hard, putting in hours of canvassing at several by-elections that year. The first was in Limerick, where the republican movement was getting back on its feet. To a friend she wrote:

> I never saw worse slums or met nicer people. Don't talk to me
> about politics, tell me how to get bread for the children was the

general cry. If one could only get the people to understand that politics ought to be nothing more or less than the organisation of food, clothes, housing and transit of every unit of the nation, one would get a lot further. Also if they would only learn to watch and heckle their leaders, aye, and distrust them, fear them more than their opponents.

She wished people would read, study and make up their own minds about their lives and how to run them, 'but alas it's always their impulse to get behind some idol, let him do all the thinking for them and then be surprised when he leads them all wrong'. She never lost belief in the power of education, organisation, co-operation, honour and courage as the cornerstones of a working republic.

In the summer, her pamphlet 'James Connolly's Policy and Catholic Doctrine' was published by Sinn Féin. A priest, Dr Peter Coffey of Maynooth, had written an article on 'James Connolly's Campaign against Capitalism, in the light of Catholic Teaching' for the *Catholic Bulletin* of 1920. In her article, Constance defends Connolly and makes a strenuous attempt to reconcile her socialism with the Catholicism she had adopted, referring to Pope Leo XIII's 1891 *Encyclical on the Condition of the Working Class* as well as to Dr Coffey's article.

In the first half of the closely written 45-page document, she outlines Connolly's socialism and concludes that 'state socialism', with all citizens as employees of the state, would be condemned by both Connolly and Pope Leo XIII. Regarding what Dr Coffey had called Connolly's 'anti-clericalism' she argues that Connolly had been misunderstood. Although the Catholic Church might recognise a de facto state and social order, individual citizens could still fight for a better world, without being any less Catholic.

In the second half of the pamphlet on 'Connolly's Programmes and Catholic Doctrine', Constance begins by considering his 1896 programme for the Irish Socialist Republican Party. She argues that Connolly's fundamental idea of Ireland as an independent republic based on Gaelic ideals never changed, although he reconsidered the tactics by which this could be achieved depending on circumstances. She examines his ideas on education and on state banks and the relationship between his nationalism and internationalism. To Connolly, Home Rule meant accepting capitalism and imperialism. She points out that the clergy who had attacked the republic had said nothing about the 'treacherous and unprovoked' attack on the Four Courts, and had ignored the cruel treatment of prisoners. She concludes with the personal belief that the writings left by Connolly would always be Gospel for his friends and those who fought under his leadership. 'The writings he has left us are the marching orders of a risen people.'

Casimir came to London from Poland that year on a diplomatic mission and travelled on to Dublin, the city he had left eleven years previously. In Warsaw, his plays were keeping him solvent. Constance was excited and full of joy at the news that her estranged husband was coming. Although she had aged greatly since he had last seen her, he found that, in many ways, she was the same old Con, full of energy and optimism. Dublin, in the middle of an economic depression, had changed and he found the post-war city dreary and most of his friends scattered. Although Constance usually scraped by, she worried about her friends who were not so well off, as she wrote to Staskou after Casimir had returned to Poland. 'All the small businesses here are heading for ruin and the farmers are in a bad way ... Taxes are awful and food prices are daily rising and rents are wicked.'

Constance continued to speak whenever she was asked for Sinn Féin, Cumann na mBan, the Women's Prisoners' Defence League, the Fianna and the labour movement. In June, the remaining political prisoners were finally released, although the government was determined to stick to a strict law-and-order policy. A few weeks later, Constance went with de Valera to Sligo for a monster meeting to celebrate his release after almost eleven months in Kilmainham Gaol. He was the last prisoner ever held in that grim place. In her native county, Constance had a happy reunion with the Bohan sisters and, at a *céilí* in the town hall, she danced the night away. Now a local celebrity, she threw out the ball at a football match between ex-internees of Dublin and Sligo.

In Dublin, Constance presided over the Cumann na mBan convention on 3 November. A day later, she attended the Sinn Féin *ard fheis* where, in his absence, 1,300 delegates re-elected de Valera as president; he had been detained in Belfast after crossing the border to speak in Derry. In 1925, Sinn Féin won only two of the nine seats at the seven by-elections held on 11 March. Oscar Traynor was elected in North Dublin and

Samuel Holt took one of two vacant seats in Sligo-Leitrim. Constance had spoken in support of Holt at a rally in Ballymote.

Casimir's visit had revived Constance's interest in the theatre and, in September 1925, she helped establish the Republican Players Dramatic Society. Within a year, the players had produced a dozen plays, including two one-act plays she had written. *The Invincible Mother* was set in Kilmainham Gaol in the 1880s and, along with *Blood Money*, set in 1798, it was performed at the Abbey on 1 March 1925. She had begun a full-length play, *Broken Dreams*, based on her own disillusioning experiences during the Black and Tan war and scribbled at it in a copy book whenever she had a spare few minutes.

Broken Dreams tells the story of 'an incident in the Black and Tan war'. The heroine, Eileen O'Rourke, a Cumann na mBan officer, is tall and slim, with short brown hair and a striking face. In manner she is like a young boy and she wears practical clothes – just as Constance did. Her troubles begin when her cruel drunkard husband, Seamus, jealous of Eileen's friendship with another man called Eamon, is shot dead after a drunken row with Eileen. Eileen is blamed for the killing because she is known to be a good shot. After various adventures, she discovers that Seamus had been an informer. Standing by is Eamon, who remains honourable throughout. In his curtain speech he says: 'God only gives happiness to those who give all. It is only where there is no self, there is God.' The play was was never performed during Constance's life; it had its first performance on 11 December 1927.

Mary Colum described meeting her old friend around this period and the portrait was unflinching: 'she was like an extinct volcano, her former violent self reduced to something burnt out ... haggard and old, dressed in ancient demoded clothes'. The long years of fighting, imprisonment and bad food had worn her down and she was obviously failing, with the old fire and eagerness gone from her eyes. In Colum's view, Constance was a disappointed woman. 'What she had fought for had not really come into being; maybe nothing on earth could have brought it into being so romantic and heroic was it.'

The delight of her life in those later years was her car – a battered 'Tin Lizzie' she had picked up at an army sale. As often as she could, she would pack paints, food, children, friends and dog into the car and head for the countryside. Constance in her car – or indeed under her car – became as familiar a sight as Constance on her bicycle in earlier days. Because it broke down frequently, she never travelled without a ball of twine for emergency repairs. Máire Nic Shiubhlaigh remembered Constance's daredevil driving: 'She used to drive this [car] around the city as fast as it would go. Its joints rattled and clanked but Madame sat at the wheel, every bit of her enjoying it.'

At the Coghlan's, she had free run of the garden, which was her other delight, especially after a long day of meetings. She saw her mother when she came to Dublin for shopping, while her daughter Maeve, who had grown tall and pretty, was a joy to her.

In June 1925, she was co-opted to the Rathmines and Rathgar Urban District Council. As a member of the Housing, Public Health, Old Age Pensions and Child Welfare committees, she dealt with everything from keeping pigs in the backyard to job discrimination. She would stand at the back wall, a restless presence, shouting 'Ahoy there, you!' to anyone whose attention she wished to attract. Her presence ensured that many of the meetings were stormy; she fought against the need for taking an oath before securing a job and demanded to know why the Boy Scouts were allowed to use public grounds when the Fianna boys were not. She worked hard to get a swimming pool opened at Williams Park in Rathmines and battled on for the poor or for those who were too sick, too young or too old to fight for themselves.

The Fianna was taking up much of her time after it was reorganised in 1925 on less military lines and reverted to the *sluagh* system. She was still chief scout. An ambitious programme included classes in the Irish language, archaeology, botany, woodcraft, arts and music, as well as games, physical drill, scouting and first aid. The new Irish Free State government was not prepared to believe that an organisation closely allied with the Volunteers only a few years earlier had given up its militaristic ways. On 3 December 1925, twelve boys who were drilling were arrested in Wexford under the Treasonable Offences Act 1925. One was released and Constance was a witness at the trial of the eleven others two months later.

She reported on the trial for *An Phobhlacht*. When sworn in, she had added to the formal oath, 'I will swear the truth on my allegiance to the Irish Republic'. The judges reprimanded her and asked that she behave with propriety. 'I always behave with propriety, for I am a most proper person, I assure your honour,' she replied, to hoots of appreciation from the Fianna boys in the packed court room.

The defence insisted that the boys were drilling in preparation for a march to the grave of Liam Mellows on 13 December and that if everyone who marched at a funeral procession was accused of military drilling, the jails would be full to overflowing. Not only that, but the Baden Powell scouts drilled in public and could indulge in revolver and musketry practise, while the Fianna forbade the use of firearms. The jury returned a verdict of not guilty.

It was by no means the last time a Fianna boy would be arrested. The Treasonable Offences Act proved an effective weapon in the Free State's fight against republicanism, and the raids, beatings and searches continued. Republicans lucky enough to find work faced possible arrest at any time, which meant they lost their jobs. Thousands were forced to emigrate. With poverty and unemployment rising, a new and more flexible political approach was needed if the fledgling Irish state was to flourish.

That same December, Constance resigned from her position as president of Cumann na mBan after discussions with de Valera about founding a new political party. Because of its abstentionist policy, Sinn Féin had not been able to make its case against the signing of the Boundary Agreement that confirmed the division of Ireland in two. It was time to move on. At the annual convention, Constance withheld her inside knowledge of de Valera's intentions. When a motion condemning any TD who entered the newly formed parliament was passed, Constance was the only dissenter. She announced that she was resigning from her position as Cumann na mBan president since the passing of the resolution would tie her hands 'in the event of certain circumstances arising'.

Without Constance, the Cumann meetings lost some of their sparkle; Sighle Humphreys reported that it nearly broke their hearts to accept her resignation. She was not the ideal chairwoman, drawing caricatures when she was bored and only brightening up when a subject interested her, but she was much loved and respected and an inspirational figure for younger members, especially those who had shared a prison cell with her. A month later, plans to make her a presentation came to nothing on the dubious grounds that she had never been a signed-up member of any Cumann na mBan branch. When elected president in 1916, she was a member of Inghinidhe na hÉireann and had come to Cumann na mBan when Inghinidhe formed a branch of the organisation.

In a letter to Staskou in autumn 1925, Constance admitted that she had been 'very sick' but assured him that her health was now wonderful. She spent most of her spare time driving out to the country and sketching: 'I have been struggling to teach myself water-colours these last few years and am just beginning to express myself in them. Oils were too expensive for me to continue, unless I gave up politics and tried to earn money by them.' She had begun using watercolours when in jail in England where, because she was living in such close quarters with other prisoners, she could could not use oil paints because of their strong smell. An exhibition of forty-one of her paintings from her time in Holloway was well received around this time.

In January, Constance wrote to Staskou again, recommending the novels of Joseph Conrad and telling him that she had cut off her hair. 'I don't see why old women should not be as comfortable as young.' Because there was a fashion for Russian boots, she had fished out the old red boots from Zywotowka and she thought they were the smartest pair in Dublin. Eva, she wrote, was the only real relation she has left. She never saw Josslyn and never wanted to. She did not mention her mother, who had kept in touch with her even through the troubled times by means of assignations at Mespil House, the home of Sarah Purser.

On 8 February 1926, Seán O'Casey's 'immoral' play *The Plough and the Stars* caused riots in the Abbey Theatre. Republicans revealed their latent puritanism by expressing their horror at the sight of a prostitute on stage and an Irish flag in a public house. Even more upsetting was the use of Pearse's words in a manner that was seen as a slur on the men of 1916. Hanna Sheehy Skeffington, Kathleen Clarke and Margaret Pearse were among those protesting, although each had different reasons for their action. Constance stayed away. So bruised was O'Casey by the controversy that he left for London, never to return.

An extraordinary meeting of Sinn Féin was held at Dublin's Rotunda from 9 to 11 March to discuss the future of the party. De Valera argued that, because the government's oppressive policies were going unopposed, the party should take its place in the Dáil and fight those policies; the only remaining stumbling block was the oath. After a furious debate, de Valera's resolution narrowly failed by 223 to 218 votes. De Valera resigned and set about forming a new party to be called Fianna Fáil after the first standing army of Celtic Ireland.

Constance kept herself busy with the new political party, as well as with the Fianna, the Republican Dramatic Society and the Prisoners' Defence League. She continued to speak out against injustice. She supported the State Pension Scheme for Necessitous Mothers. She was closely connected to St Ultan's Infant Hospital, where Kathleen Lynn was vice-chairman and Madeleine ffrench-Mullen secretary. She was tired, but soldiering on. She loved young people and would bring the Coghlan children to Grafton Street, stopping her car outside Woolworth's and making lots of noise, to their great embarrassment. She visited Francis Stuart and Iseult Gonne at their cottage in Glencree. They found her likeable: 'She was warm-hearted, natural, very interested in practical things like how we were living and how we were managing'.

On 16 May 1926, Constance chaired the inaugural meeting of Fianna Fáil, the Soldiers of Destiny, in the La Scala Theatre, off Dublin's O'Connell Street, as Sackville Street was now known. She introduced the main speaker as 'President de Valera'. After the applause had died down, de Valera corrected her, stating 'I am not here as president'. He outlined his plan to get rid of the oath of allegiance and cut the bonds of foreign interference. 'Today we are making a new start for another attempt to get the nation out of the paralysing "Treaty dilemma"', he said. Constitutional methods were to be preferred to physical force; the people of Ireland were tired of bloodshed and conflict.

Writing to Eva around that time, Constance wondered whether 'people get rather mad when they go in for politics'. She gave her opinion on 'the oath', which 'made it absolutely impossible for an honourable person to enter the Free State parliament. De Valera had said he would 'go in' if there was no oath and believed the time had come to demand its removal. She commented that some 'unlogical persons' are howling. These 'self-righteous fools' stood 'for principle and for the honour of the Republic'. How her views had changed!

During this period Constance was unaware that her sister was gravely ill with colon cancer. Eva and Esther had told no one and, in her final eighteen months, Eva devoted herself to writing on religious topics and giving talks to theosophical societies. By January, she was bedridden and Esther's brother Reginald was helping to nurse her.

An office was found on O'Connell Street for the new party, with expenses paid for by friends. Meetings were held all over the country and when the first *ard fheis* was held on 24 November at the Rotunda Buildings in Dublin, more than 500 delegates attended. De Valera was unanimously elected president and Constance was elected to the sixteen-person executive, along with P.J. Routledge and Seán T. O'Kelly (vice-presidents); Seán Lemass and Gerald Boland (honorary secretaries) and Dr James Ryan and Seán McEntee (honorary treasurers). The first executive of Fianna Fáil included six women – Margaret Pearse, Kathleen Clarke, Hanna Sheehy Skeffington, Dorothy Macardle and Linda Kearns, as well as Constance. Apart from Sheehy Skeffington, all would remain staunch members of the party. Writing about the possibility of Constance taking the oath, Eithne Coyle pointed out that 'Madame was no fool ... she had more than average intelligence to realise all the implications involved'.

On 30 June 1926, a month after her fifty-sixth birthday, Eva died; she had taken a turn for the worse two days earlier. Constance, who knew nothing of what was going on, had been away at the seashore for a few days and did not get the telegram with its shattering news until she returned to Frankfort House. She had been depressed for several days, not knowing why until she received the news. 'Everything seemed to go from under me,' she wrote to Esther Roper. Her sister had been her mentor and her guide all their lives. 'She was something wonderful and beautiful, and so simple and thought so little of herself. Her gentleness prevented me getting very callous in a war. I once held out and stopped a man being shot because of her.'

Since her time in Aylesbury Jail, she had developed a habit of imagining her sister's opinion on anything she did. 'Every sketch I made I wondered how she would like it, and I looked forward to showing it to her. If I saw anything beautiful, I thought of her and wished she was there to enjoy it.' In recent times, she had begun her feel her sister's presence again:

> When I'm painting she seems to look at me and help me from the clouds. I wake suddenly and it is just as if she was there. Last

Sunday at Mass, when I wasn't thinking of her at all, she suddenly seemed to smile at me from behind the priest, and I know it is real and that she, the real Eva, is somewhere very near.

She did not go to the funeral, telling a friend that she could not face the family. Mabel and Mordaunt attended but their mother was too ill to travel.

In September, Constance visited Esther Roper in London. She felt her sister's loss deeply but was determined to drive herself on. In the winter of 1926–7, a prolonged coal strike in England meant that Dublin's poor were again starving and freezing. Constance made frequent trips into the Dublin and Wicklow mountains in her old car to collect turf, and she arranged for her friend Lady Albina Broderick, also known as Gobnait Ní Bhrudair, to send turf from Kerry. Men would hold meetings while people froze, she would say. She had come to the belief that meetings were politics as practised by men. She delivered the turf to those who needed it, carrying the heavy bags herself up the dark tenement stairs and then helping to light the fire and tidy up the room.

She continued to charm her admirers: the street traders of Moore Street, the ardent republicans, and a group of hecklers known as 'Madame's Wans'. There was a day out at a holy well in County Meath with the future Fianna Fáil Minister Michael Hilliard, where she sketched for several hours. He remembered her beautiful eyes and distinguished bearing.

In October, the Sinn Féin *ard fheis* attracted only 200 delegates. Women were well represented, or perhaps their presence was more obvious because of the overall drop in numbers. Mary MacSwiney was elected vice-president and Caitlín Brugha became secretary for Dublin. Others elected included Kathleen Lynn, Margaret Buckley, Lily Coventry, Máire Comerford, Dulcibella Barton, Kate O'Callaghan, and Gobnait Ní Bhrudair.

On 11 November 1926, Constance spoke at an anti-Remembrance Day rally along with Maud Gonne MacBride, Charlotte Despard and Tom Kelly. A few weeks later, she unveiled a cross in memory of two Fianna boys, Alf Colley and Seán Cole, captured and killed during the Civil War. She seemed tired.

On 23 January 1927, Constance's mother Georgina died at her home in County Sligo at the age of eighty-five. Constance and her daughter Maeve attended the funeral in Lissadell. She had not seen her brother Josslyn since 1917, although she corresponded with him. She occasionally gave way to sadness at the deaths of her mother and sister. Once a friend entered her room without knocking because she thought Constance had gone out. She found her sitting quietly at the window looking out at the rainy twilight with tears running down her cheeks.

Her last notable outing came at a protest meeting in Rathmines against the government's proposed Electricity Supply Bill in February 1927, where she argued that such a bill would create a state-owned monopoly. In chaotic scenes, and with her dog running around the hall, Constance was ordered by the chairman to sit down. 'I am afraid of no man,' she retorted. 'No one says you are,' was the response. The meeting ended with opposing sides belting out 'God Save the King' and 'The Red Flag'.

In June 1927 came Constance's final general election – the first for the fledgling Fianna Fáil party. The programme included tariffs to promote Irish self-sufficiency, which appealed to Constance. She was fully involved in the campaigning, despite breaking both bones in her lower arm while cranking her beloved car. 'Glory be it's not my jaw, I can still talk,' she said while it was being set. With her arm in a sling, she went on to her meeting and made her speech. However, the broken arm restricted her – she could not paint nor could she drive, and dressing and combing her hair were difficult. In the election, she stood for her old South Dublin City constituency and was elected. The party in power won forty-seven seats – a big drop of sixteen. Fianna Fáil was only three seats behind with forty-four. Sinn Féin had a disaster, winning only five seats – a loss of thirty-nine. Labour took a respectable twenty-two seats, up by eight.

On 23 June, with her arm in a black sling, Constance walked with de Valera to Leinster House to demand admission to the Dáil. She was as tall and imposing as ever, but looked frail. The doors to the chamber inside were locked and they could go no further without taking the despised oath. They returned to their headquarters and addressed a large crowd.

The last in a lifetime of meetings was a gathering of the Fianna Fáil executive in early July. She looked so poorly that one of the young men present suggested she go home but, as he said, 'She was a peculiar woman. She'd sit a meeting out even if she dropped dead.' Still concerned, he surreptitiously asked the chairman to cut the agenda short and took her home to Frankfort House on the tram. Dr Lynn was called and immediately sent her to Sir Patrick Dun's Hospital, where Dr William Taylor, a much-respected medical man, performed an appendectomy. At first she seemed to be recovering. He joked with her about the great streak of antiseptic on her stomach. 'Well, Madame, I never thought I'd see you painted orange.' She responded in kind.

On 7 July, a message broadcast on the radio summoned her family. After a second operation for peritonitis, her condition was critical, though she remained alert and calm. Dorothy Macardle sent a telegram to Josslyn at Lissadell.

She was in a public ward with no privacy and when Éamon de Valera visited; he suggested that she might prefer a private room. He got short shrift. 'She was angry with me because she felt that I was suggesting that what was good enough for the ordinary poor was not good enough for her. She had always helped the worker and the needy and she wanted to be identified with them.' Her daughter Maeve arrived at her bedside as did Esther Roper from London. Along with Helena Molony, Marie Perolz, May Coghlan and Florrie O'Connell, they undertook a vigil on the Saturday, praying for her in the hospital board room.

Constance rallied briefly. Sighle Humphreys came to visit wearing a new pink dress she had bought in Paris, knowing how Constance loved pretty things. In the streets, Esther Roper was stopped by strangers looking for news. 'Ah what would the people in the slums do without her,' said one tearful woman. 'She's given up everything for us and she thinks that what's good enough for us is good enough for her. Please God she'll get better.'

To Constance's great joy, her husband Casimir hurried to Dublin from Warsaw, bringing with him Staskou, the beloved stepson she had not seen for years. She was cheerful and happy. 'This is the happiest day of my life,' she said. When they arrived, Esther Roper was with her. Constance insisted on opening a bunch of roses sent by Josslyn, though her hands were shaking. She did not fear death. 'It is so beautiful to have this love and kindness before I go.' On her last day, she showed May Coghlan how she could lift her tea cup with her right hand. Her broken bone had healed.

Casimir was staying with the Starkeys, artist friends from the old days. At ten o'clock on 14 July, he got a message to come quickly. Constance was drifting away; she spoke of seeing bright lights and said she felt she was being lifted upwards. He was with her when she sank into a coma and, with her face radiant, she died at 1.30am on Friday 15 July. Also at her bedside were Éamon de Valera, Hanna Sheehy Skeffington and May Coghlan. Esther Roper was back in London when she heard the news.

Between the pages of the Catholic bible beside her bed was a typewritten verse 'To Mother and Eva 1927' adapted from Shelley's *Adonais* verses 39 and 40.

They are not dead, they do not sleep;
They have awakened from the dream of life,
They have outsoared the shadow of our night.
Envy and calumny and hate and pain,
And that unrest which men miscall delight,
Can touch them not, nor torture them again.

While ordinary Dubliners mourned one of their champions, both City Hall and the Mansion House, as public properties, were refused for her lying-in-state. She was managing to cause trouble even in death. Instead, her body was taken from St Andrew's Church on Westland Row to the familiar surroundings of the Rotunda, where her casket was guarded by Fianna boys, and long streams passed by to say their final farewell. It was an emotionally charged time in Dublin. Five days before her death, one of her political enemies, Kevin O'Higgins, had been murdered near his home in Booterstown; he was given a full state funeral with children getting the day off school.

Constance's funeral on Sunday, 17 July was one of the biggest ever seen in Dublin. Thousands followed the coffin and thousands more lined the route to Glasnevin Cemetery to say goodbye to their 'Madame'. Leading the procession was her family – Casimir, Stanislaus, Maeve, Sir Josslyn and his wife, Lady Mary Gore-Booth. Eight motor tenders were needed for the wreaths and flowers, sent not only by all the organisations to which she had given such energy, but also by childhood companions, society friends, the rich and the poor of Dublin. Among the donations –

allegedly – were the two dozen eggs one countrywoman had promised she would give Constance when she came out of hospital.

The funeral took two hours to make it through O'Connell Street. Behind the advance guard of Fianna boys came a band, followed by representatives of the Irish Citizen Army, and then another band. More Fianna preceded the coffin wrapped in a tricolour, along with members of the clergy. One of the priests was Father Tom Ryan, chaplain at Kilmainham in 1916 when Constance had asked him to be with her at the end, thinking it would be then. He kept his promise to her eleven years later. Fianna Fáil and Republican deputies followed, with more bands, several contingents of Volunteers, members of the Workers' Union, Cumann na mBan, Clan na nGaedheal, and the Women's Defence League, led by Maud Gonne MacBride and Charlotte Despard. Mary MacSwiney and J.J. O'Kelly led the Sinn Féin representatives.

In the crowd were members of the old Citizen Army, mothers from the poorer parts of Dublin, and thousands more whose lives had been touched by a big-hearted, generous and brave woman, whose essential humanity had sometimes found her at odds with the harsh and often brutal reality of Irish politics. At three o'clock, when the advance guard reached Glasnevin, one hundred Free State soldiers with rifles had taken up position a short distance from her grave, while a number of detectives mingled with the crowd. At the chapel, the rosary was recited in Irish and the coffin taken to the vault.

Éamon de Valera gave the oration:

> Madame Markievicz is gone from us, Madame, the friend of the toiler, the lover of the poor. Ease and station she put aside, and took the hard way of service with the weak and the down-trodden. Sacrifice, misunderstanding and scorn lay on the road she adopted, but she trod it unflinchingly.

He applauded

> this wonderful outcrop of Irish landlordism and Dublin Castle, this brilliant, fascinating, incomprehensible rebel ... consumed with the fires of a burning devotion to whatever cause happened to capture her restless and enthusiastic, intellectual personality.

She now lies at rest with her fellow champions of the right – mourned by the people whose liberties she fought for; blessed by the loving prayers of the poor she tried so hard to befriend. The world knew her only as a soldier of Ireland, but we knew her as a colleague and comrade.

We knew the kindliness, the great woman's heart of her, the great Irish soul of her, and we know the loss we have suffered is not to be repaired. It is sadly we take our leave, but we pray high heaven that all she longed for may one day be achieved.

The burial was postponed because gravediggers did not work on Sundays. A day later, Constance was laid to rest, watched by Free State military, uniformed police and detectives. They had remained on duty at the cemetery all day. The last post was sounded by buglers of Fianna Éireann and the uniform Constance wore at the Royal College of Surgeons in 1916 was lowered into the grave with her. For weeks after, the family received letters of condolence from public bodies, those who had worked with her and many ordinary people who had loved and admired her, even those who felt that her life had followed an unfortunate path.

On 11 August 1927, having signed the Oath of Allegiance in front of a representative of the governor general of the Irish Free State, the Fianna Fáil TDs entered the Dáil. De Valera took the Oath while claiming that he was simply signing a slip of paper to gain a right of participation in the Dáil. An election was called on 15 September; Cumann na nGaedheal was returned to power but with a reduced majority. Sinn Féin, clinging to the fantasy that the surviving members of the Second Dáil constituted the legitimate government of Ireland, opted not to contest the election, distancing itself from the political mainstream for decades to come.

After ten years of Cumann na nGaedheal, which had brought the country bloodshed, repression, unemployment, a drop in pensions and public pay, and a reduced role for women in public life, Fianna Fáil came to power in 1932. In the years following, xenophobia, economic protectionism and an authoritarian government helped ensure that women's rights were further eroded. Those with a wider vision emigrated. The Oireachtas enacted a marriage bar for civil servants, including widows; it brought in lower pay rates for women teachers and made jury service non-compulsory for women, which meant that women who had the misfortune to fall foul of the law would be judged by all-male juries. There was a ban on contraceptives, strictly no divorce, and a limit on female employment in industry. Women's primary role as 'housewives and mothers' was enshrined in de Valera's 1937 Constitution. Feminists found little support in a world where women, wearied by war, returned to a more traditional way of life, and regarded any foreign influence with suspicion, especially in matters of morality. All over Europe, the gains made by strong, brave women like Constance Markievicz were eradicated.

Romantic Ireland was – emphatically – dead and gone.

Sources and Bibliography

By Constance Markievicz

Diary 1892–93 (National Museum, Collins Barracks).

Prison Letters of Countess Markievicz, ed. Esther Roper (London: Virago Press, 1987).

What Irish Republicans Stand For (Glasgow: Civic Press, 1922).

James Connolly's Policy and Catholic Doctrine (1924).

Free Women in a Free Nation (*Bean na hÉireann*, February 1909).

The Women of '98 (*Irish Citizen*, 6, 13, 20, 27 November and 4 December 1915).

A Call to the Women of Ireland (Dublin, Fergus O'Connor, 1918).

Break Down the Bastilles (*Voice of Labour*, 1 May 1919).

On the Run, undated, hand written article.

The Police, 16 December 1919, handwritten article.

Peace with Honour (*Phoblacht na hÉireann*, 3 January 1922).

Women in the Fight, Roger McHugh (ed.) Dublin 1916 (1966).

Conditions of Women in English Jails (*New Ireland*, 8 and 15 October 1922).

Tom Clarke and the first Day of the Republic (*Éire*, 26 May 1923).

Na Fianna (*Éire*, 9 June 1923).

Larkin, the Fianna and the King's Visit (*Éire*, 16 June 1923).

Memories of the King's Visit, 1911 (*Éire*, 14, 21, 28 July; 4 August 1923).

Mr. Arthur Griffith and the Sinn Féin Organisation (*Éire*, 18 and 25 August 1923).

Fianna Éireann and the 1921 Treaty (*Sinn Féin*, 21 June 1924).

Wolfe Tone's Ideals of Democracy (*An Phoblacht*, 26 June 1925).

How We Won the Fianna Trials (*An Phoblacht*, 5 March 1926).

Liam Mellows (*An Phoblacht*, 28 May 1926).

James Connolly as I Knew Him (*The Nation*, 26 March 1927).

1916 (*The Nation*, 23 April 1927).

Citizenship (*Éire*, 13 August 1927).

Blood Money: A One-Act Play (1925).

The Invincible Mother: A One-Act Play (1925).

Broken Dreams: A Three-Act Play (1927).

Books

Andrews, C.S., *Dublin Made Me* (Dublin: Mercier Press, 1979).

Arrington, Laurie, *Revolutionary Lives – Constance and Casimir Markievicz* (New Jersey: Princeton University Press, 2016).

Barton, Brian, *The Secret Court Martial Records of the Easter Rising* (Stroud: The History Press, 2010).

Bowen, Elizabeth, *The Shelbourne* (London: George G Harrap, 1951).

Boylan, Patricia, *All Cultivated People: A History of the United Arts Club Dublin* (London: Colin Smythe, 1988).

Brennan, Robert, Allegiance (Dublin: Brown and Nolan, 1950)

Breen, Timothy Murphy, *The Government's Executions Policy during the Irish Civil War 1922–1923* (NUI, Maynooth, PhD thesis, 2010).

Clarke, Kathleen, *Revolutionary Woman: An Autobiography 1878–1972* (Dublin: O'Brien Press, 2008).

Clare, Anne, *Unlikely Rebels: The Gifford Girls and the Fight for Irish Freedom* (Cork: Mercier Press, 2011).

Coldrey, Barry M, *Faith and Fatherland – the Christian Brothers and the Development of Irish Nationalism 1838–1921* (Dublin: Gill and Macmillan, 1988)

Colum, Mary, *Life and the Dream* (London: Macmillan, 1947)

Connell, Joseph E.A., *Dublin in Rebellion: A directory 1913–1923* (Dublin: The Lilliput Press, 2009).

Connolly, James, *The Re-Conquest of Ireland* (Dublin: New Book Publications, 1972).

—, *Labour in Irish History* (Dublin: New Book Publications, 1971).

—, *Labour, Nationality and Religion* (Dublin: New Book Publications, 1969).

—, *Selected Writings* (ed. P. Beresford Ellis) (London: Pelican, 1975).

Connolly-O'Brien, Nora, *Portrait of a Rebel Father* (Dublin: Four Masters, 1975).

Coogan, Tim Pat, *De Valera: Long Fellow, Long Shadow* (London: Hutchinson, 1993).

Coxhead, Erin, *Daughters of Erin* (London: Colin Smythe, 1979).

Cullen, Clara (ed.), *The World Upturning: Elsie Henry's Irish Wartime Diaries 1913–1919* (Dublin: Merrion Press, 2013).

Cullen Owens, Rosemary, *Louie Bennett* (Cork: Cork University Press, 2001).

Curry, James, *Artist of the Revolution: The Cartoons of Ernest Kavanagh* (Cork: Mercier Press, 2012).

Czira, Sidney Gifford, *The Years Flew By* (Dublin: Gifford and Craven, 1974).

Dangerfield, George, *The Damnable Question: A Study in Anglo-Irish Relations* (London: Constable, 1977).

Davis, Graham (ed.), *In Search of a Better Life: British and Irish Migration* (Stroud: The History Press, 2011).

Dickinson, P.L., *Dublin of Yesteryear* (London: Methuen, 1929)

Dooley, Chris, *Redmond: A Life Undone* (Dublin: Gill and Macmillan, 2015).

Fanning, Ronan, *Fatal Path: British Government and Irish Revolutions 1910–1922* (London: Faber and Faber, 2013).

—, *Eamon de Valera: A Will to Power* (London: Faber and Faber, 2015)

Feeney, Brian, *16 Lives: Seán Mac Diarmada* (Dublin: O'Brien Press, 2014).

Ferriter, Diarmaid, *The Transformation of Ireland 1900–2000* (London: Profile Press, 2004).

—, *Judging Dev* (Dublin: Royal Irish Academy, 2007).

—, *A Nation and not a Rabble: The Irish Revolution 1913–1923* (London: Profile Books, 2015).

Figgis, Darrell, *AE (George W. Russell)* (New York: Dodd, Mead and Company, 1916).

Fingall, Elizabeth, Countess of, *Seventy Years Young* (Dublin: The Lilliput Press, 1991).

Fitz-Simons, Christopher, *Eleven Houses* (London: Penguin Ireland, 2007).

Forester, Margery, *Michael Collins, Lost Leader* (London: Sphere Books, 1972).

Foster, R.F., *Vivid Faces – The Revolutionary Generation in Ireland 1890–1923* (London: Allen Lane, 2014).

—, *Modern Ireland 1600–1972* (London: Penguin, 1989).

—, *W.B. Yeats: A Life, Vol 1: The Apprentice Mage 1865–1914* (Oxford: University Press, 1997).

—, *W.B. Yeats: A Life, Vol 2: The Arch-Poet 1915–1939* (Oxford: University Press, 2003).

Foy, Michael T. and Barton, Brian, *The Easter Rising* (Stroud: The History Press, 2011).

Fox, R.M., *Rebel Irishwomen* (Dublin and Cork: The Talbot Press, 1935).

—, *The History of the Irish Citizen Army* (Dublin: J. Duffy, 1944).

Gaughan, J. Anthony, *Scouting in Ireland* (Dublin: Kingdom Books, 2006).

—, *The Memories of Constable Jeremiah Mee RIC* (Cork: Mercier Press, 2012).

Gore-Booth, Eva, *Death of Fionavar* (London: Erskine Macdonald, 1916).

Gregory, Augusta, Lady, *Lady Gregory's Journals 1916–1930*, ed. Lennox Robinson (London: Putnam and Company, 1946).

Haverty, Anne, *Constance Markievicz: An Independent Life* (London: Pandora, 1993).

Hay, Marnie, *Bulmer Hobson and the Nationalist Movement in Twentieth-Century Ireland* (Manchester: Manchester University Press, 2009).

Hobson, Bulmer, *A Short History of the Irish Volunteers* (Dublin: The Candle Press, 1918).

Hughes, Brian, *16 Lives: Michael Mallin* (Dublin: O'Brien Press, 2012).

James, Dermot, *The Gore-Booths of Lissadell* (Dublin: Woodfield Press, 2004).

Keohane, Leo, *Captain Jack White, Imperialism, Anarchism and the Irish Citizen Army* (Dublin: Merrion Press, 2014).

Knirck, Jason, *Women of the Dáil* (Dublin: Irish Academic Press, 2006).

Lee, J.J, *Ireland 1912–1986: Politics and Society* (Cambridge: Cambridge University Press, 1993).

Lyons, F.S.L., *Ireland since the Famine* (London: Fontana, 1986).

MacBride, Maud Gonne, *A Servant of the Queen* (London: Victor Gollancz, 1992).

Marreco, Anne, *The Rebel Countess: The Life and Times of Constance Markievicz* (London: Phoenix Press, 1967).

Martin, F.X. (ed.), *The Irish Volunteers 1913–1915: Recollections and Documents* (Dublin: Merrion Press, 2013).

— (ed.), *The Howth Gun Running and the Kilcoole Gun Running: Recollections and Documents* (Dublin: Merrion Press, 2014).

— (ed.), *Leaders and Men of the Easter Rising: Dublin 1916* (London: Methuen, 1967).

Martin, F.X. and F. J. Byrne (eds), *The Scholar Revolutionary: Eoin MacNeill 1867–1945 and the Making of the New Ireland* (Shannon: Irish University Press, 1973).

Matthews, Anne, *Renegades – Irish Republican Women 1900–1922* (Cork: Mercier Press, 2010).

—, *Dissidents - Irish Republican Women 1923-1941* (Cork: Mercier Press, 2012).

—, *The Irish Citizen Army* (Cork: Mercier Press, 2014).

McCarthy, Cal, *Cumann na mBan and the Irish Revolution* (Cork: Collins Press, 2007).

McConville, Michael, *Ascendancy to Oblivion: The Story of the Anglo Irish* (London: Quartet, 1986).

McConville, Seán, *Irish Political Prisoners 1848-1922* (London: Routledge, 2003).

McCoole, Sinead, *No Ordinary Women: Irish Female Activists in the Revolutionary Years 1900-1923* (Dublin: O'Brien Press, 2008).

—, *Easter Widows* (London: Doubleday Ireland, 2014).

McGowan, Joe (ed.), *Constance Markievicz: The People's Countess* (Sligo: Constance Markievicz Millennium Committee, 2003).

Mitchell, Arthur, *Revolutionary Government in Ireland: Dáil Éireann 1919-1921* (Dublin: Gill and Macmillan, 1993).

Nevin, Donal, *James Connolly: A Full Life* (Dublin: Gill and Macmillan, 2005).

— (ed.), *James Larkin Lion of the Fold* (Dublin: Gill and Macmillan, 2006).

Nic Shuibhlaigh, Máire, *The Splendid Years* (Dublin: Duffy, 1955).

Norman, Diana, *Terrible Beauty: A Life of Constance Markievicz, 1868-1927* (Swords: Poolbeg Press, 1987).

O'Brien, Paul, *1916 in Focus: Shootout: The Battle for St Stephen's Green 1916* (Dublin: New Island, 2013).

O'Casey, Seán, *The Story of the Irish Citizen Army, 1913-1916* (Libcom. org/library/story-irish-citizen-army-sean-ocasey).

—, *Three Dublin Plays* (London: Faber and Faber, 1988).

—, *Autobiography Volume 3: Drums Under the Windows* (London: Pan Books, 1972).

O'Connor, Emmett, *A Labour History of Ireland 1824-2000* (Dublin: UCD Press, 2011).

O'Faolain, Nuala, *The Story of Chicago May* (London: Michael Joseph, 2005).

O'Faolain, Seán, *Constance Markievicz* (London: Cresset Library, 1987).

—, *The Irish* (London: Pelican, 1969).

Ó hÓgartaigh, Margaret, *Kathleen Lynn: Irishwoman, Patriot, Doctor* (Dublin: Irish Academic Press, 2006).

Oikarinin, Sari, *A Dream of Liberty: Constance Markievicz's Vision of Ireland 1908–1927* (Helsinki: Suomen Historiallinem Seura, 1998).

O'Neill, Marie, *From Parnell to de Valera – a Biography of Jennie Wyse Power* (Dublin: Blackwater Press, 1991).

O'Rahilly, Aodogán, *The O'Rahilly: A Secret History of the Rebellion of 1916* (Dublin: The Lilliput Press, 1991 and 2016).

Pearse, Patrick, *The Coming Revolution: The Political Writings and Speeches of Patrick Pearse* (Cork: Mercier, 2012).

Pešeta, Sonia, *Irish Nationalist Women 1900–1918* (Cambridge: Cambridge University Press, 2013).

Plunkett Dillon, Geraldine, *All in the Blood* (ed. Honor Ó Brolchain) (Dublin: A & A Farmar, 2006).

Quigley, Patrick, *The Polish Irishman – the Life and Times of Count Casimir Markievicz* (Dublin: Liffey Press, 2012).

Quinlan, Carmel, *Genteel Revolutionaries: Anna and Thomas Haslam and the Irish Women's Movement* (Cork: Cork University Press, 2005).

Ryan, Desmond, *Remembering Sion* (London: Arthur Baker, 1934) Desmond

—, *The Rising* (Dublin: Golden Eagle, 1957)

Ryan, Louise and Ward, Margaret (eds), *Irish Women and the Vote: Becoming Citizens* (Dublin: Irish Academic Press, 2007).

Scourer, Clive, *Maeve de Markievicz – Daughter of Constance* (Killyleagh, Co Down: Clive Scourer, 2003)

Skinnider, Margaret, *Doing My Bit for Ireland* (New York: The Century Company, 1917).

Smith, Nadia Clare, *Dorothy Macardle – A Life* (Dublin: Woodfield Press, 2007)

Stephens, James, *The Insurrection in Dublin* (MacMillan: New York, 1917).

Tiernan, Sonja, *Eva Gore-Booth – an Image of Such Politics* (Manchester: Manchester University Press, 2012).

— (ed.), *The Political Writings of Eva Gore Booth* (Manchester: Manchester University Press, 2015).

Torchiana, Donald T., *W.B. Yeats and Georgian Ireland* (Evanston, Illinois: Northwestern University Press, 1966).

Townshend, Charles, *Easter 1916* (London: Allen Lane, 2005).

—, *The Republic* (London: Allen Lane, 2013).

Van Voris, Jacqueline, *Constance de Markievicz in the Cause of Ireland* (Amherst: University of Massachusetts Press, 1967).

Walsh, Maurice, *Bitter Freedom – Ireland in a Revolutioanry World 1918–1923* (London: Faber and Faber, 2015).

—, *The News from Ireland* (London: I.B. Tauris, 2008).

Ward, Margaret, *Maud Gonne: Ireland's Joan of Arc* (London: Pandora, 1990).

—, *Unmanageable Revolutionaries* (London: Pluto Press, 1995).

—, *Hanna Sheehy Skeffington: A Life* (Cork: Attic Press, 1997).

— (ed.), *In Their Own Voices: Women and Irish Nationalism* (Cork: Attic Press, 2001).

Wheeler, Charles Newton, *The Irish Republic* (Chicago: Cahill-Igoe Company, 1919).

Yeates, Padraig, *Lock-Out: Dublin 1913* (Dublin: Gill and Macmillan, 2000).

Yeats, W.B., *Selected Poetry* (ed. A. Norman Jeffares) (London: Papermac, 1971).

—, *The Autobiography* (New York: Collier Books, 1965).

—, *The Collected Letters* Vols, 1, 2, 3 (general ed. John Kelly) (Oxford: Clarendon Press, 1997).

Articles

Farrell, Brian, 'Markievicz and the women of the revolution' in F.X. Martin (ed.), *Leaders and Men of the Easter Rising: Dublin 1916* (London: Methuen, 1967).

Hay, Marnie, 'The Foundation and Development of Na Fianna Éireann, 1909–16 ', *Irish Historical Studies*, May 2008.

O Briain, Liam, 'Saint Stephen's Green Area', *Capuchin Annual*, 1966.

Rooney, Philip, 'The Green Jacket – the Story of the Countess' (serialised *Sunday Press*, Dublin, 11 September to 30 October 1960).

Sheehy Skeffington, Hanna, 'British Militarism as I Have Known It', Tralee: *Kerryman*, 1946.

—, 'Constance Markievicz and What She Stood for', *An Phoblacht*, 16 July 1932, pp. 7–8.

—, 'Reminiscences of an Irish Suffragette', *The Field Day Anthology of Irish Writing*, Vols IV/V (Cork University Press, 1991; ed. Angela Bourke).

Other Sources

Royal Commission on the Rebellion in Ireland (London, 1916).

The Peace Treaty with Germany

Dáil Reports, 1918–1925.

Newspapers and Periodicals

Bean na hÉireann

Capuchin Annual 1966

The Fenian

Freeman's Journal

History Ireland

Irish Citizen

Irish Independent

Irish Times

Irish Worker

The Nation

An Phoblacht

Sinn Féin

Sligo Champion

Sunday Press

The Times

Bureau of Military History Witness Statements

St Stephen's Green:

WS 258 Maeve Cavanagh

WS 256 Nellie Donnelly

WS 382, Thomas Mallin

WS 505 Seán Moylan

WS 907 Laurence Nugent

WS 296 Harry Nicholls

WS 6 Liam Ó Briain

WS 1766 William O'Brien

WS1666 Thomas O'Donoghue

WS 421 William Oman

WS 733 James O'Shea

WS 585 Frank Robbins

WS 246 Marie Perolz

Other

WS 483 Maurice Aherne

WS 645 Nora Ashe

WS 251 Richard Balfe

WS 723 Alice Barry

WS 1754 Leslie Bean Ui Barry (Leslie Price)

WS 936 Dulcibella Barton

WS 979 Robert C. Barton

WS 385 Mrs Seán Beaumont (Maureen McGavock)

WS 939 Ernest Blythe

WS 779 Robert Brennan

WS 1,019 Alfred Bucknill

WS 58 Seamus Cashin

WS 258 Maeve Cavanagh (Mrs Mac Donnell)

WS 266 Áine Ceannt

WS 919 Ina Connolly-Heron

WS 1,349 Daniel Conway

WS 179 Elizabeth and Nell Corr

WS 750 Eithne Coyle

WS 909 Sidney Czira

WS 327 Patrick Egan

WS 216 Louise Gavan Duffy

WS 700 St John Gogarty

WS 546 Rose Hackett

WS 76 John Hanratty

WS 30, 31, 51 Bulmer Hobson

WS 280 Robert Holland

WS 328 Garry Holohan

WS 217 John J. Keegan

WS 842 Seán Kennedy

WS 494 Peter Kiernan

WS 357 Kathleen Lynn

WS 317 Maud Gonne MacBride

WS 219 John MacDonagh

WS 1,377 Hugo (Aodh) MacNeill

WS 382 Thomas Mann

WS 100 Patrick McCartan

WS 1,497 Joseph McCarthy

WS 290 Seán McLoughlin

WS 306 Michael McDunphy

WS 1,013 P.J. McElligott

WS 244 John McGallogly

WS 379 Jeremiah Mee

WS 391 Helena Molony

WS 11080 Patrick Mullolly

WS 296 Harry Nicholls

WS 1,369 James Nolan

WS 323 Liam O'Brien

WS 1766 William O'Brien

WS 321 Máire Ó Brolchain

WS 1,666 Father Thomas O'Donoghue

WS 193 Senator Seamus O'Farrell

WS 1235 William O'Flynn

WS 161 Donal O'Hannigan

WS 5841 Patrick Sarsfield O'Hegarty

WS 384 J.J. O'Kelly ("Sceilg")

WS 180 Kathleen O'Kelly

WS 1,108 Jeremiah J. (Diarmuid) O'Leary

WS 1,219 Seán O'Neill

WS 1728 Nioclas O Nuallain

WS 333 Áine O'Rahilly

WS 246 Marie Perolz

WS 257 Grace Plunkett

WS 267 Seamus Pounch

WS 191 Joseph Reynolds

WS 817 Seán Saunders

WS 288 Lieutenant Colonel Charles Saurin

WS 892 Very Reverend T.J. Shanley

WS 334 Eugene Smith

WS 0230 John Southwell

WS 139 Michael Walker

WS 1,140 Patrick Ward

WS 1420 Patrick Whelan

WS 1,207 Alfred White (Ailfred de Faoite)

Public Records Office of Northern Ireland

Lissadell Papers

National Library of Ireland

Constance Markievicz papers

Joseph McGarrity papers

Hanna Sheehy Skeffington papers

Public Records Office, London

Sinn Féin and Republican Suspects 1899–1921: Dublin Special Branch Files CO 904 (193–216)

Home Office, Activities of Countess Markievicz 1916–1920 HO 144/1580/316818

War Office: Army of Ireland: Administrative and Easter Rising Records 1 June 1918-30 June 1919 WO 35/210

Websites

www.theirishrevolution.wordpress.com

www.garda.ie

www.bureauofmilitaryhistory.ie

www.warofindependence.info

www.firstworldwar.com

www.fiannaeireannhistory.wordpress.com

Index